VN BROWN

TION

THE TELL-TALE HEART
THE PIT & THE PENDULUM
THE MASQUE OF THE RED DEATH
WILLIAM WILSON
THE RAVEN

WRITTEN BY EDGAR ALLAN POE
ILLUSTRATED BY DAWN BROWN

Please visit us on the web:

www.dawnbrown.net
www.speakeasycomics.com

RAVENOUS. May 2005. FIRST PRINTING. Published by Speakeasy Comics P.O. Box
159 Station P 704 Spadina Ave. Toronto, Ontario M5S 2S7 Canada. Copyright © 2005
Dawn Brown. All rights reserved. Any similarities to any persons living or dead are purely
coincidental. With the exception of artwork used for the purposes of review, none of the
contents of this publication may be used or reproduced without permission of Dawn Brown.
Printed in Canada.

for my
dad.

chapter one

Cap's last stand.

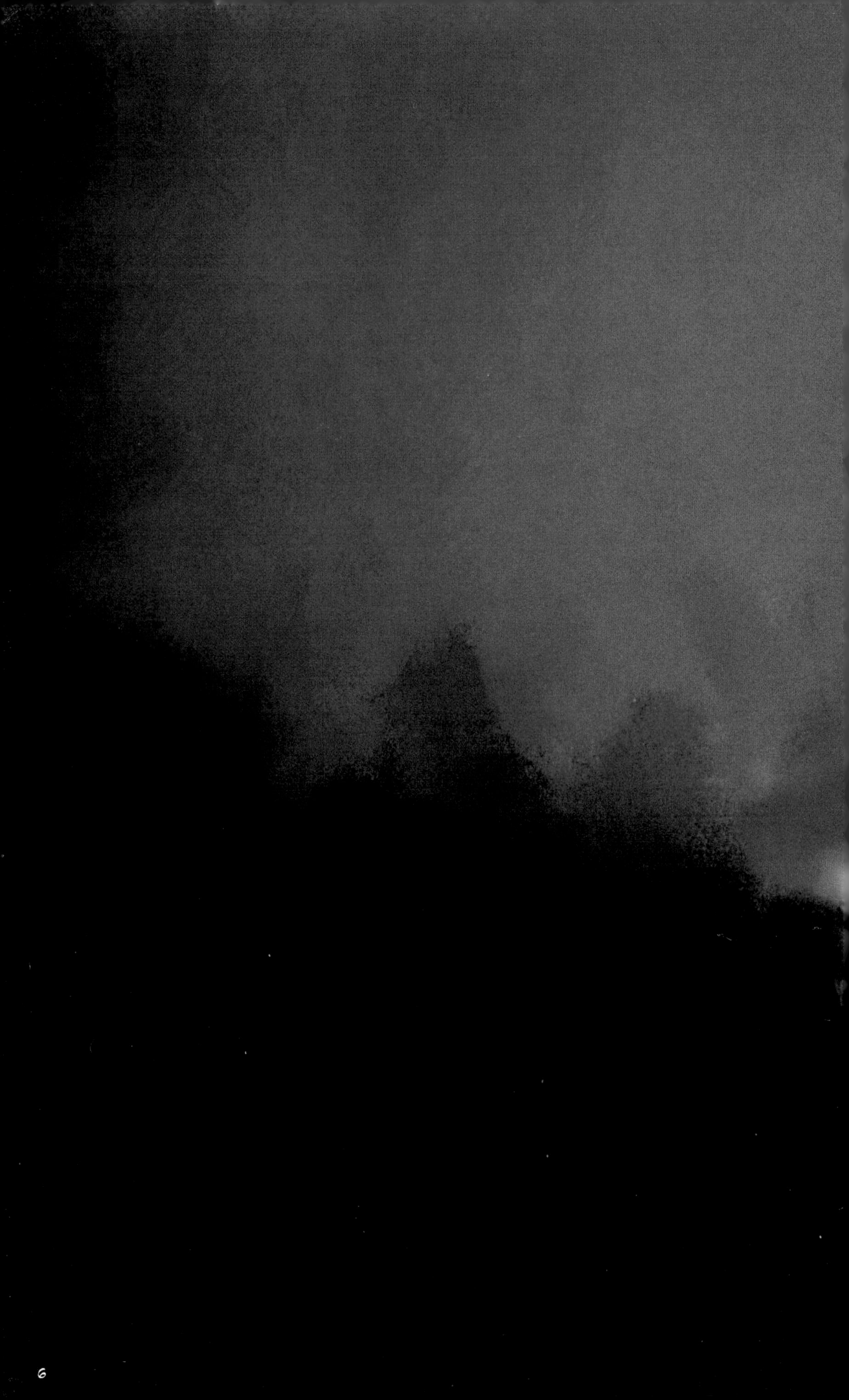

"TONIGHT IS A GOOD NIGHT FOR A STORY."

"NO THANKS."

"YOU'LL LIKE THIS ONE. IT'S ABOUT A *WEREWOLF!*

THE HORRORS WE INFLICT UPON EACH OTHER HAVE
LONG BEEN THE CONSEQUENCE OF *ONE THING...*

FREE WILL.

THERE'S A *LINE* BETWEEN GOOD AND EVIL THAT EXISTS
IN ALL OF US; A DUALITY BUILT INTO OUR NATURE.
YOU SEE, WE ALL EXIST WITHOUT ANY REAL CERTAINTY
THAT GIVEN THE *RIGHT* TO *CHOOSE*, WE WILL *CHOOSE*
WHAT IS *RIGHT."*

"OH JEEZ, HERE WE GO."

"THIS IS WHAT THE WOLF-MAN SAID AS HE GRABBED
THE LITTLE GIRL AND BIT OFF HER HEAD!"

"DAMMIT, MASON! IT FREAKS ME OUT
WHEN YOU TALK LIKE THAT. I DON'T WANT
TO HEAR THAT GARBAGE ANYMORE!

KEEP THE CREEPY LITTLE STORIES
TO YOURSELF!"

We are all but **consumed** by the endless midnight dreary.
Here in **Good Fortune**, no one is happy. No one is cheery.

For now, the story stays tucked inside my head.
In total silence, we race to meet the dead.

For the third time this week.

Just beyond the riches and
resources of civilization, we
are forced to fend for
ourselves.

Even the moon and stars
have abandoned us.

As bad as it's getting, I'd still take this over the **boredom** that was **before**.

As cops, it is our sworn duty to investigate these horrible things we inflict upon each other, and I'm excited about being useful once more.

My partner, all doom and dowdy, is the world famous **Captain Howdy**. He does not share my enthusiasm.

He's facing retirement in two days, But there will be no ticker-tape parade, no thanks or praise.

An honorable career has been marred by this unworthy coda.

He pushes through the tall grass in a fitful and unsteady fury. The old man struggles to maintain order and procedure like he's holding onto those last few strands of thick hoary hair that snake across his broad forehead.

It has become increasingly clear he is unprepared to handle an evil of this magnitude. The men are losing faith.

In the quiet moments, I notice his hands tremble - slightly. It is so subtle - imperceptible to the others. It has become habit to offer him a cup of coffee, which he graciously accepts, and grips tightly.

I love the old man. But I am not alone in my frustration with how he is leading us into **war**...

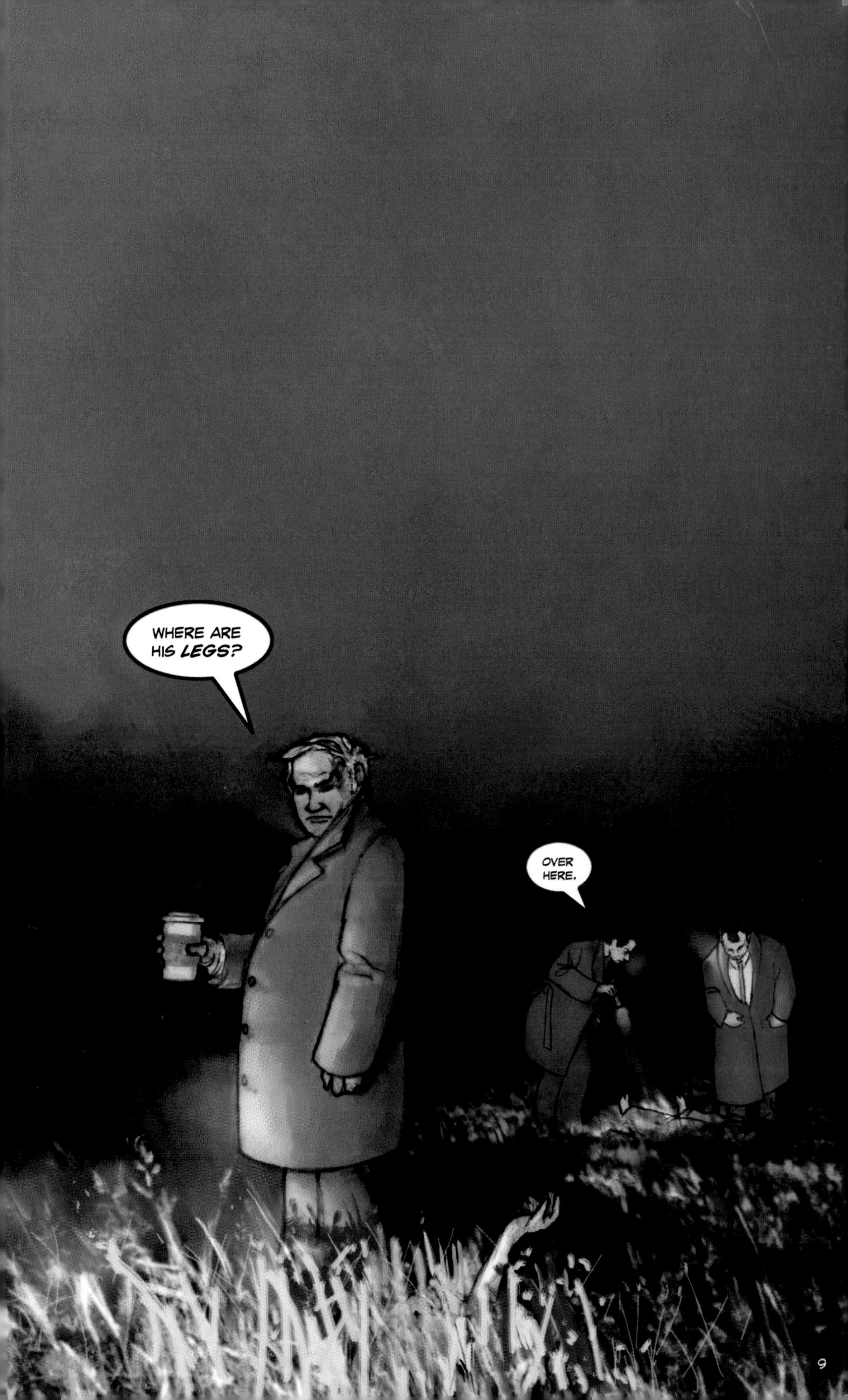
WHERE ARE HIS *LEGS?*
OVER HERE.

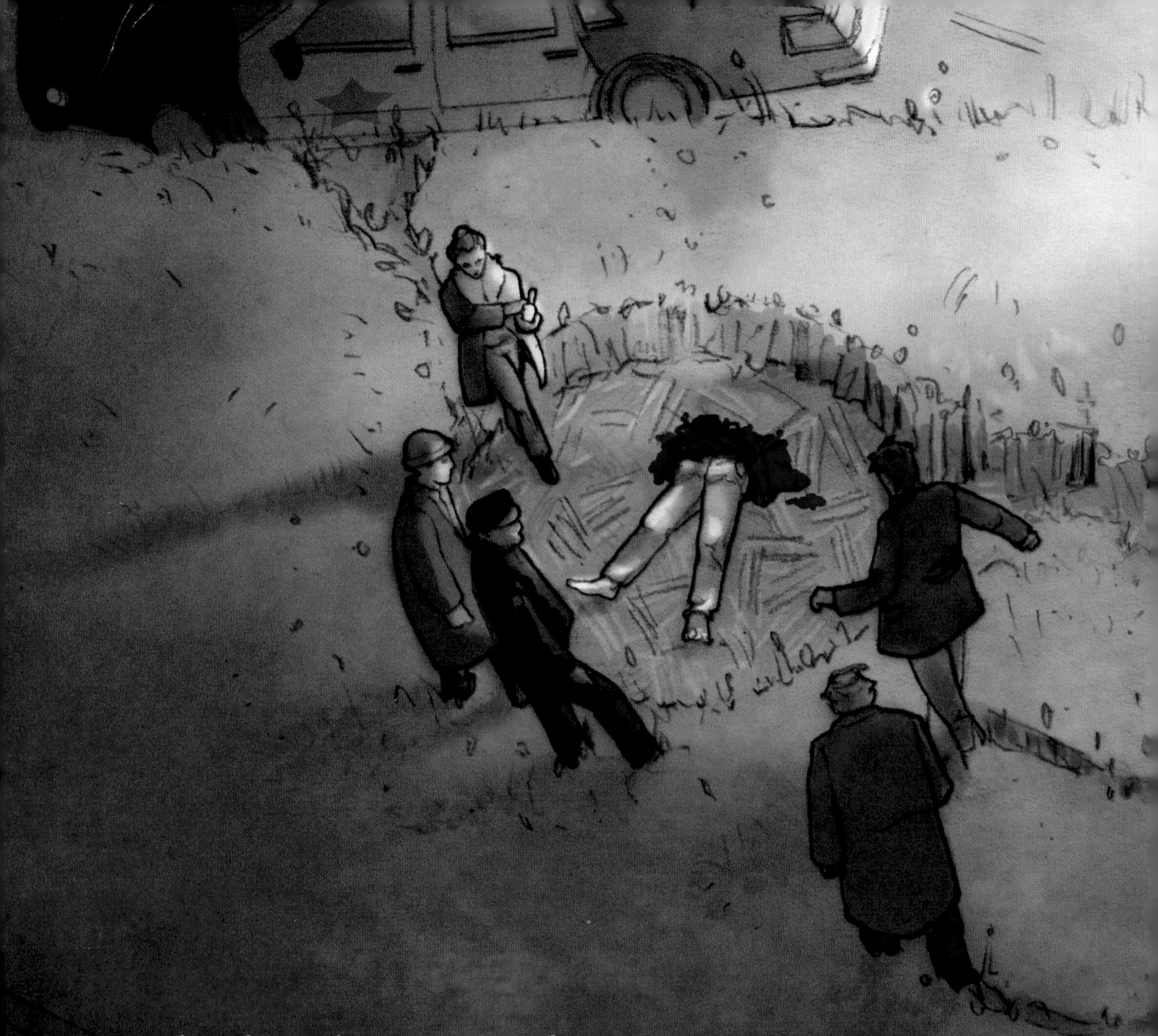

Not long after I transferred to Good Fortune, an otherwise uneventful tenure was interrupted by a string of **murders.**

A **serial killer** has awakened this sleepy hamlet! We are compelled to solve his horrible riddle.

This monster is stealing our people, without order or cause, and arranges their bodies cut width-wise through the middle!

God has allowed this invitation to match wit and will against the Devil himself. We are not prepared - no one has ever seen anything of its equal.

After we found the first body, the Captain muttered a prayer and thought nothing more.

He turned to **the bottle** for two, three, and four.

This is body number **nine**.

We are consumed by something truly evil - a fact you just can't ignore.

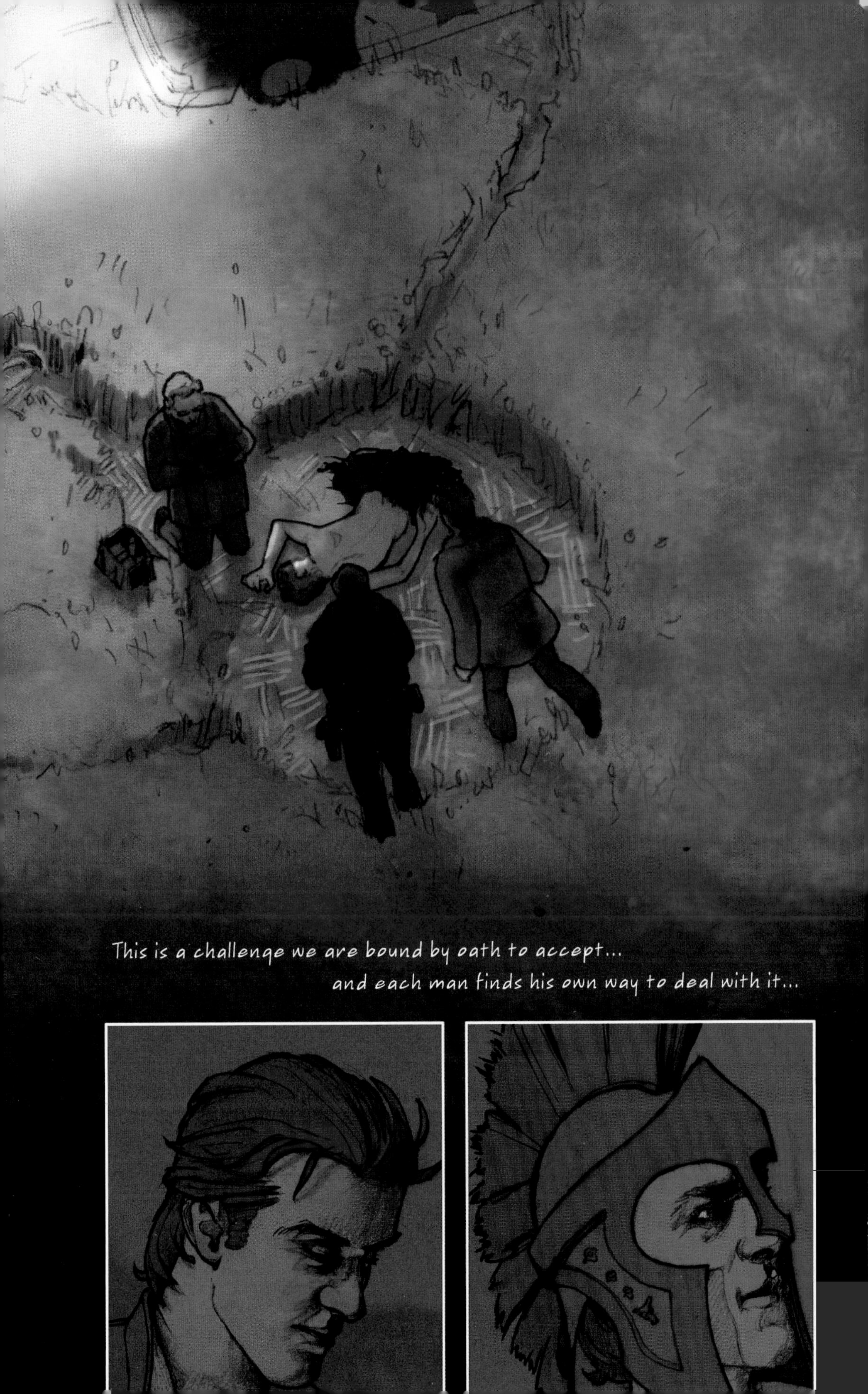
This is a challenge we are bound by oath to accept...
and each man finds his own way to deal with it...

I was sick as a kid.

A nasty gastric infection left me bedridden for a number of years, estranged from the neighborhood children.

I loitered away my youth in books. My peers were literary heroes like Lancelot, Conan, and Sinbad. Their adventures became my own.

My dreaming hours were spent on the battlefield. Eventually, all the dragons, demons and warlords kind of rolled into one monster I called **The Red Death.**

This phantasm was tall and gaunt, shrouded in a whispery, tattered cloak. His armor was woven from the claws of bears and wolves. He wore goat-skin chaps teeming with bloodthirsty fleas and mites. Between his bony shoulders sat a rotting skull. And what was left of the flesh had stiffened into a hideous sneer.

Although I haven't seen him since my boyhood days, I've always known he was still around - lurking in the shadows. Buried between the deep crevaces of my poor, wrinkled brain... he's been taunting me to join him on the front line.

The clock strikes three and I am once again standing on his battlefield - and again, a moment too late. The worms have already surfaced to gorge on the remains of his massacre.

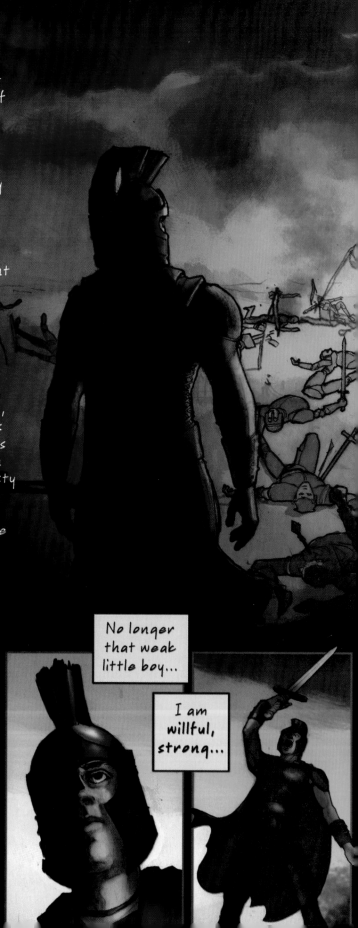

No longer that weak little boy...

I am willful, strong...

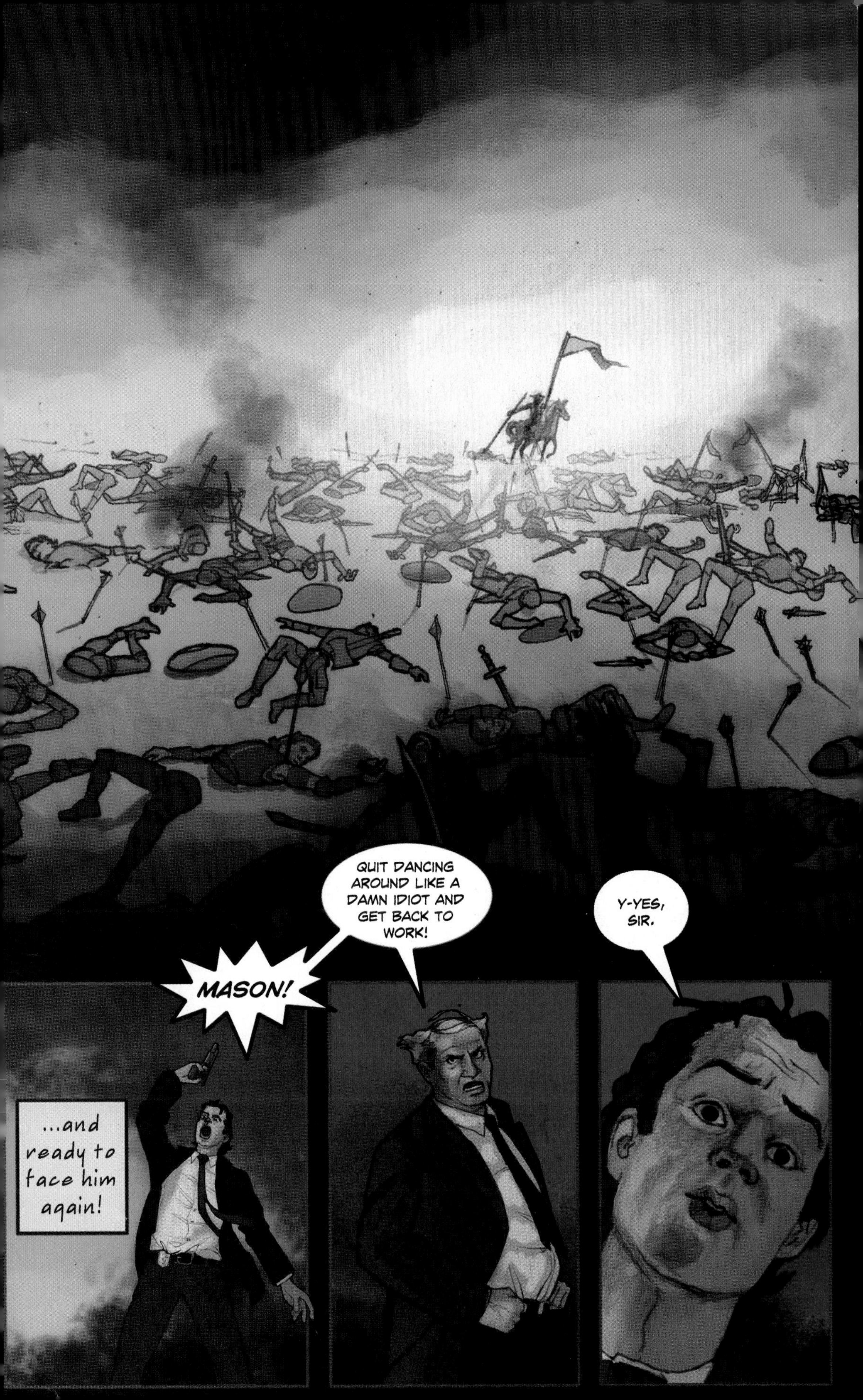
MASON!
QUIT DANCING AROUND LIKE A DAMN IDIOT AND GET BACK TO WORK!
Y-YES, SIR.
...and ready to face him again!

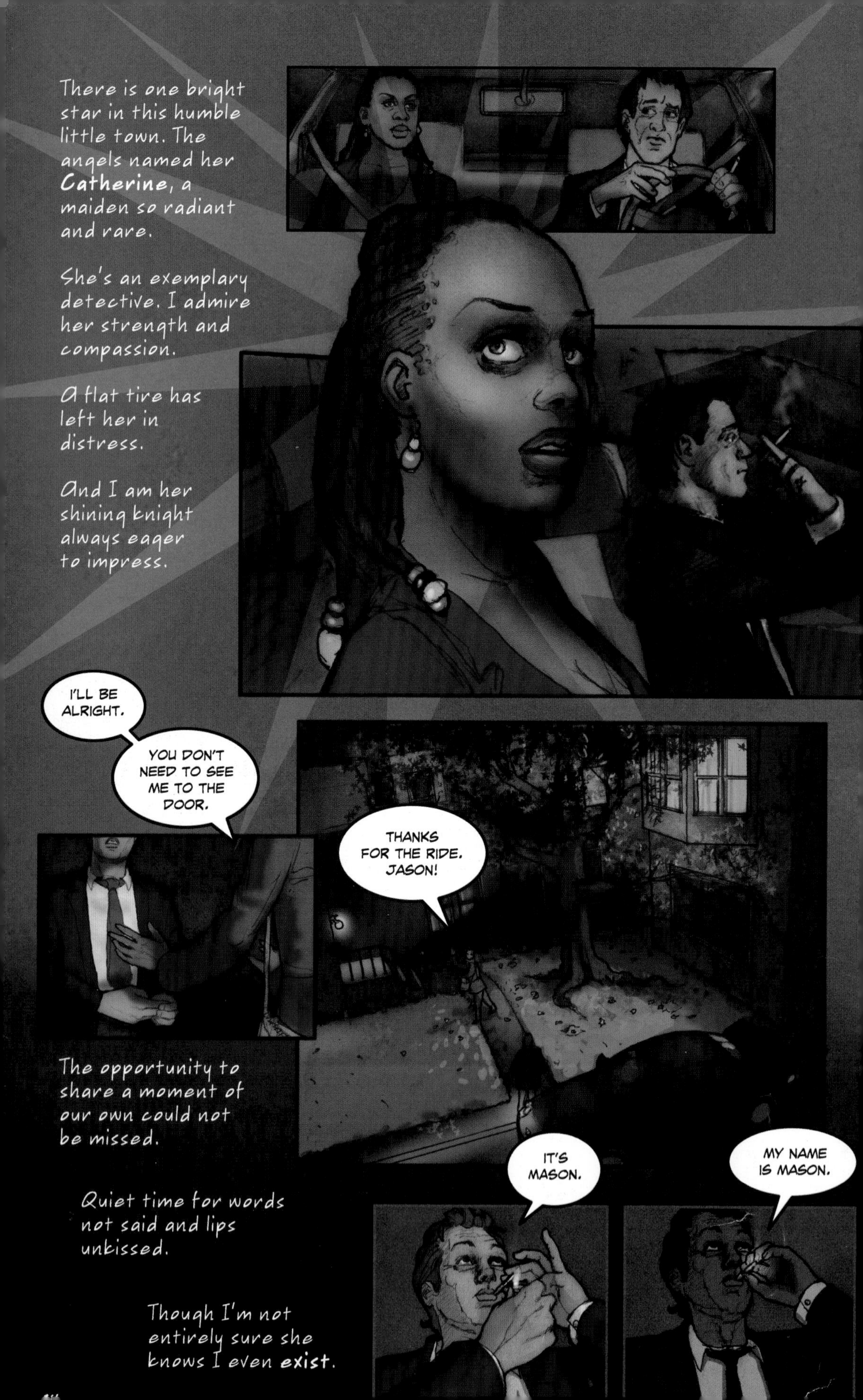

There is one bright star in this humble little town. The angels named her **Catherine**, a maiden so radiant and rare.
She's an exemplary detective. I admire her strength and compassion.
A flat tire has left her in distress.
And I am her shining knight always eager to impress.
I'LL BE ALRIGHT.
YOU DON'T NEED TO SEE ME TO THE DOOR.
THANKS FOR THE RIDE, JASON!
The opportunity to share a moment of our own could not be missed.
Quiet time for words not said and lips unkissed.
IT'S MASON.
MY NAME IS MASON.
Though I'm not entirely sure she knows I even **exist**.

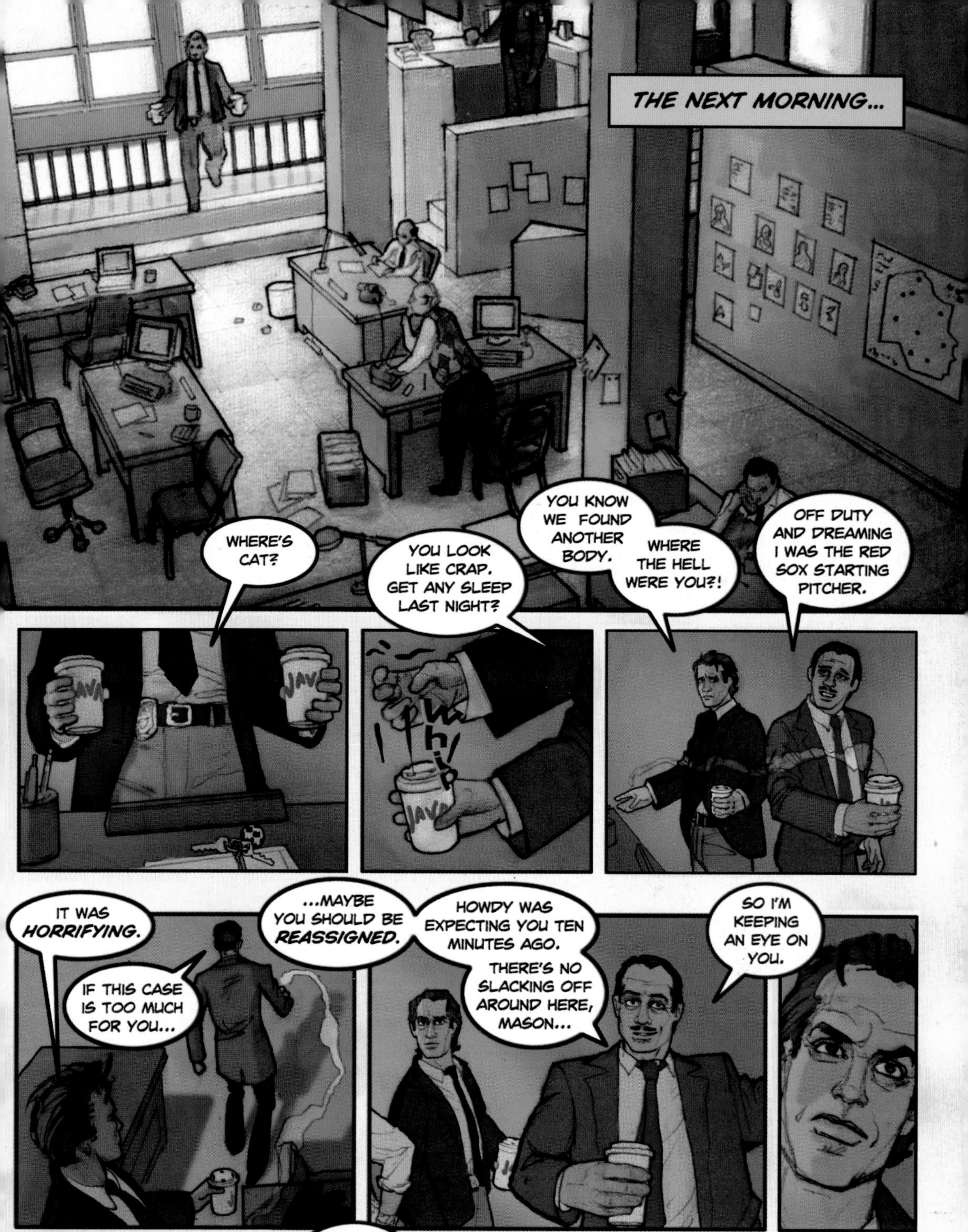
THE NEXT MORNING...
WHERE'S CAT?
YOU LOOK LIKE CRAP. GET ANY SLEEP LAST NIGHT?
YOU KNOW WE FOUND ANOTHER BODY.
WHERE THE HELL WERE YOU?!
OFF DUTY AND DREAMING I WAS THE RED SOX STARTING PITCHER.
JAVA
JAVA
whip
JAVA
IT WAS *HORRIFYING*.
IF THIS CASE IS TOO MUCH FOR YOU...
...MAYBE YOU SHOULD BE *REASSIGNED*.
HOWDY WAS EXPECTING YOU TEN MINUTES AGO.
THERE'S NO SLACKING OFF AROUND HERE, MASON...
SO I'M KEEPING AN EYE ON YOU.

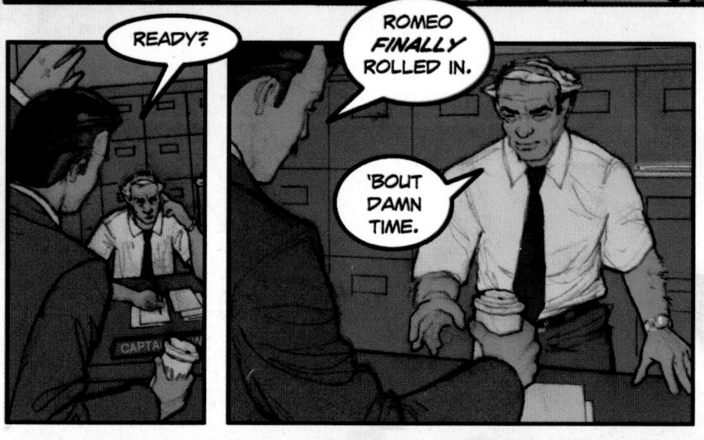
READY?
ROMEO *FINALLY* ROLLED IN.
'BOUT DAMN TIME.

With the exception of Cat, I have little to say of the other cops.

The most reprehensible is **Detective Garcia**. He's been in my face since I got here. The harassment never stops.

I have spent countless hours plotting **my revenge**!

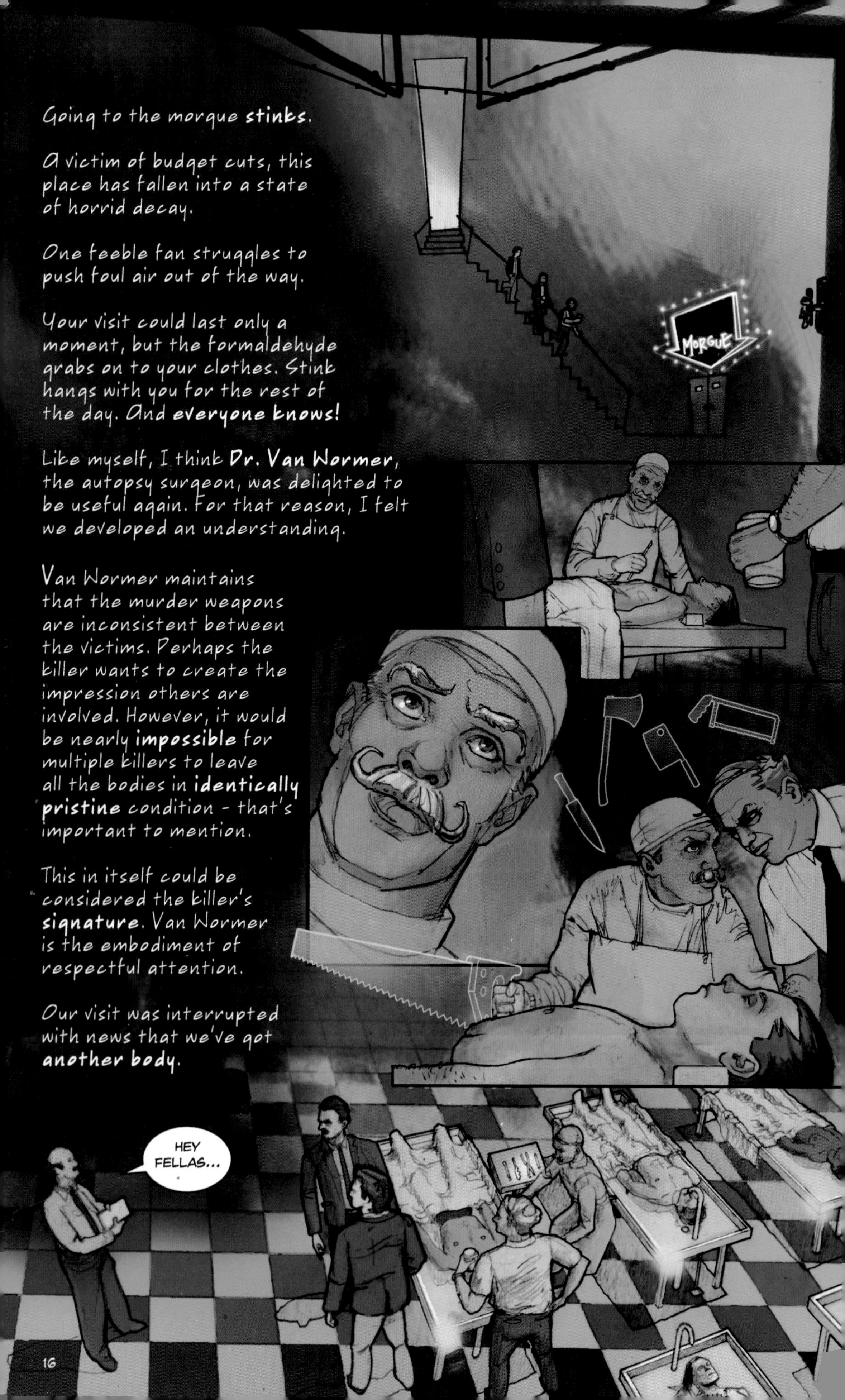
Going to the morgue **stinks**.
A victim of budget cuts, this place has fallen into a state of horrid decay.
One feeble fan struggles to push foul air out of the way.
Your visit could last only a moment, but the formaldehyde grabs on to your clothes. Stink hangs with you for the rest of the day. And **everyone knows!**
MORGUE
Like myself, I think **Dr. Van Wormer**, the autopsy surgeon, was delighted to be useful again. For that reason, I felt we developed an understanding.
Van Wormer maintains that the murder weapons are inconsistent between the victims. Perhaps the killer wants to create the impression others are involved. However, it would be nearly **impossible** for multiple killers to leave all the bodies in **identically pristine** condition - that's important to mention.
This in itself could be considered the killer's **signature**. Van Wormer is the embodiment of respectful attention.
Our visit was interrupted with news that we've got **another body**.
HEY FELLAS...

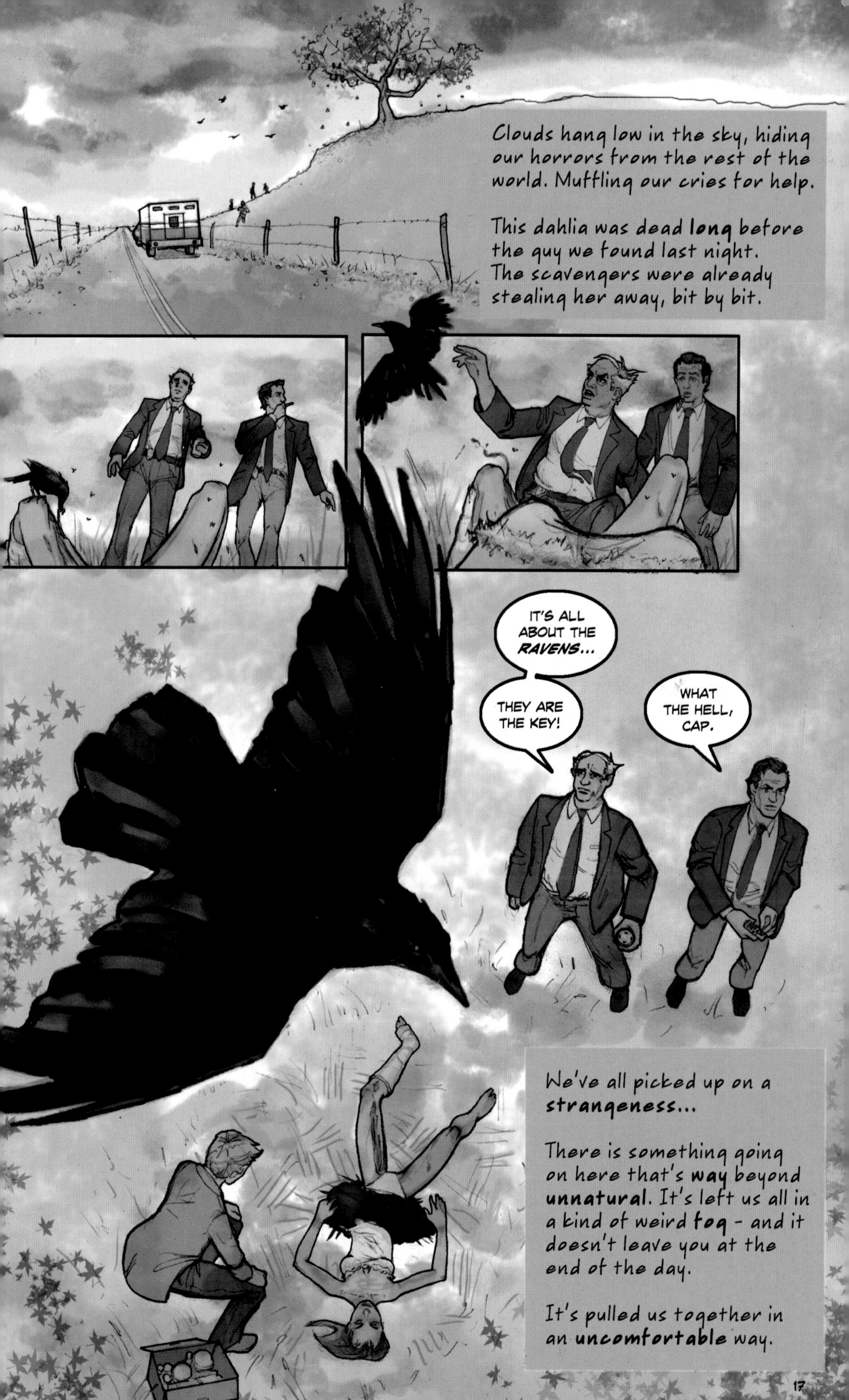
Clouds hang low in the sky, hiding our horrors from the rest of the world. Muffling our cries for help.
This dahlia was dead long before the guy we found last night. The scavengers were already stealing her away, bit by bit.
IT'S ALL ABOUT THE RAVENS...
THEY ARE THE KEY!
WHAT THE HELL, CAP.
We've all picked up on a strangeness...
There is something going on here that's way beyond unnatural. It's left us all in a kind of weird fog - and it doesn't leave you at the end of the day.
It's pulled us together in an uncomfortable way.

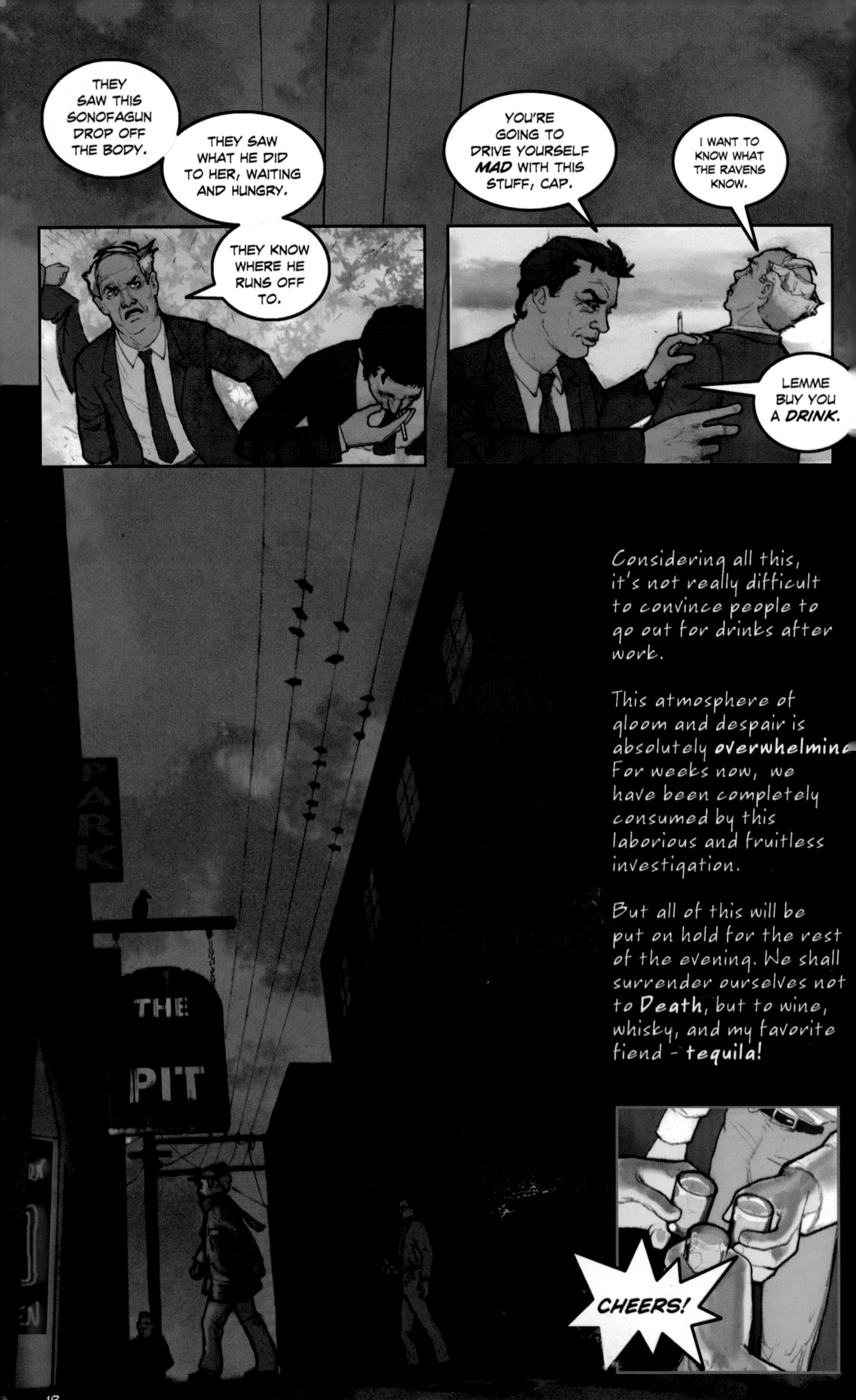
THEY SAW THIS SONOFAGUN DROP OFF THE BODY.
THEY SAW WHAT HE DID TO HER, WAITING AND HUNGRY.
THEY KNOW WHERE HE RUNS OFF TO.
YOU'RE GOING TO DRIVE YOURSELF **MAD** WITH THIS STUFF, CAP.
I WANT TO KNOW WHAT THE RAVENS KNOW.
LEMME BUY YOU A **DRINK**.
PARK
THE PIT
Considering all this, it's not really difficult to convince people to go out for drinks after work.
This atmosphere of gloom and despair is absolutely **overwhelmin** For weeks now, we have been completely consumed by this laborious and fruitless investigation.
But all of this will be put on hold for the rest of the evening. We shall surrender ourselves not to **Death**, but to wine, whisky, and my favorite fiend - **tequila!**
CHEERS!

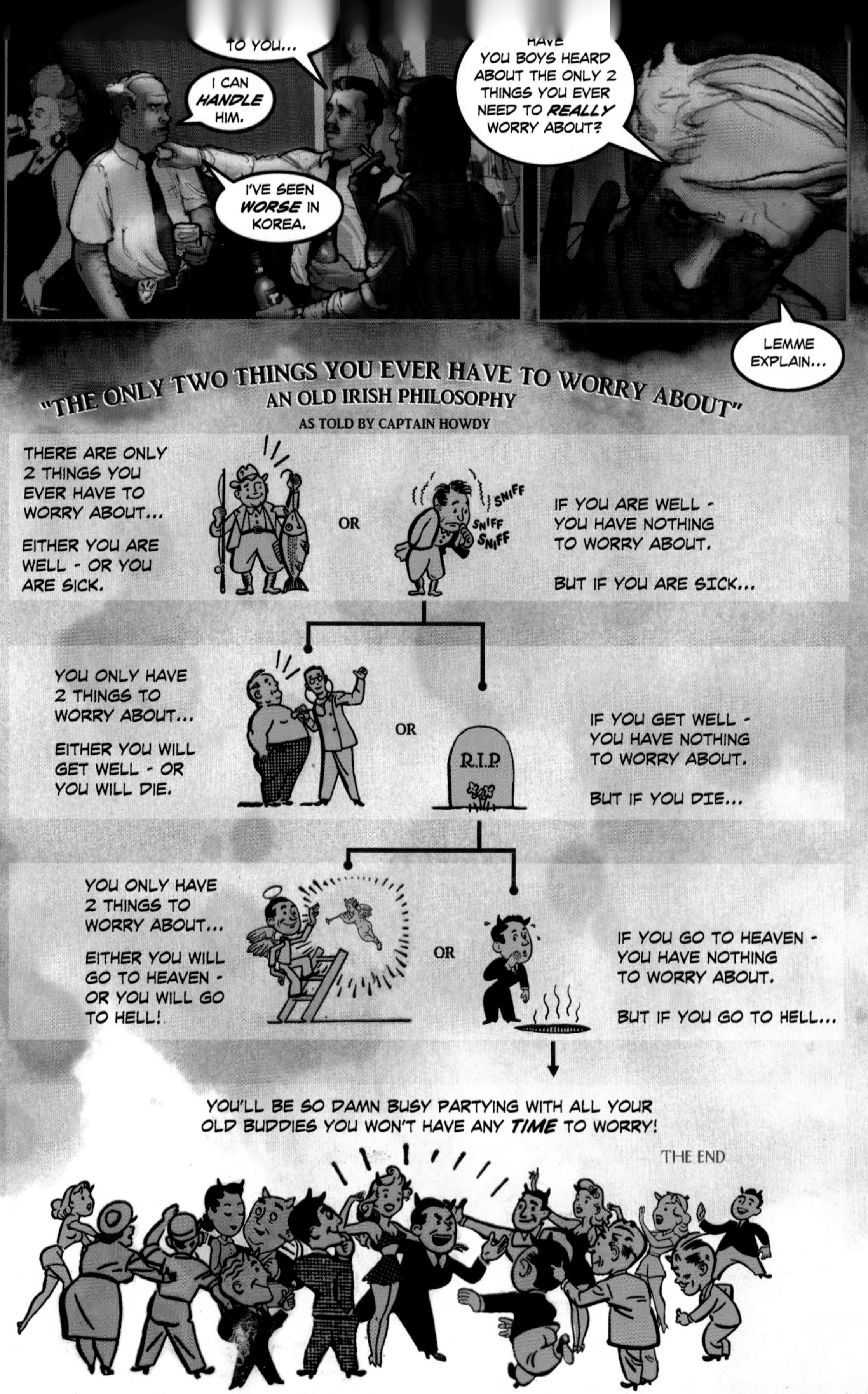

TO YOU...
I CAN HANDLE HIM.
I'VE SEEN WORSE IN KOREA.
HAVE YOU BOYS HEARD ABOUT THE ONLY 2 THINGS YOU EVER NEED TO REALLY WORRY ABOUT?
LEMME EXPLAIN...
"THE ONLY TWO THINGS YOU EVER HAVE TO WORRY ABOUT"
AN OLD IRISH PHILOSOPHY
AS TOLD BY CAPTAIN HOWDY
THERE ARE ONLY 2 THINGS YOU EVER HAVE TO WORRY ABOUT...
EITHER YOU ARE WELL - OR YOU ARE SICK.
OR
SNIFF SNIFF SNIFF
IF YOU ARE WELL - YOU HAVE NOTHING TO WORRY ABOUT.
BUT IF YOU ARE SICK...
YOU ONLY HAVE 2 THINGS TO WORRY ABOUT...
EITHER YOU WILL GET WELL - OR YOU WILL DIE.
OR
R.I.P.
IF YOU GET WELL - YOU HAVE NOTHING TO WORRY ABOUT.
BUT IF YOU DIE...
YOU ONLY HAVE 2 THINGS TO WORRY ABOUT...
EITHER YOU WILL GO TO HEAVEN - OR YOU WILL GO TO HELL!
OR
IF YOU GO TO HEAVEN - YOU HAVE NOTHING TO WORRY ABOUT.
BUT IF YOU GO TO HELL...
YOU'LL BE SO DAMN BUSY PARTYING WITH ALL YOUR OLD BUDDIES YOU WON'T HAVE ANY TIME TO WORRY!
THE END

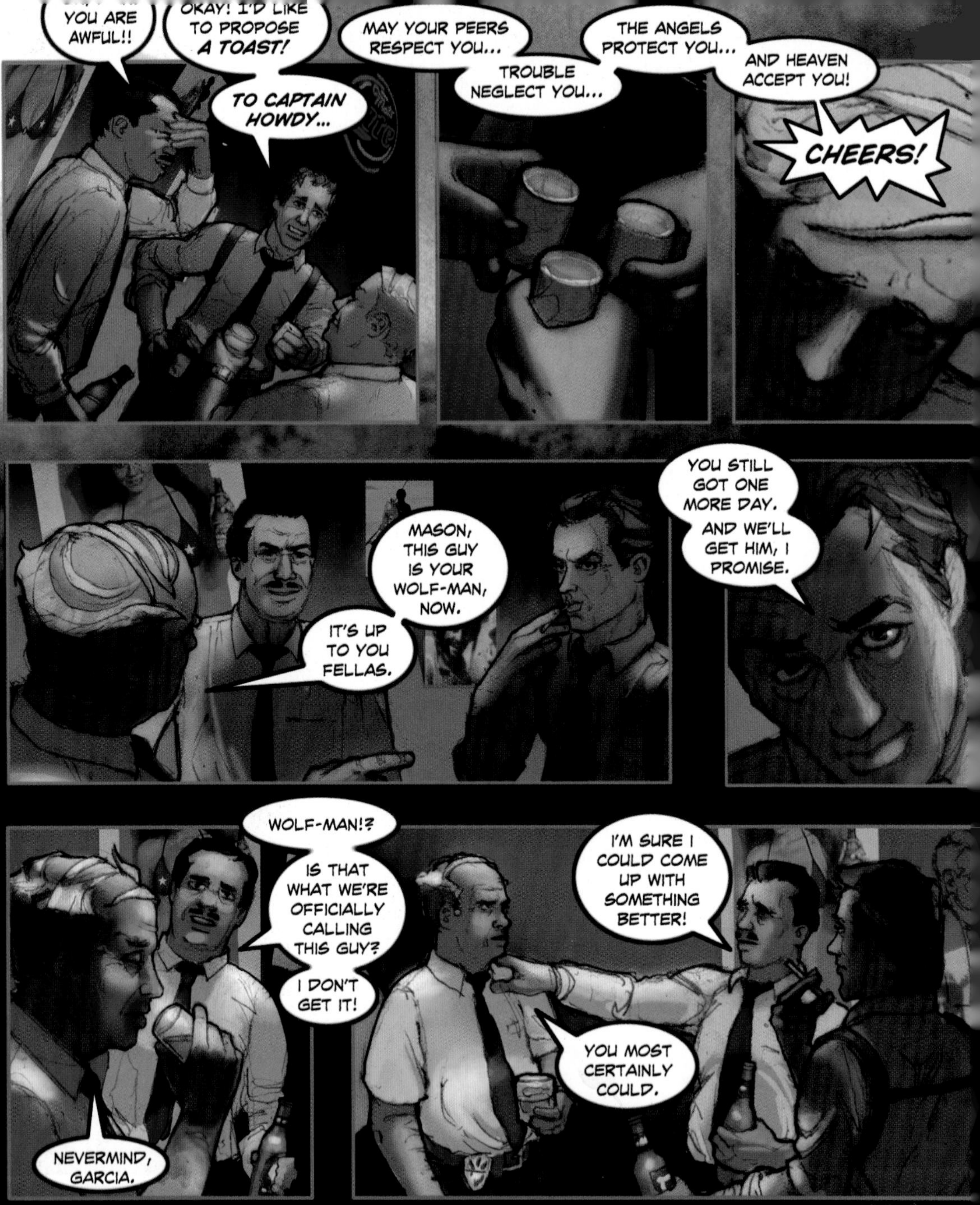
YOU ARE AWFUL!!
OKAY! I'D LIKE TO PROPOSE A TOAST!
TO CAPTAIN HOWDY...
MAY YOUR PEERS RESPECT YOU...
TROUBLE NEGLECT YOU...
THE ANGELS PROTECT YOU...
AND HEAVEN ACCEPT YOU!
CHEERS!
MASON, THIS GUY IS YOUR WOLF-MAN, NOW.
IT'S UP TO YOU FELLAS.
YOU STILL GOT ONE MORE DAY.
AND WE'LL GET HIM, I PROMISE.
WOLF-MAN!?
IS THAT WHAT WE'RE OFFICIALLY CALLING THIS GUY?
I DON'T GET IT!
NEVERMIND, GARCIA.
I'M SURE I COULD COME UP WITH SOMETHING BETTER!
YOU MOST CERTAINLY COULD.

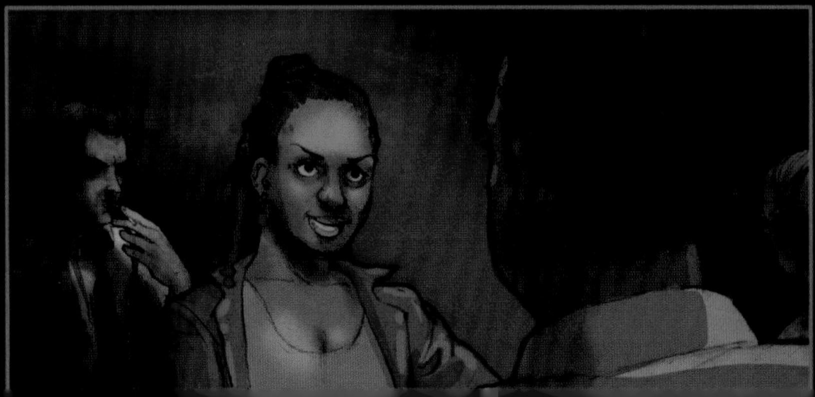

By sure degrees, the laughter and the liquor revived us. Even Catherine found comfort in a new friend. In these few hours, we knew only happiness.

The outside world could take care of itself.

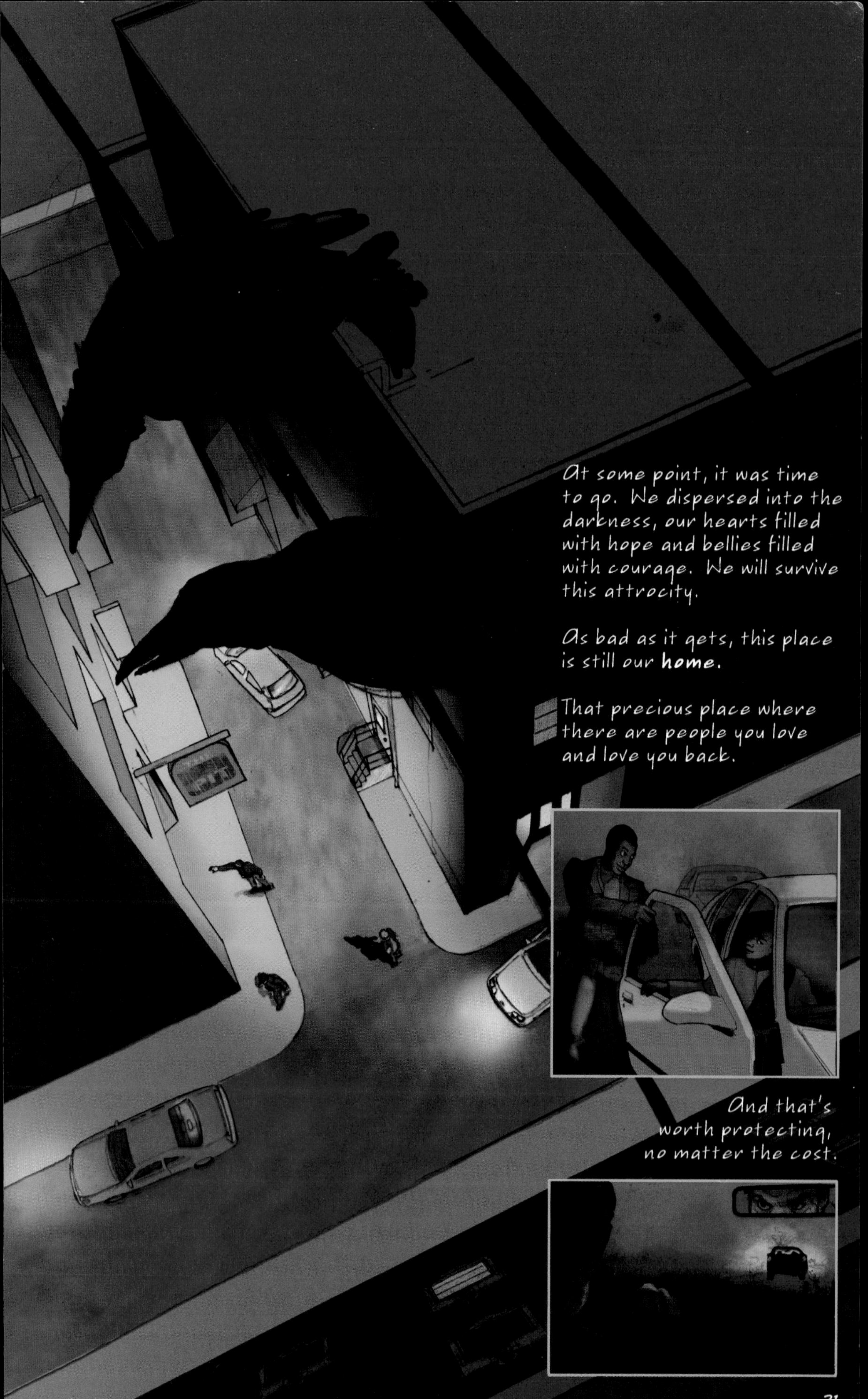
At some point, it was time to go. We dispersed into the darkness, our hearts filled with hope and bellies filled with courage. We will survive this attrocity.
As bad as it gets, this place is still our **home.**
That precious place where there are people you love and love you back.
And that's worth protecting, no matter the cost.

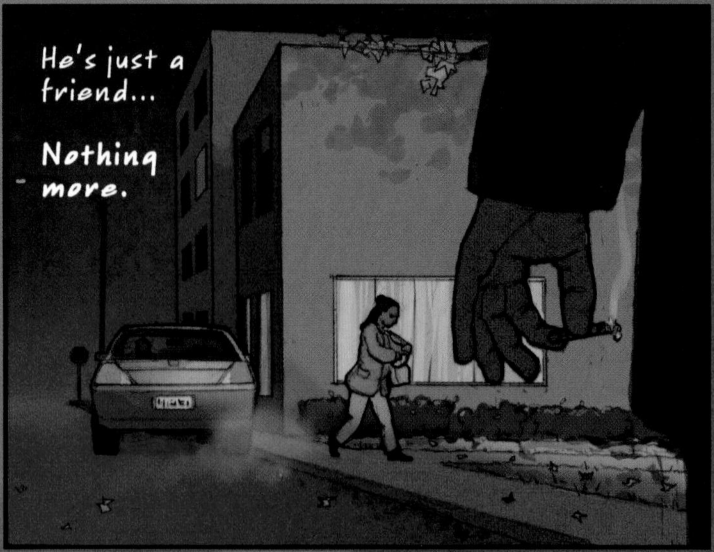
He's just a friend...
Nothing more.

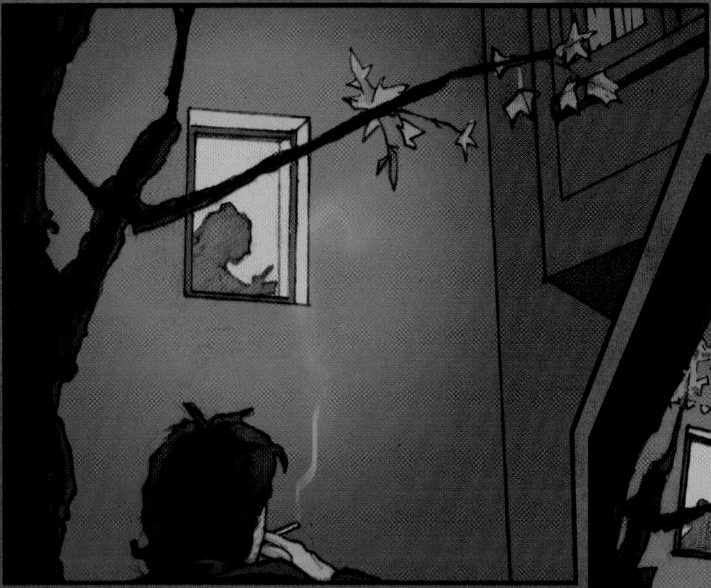

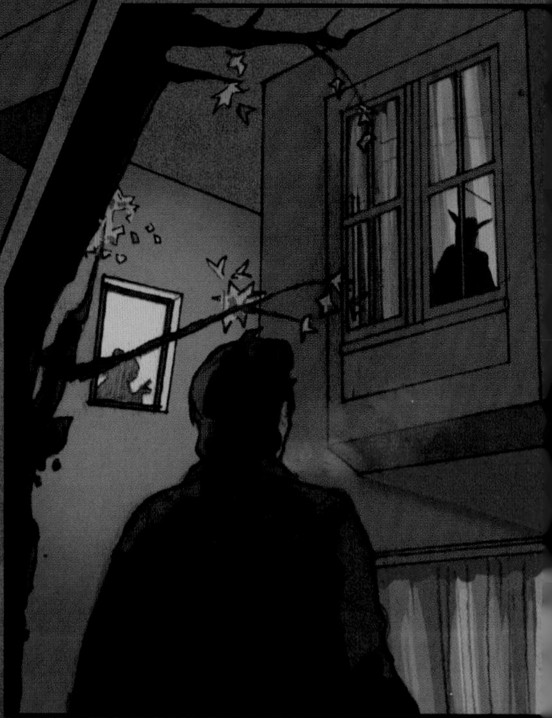

In spite of the attrocities we witnessed today, she does not divert from her usual habits. She still stops in the kitchen to thumb through the bills. Spending an extra minute to peruse a mail-order catalog, dreaming of a lifestyle she can't possibly afford.

Perhaps this is comforting... imagining somewhere else there's a better life waiting for you. All you have to do is get out of this one.

Maybe it's just that simple

The kitchen throws light down the hall and into her bedroom. The most feeble rays are strong enough to crudely define a silouette - a shadow - I had not noticed before!

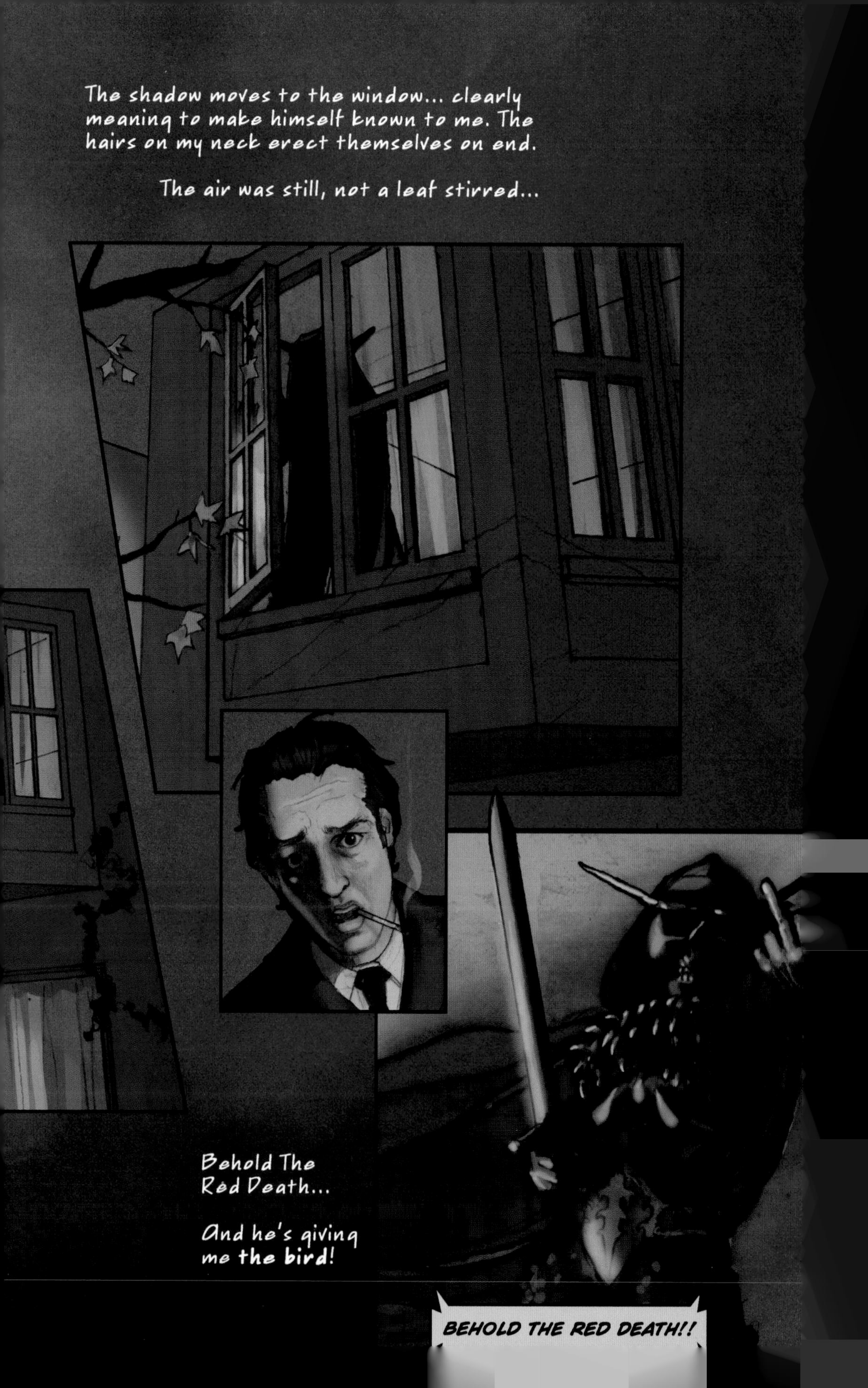
The shadow moves to the window... clearly meaning to make himself known to me. The hairs on my neck erect themselves on end.
The air was still, not a leaf stirred...
Behold The Red Death...
And he's giving me **the bird**!
BEHOLD THE RED DEATH!!

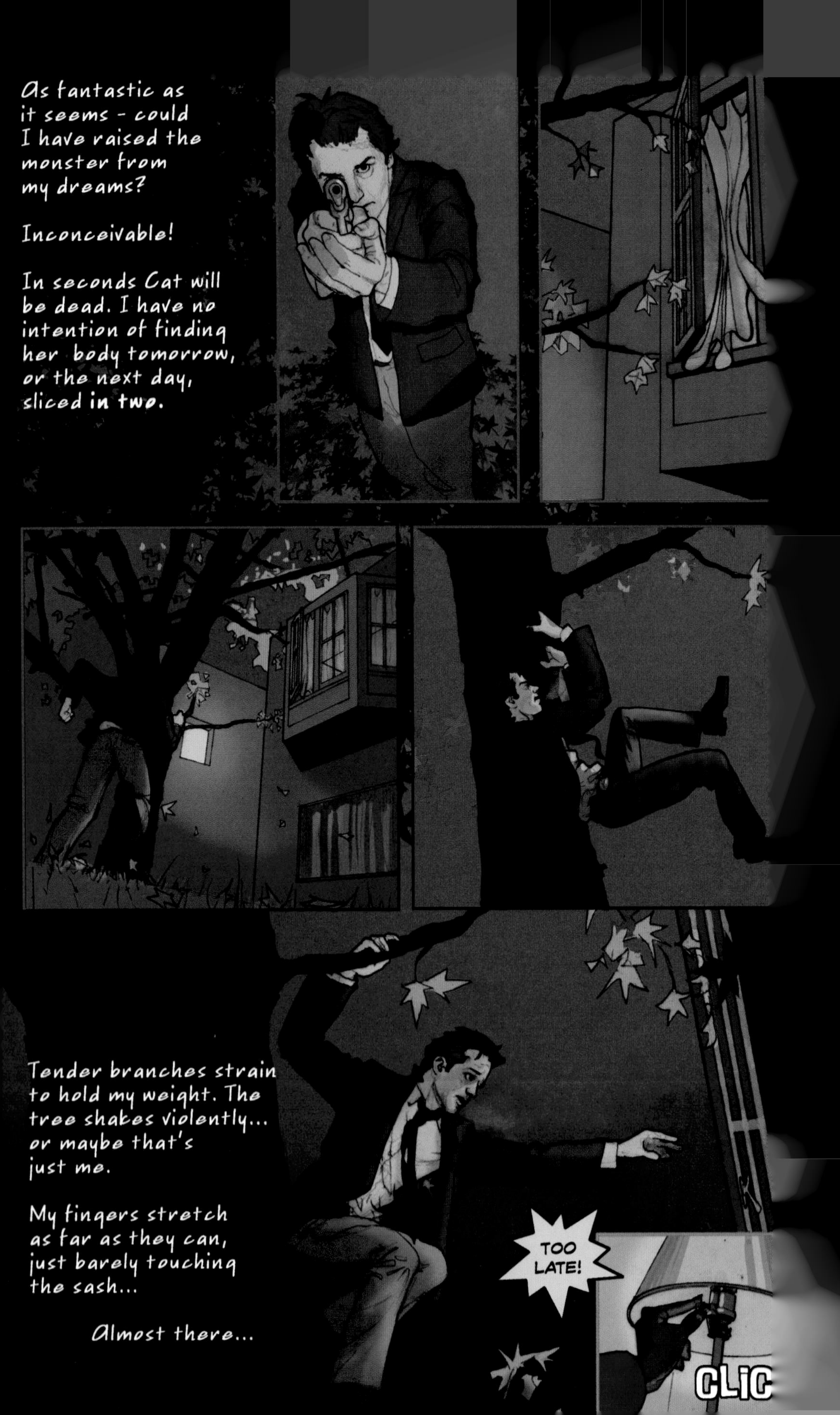
As fantastic as it seems - could I have raised the monster from my dreams?
Inconceivable!
In seconds Cat will be dead. I have no intention of finding her body tomorrow, or the next day, sliced in two.
Tender branches strain to hold my weight. The tree shakes violently... or maybe that's just me.
My fingers stretch as far as they can, just barely touching the sash...
Almost there...
TOO LATE!
CLIC

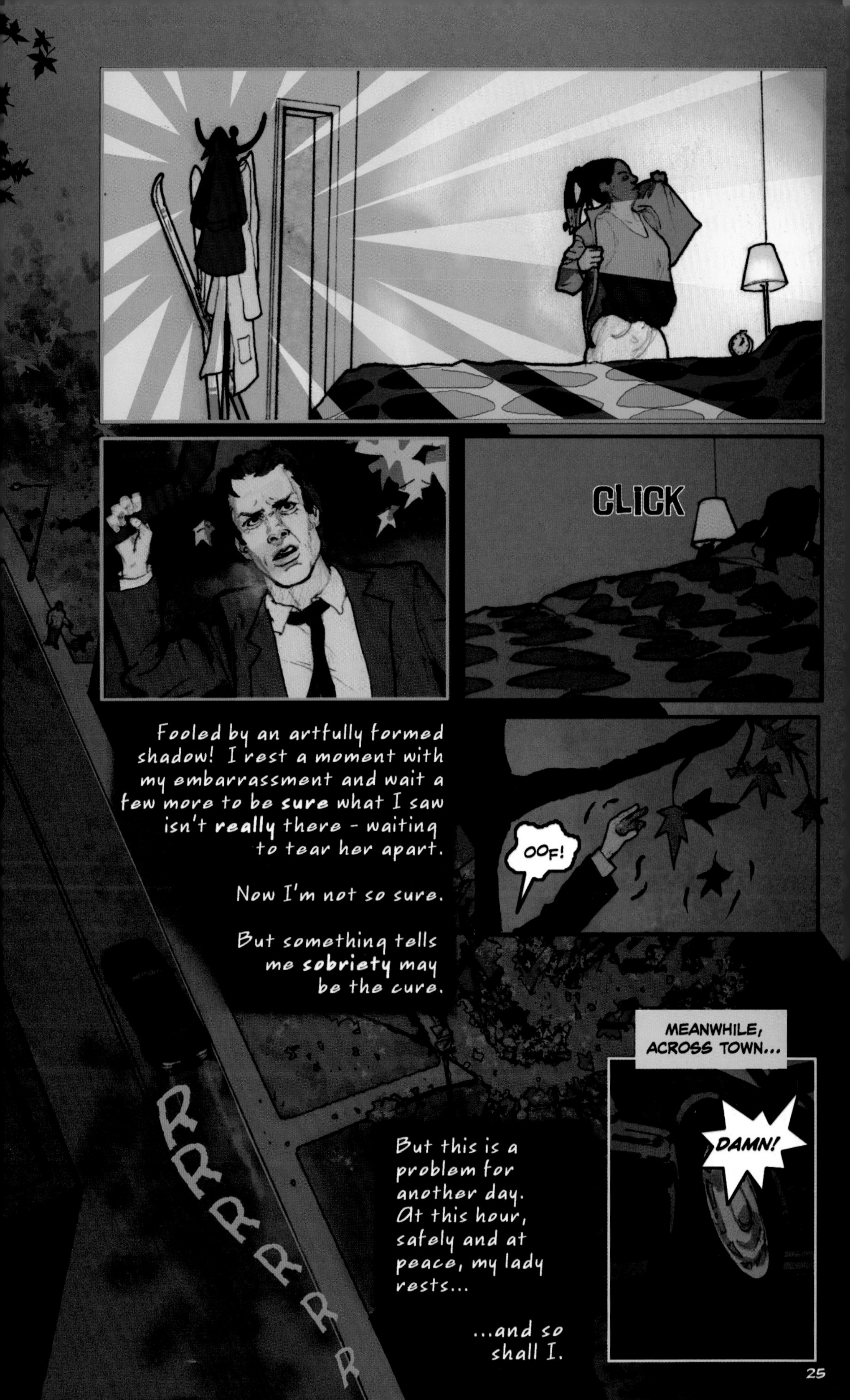
CLICK
Fooled by an artfully formed shadow! I rest a moment with my embarrassment and wait a few more to be sure what I saw isn't really there - waiting to tear her apart.
Now I'm not so sure.
But something tells me sobriety may be the cure.
OOF!
MEANWHILE, ACROSS TOWN...
DAMN!
But this is a problem for another day. At this hour, safely and at peace, my lady rests...
...and so shall I.
RRRRRRR

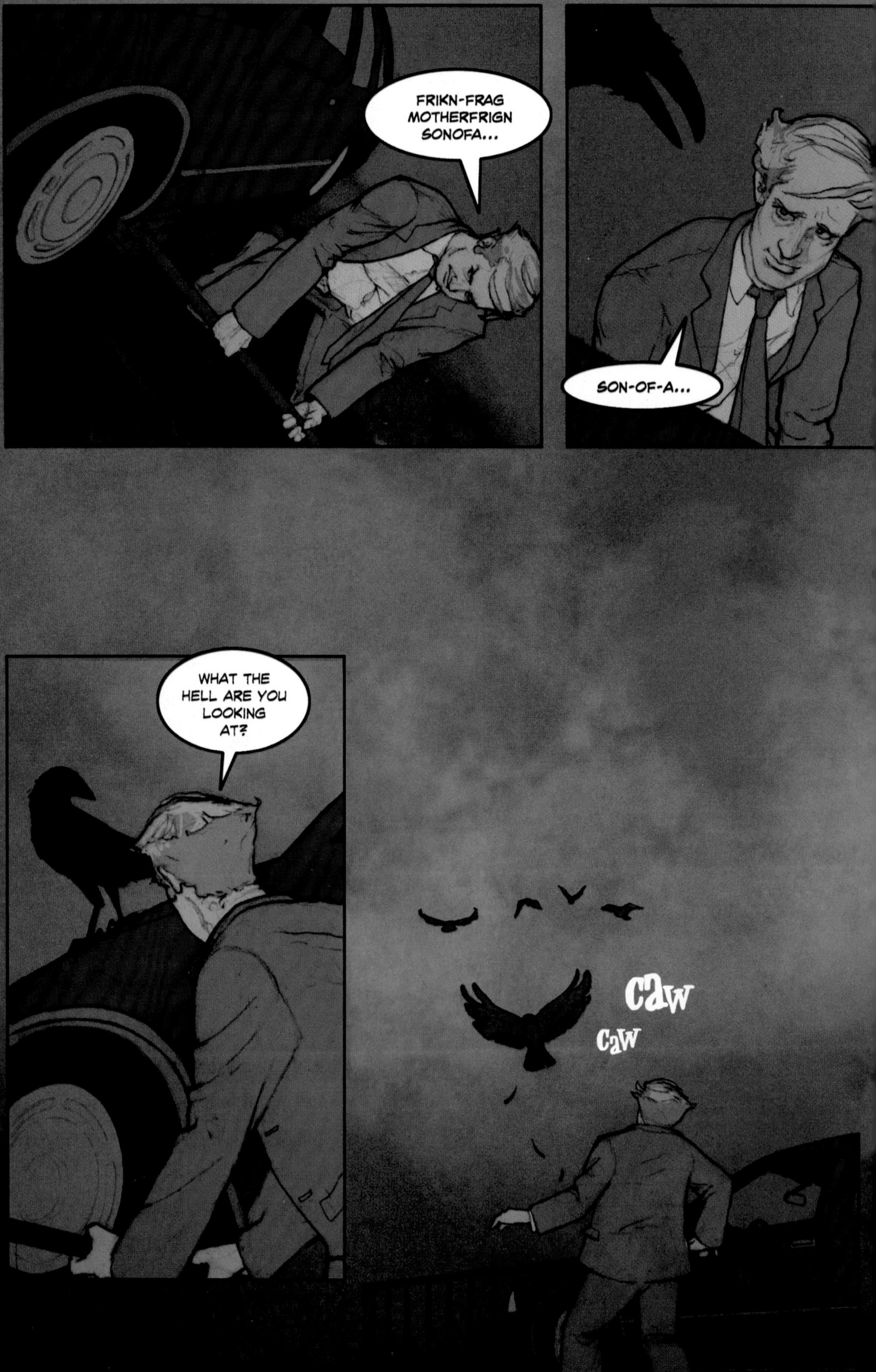
FRIKN-FRAG MOTHERFRIGN SONOFA...
SON-OF-A...
WHAT THE HELL ARE YOU LOOKING AT?
CAW
CAW

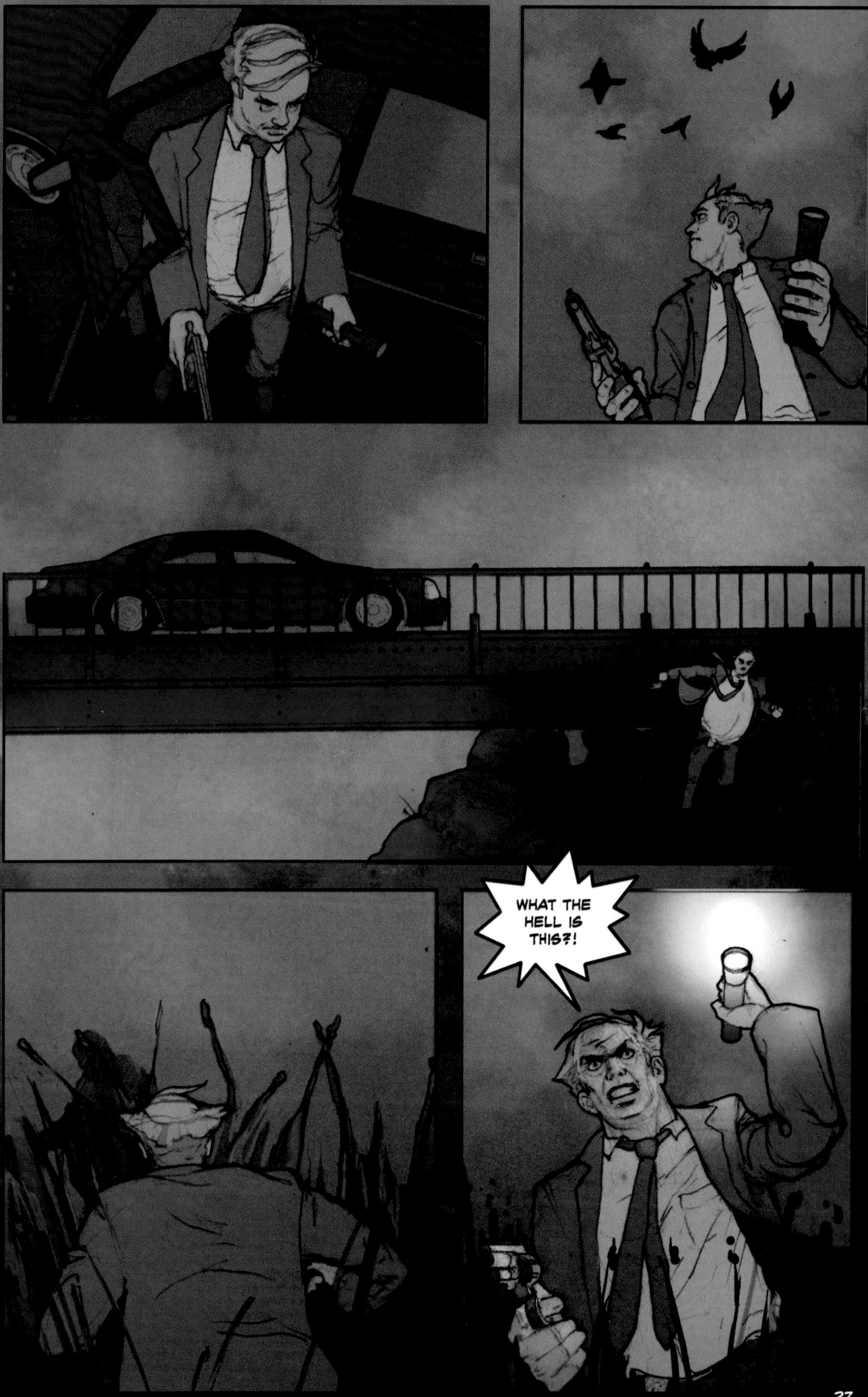
WHAT THE HELL IS THIS?!

chapter two

Casualties of war.

The sun pokes through thick clouds like the head of a boil - bathing everything in a sick yellow luster.

The air hums with flies who would brave the bitter cold for a succulent meal.

Today going to be a **bad day.**

We found Captain Howdy's body split in two. Quite a display.

Tell-tale bruises on his hands and face mean Cap put up a hell of a fight. If we're lucky, he grabbed some skin off the other guy. And **that** would be a first.

It's wasn't enough for this monster to leave his victims in a field or by the lake, now he's brought this to our **homes**... delivering a very clear message - **he is not afraid of us.**

Is this a transient demon passing through? Or perhaps a trusted brother fallen into the grasp of the devil?

Today, the place to search for these answers lies between a five-year old boy's soccer ball and his Big Wheel. Like any other crime scene, this place has become **sacred.** There is a respect - a reverence for this sacred place. Meaning, this place was last occupied by a **dead man,** and no one will ever tread there again.

If that five-year old boy dares to play in this big beautiful yard ever again, the only thing he'll see is the small patch of grass where the dead man was.

It's also the last place the players in this mystery were together - only now one is **dead** and one is **still alive.**

There is a relationship between them that is tighter than a marriage, and cannot be undone.

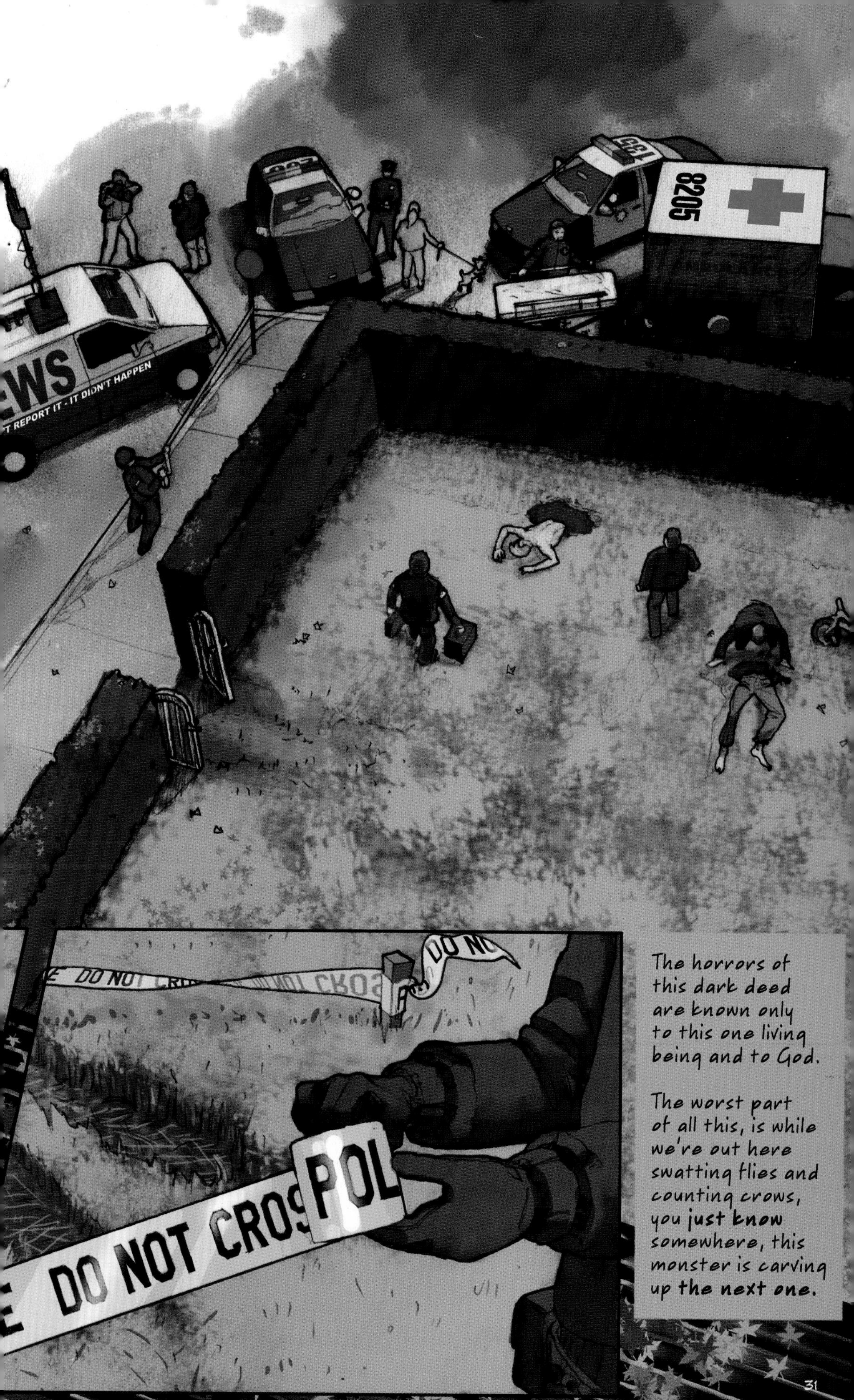
EWS
T REPORT IT - IT DIDN'T HAPPEN
8205
DO NOT CROS
DO NOT CROS
POL
The horrors of this dark deed are known only to this one living being and to God.
The worst part of all this, is while we're out here swatting flies and counting crows, you **just know** somewhere, this monster is carving up **the next one.**

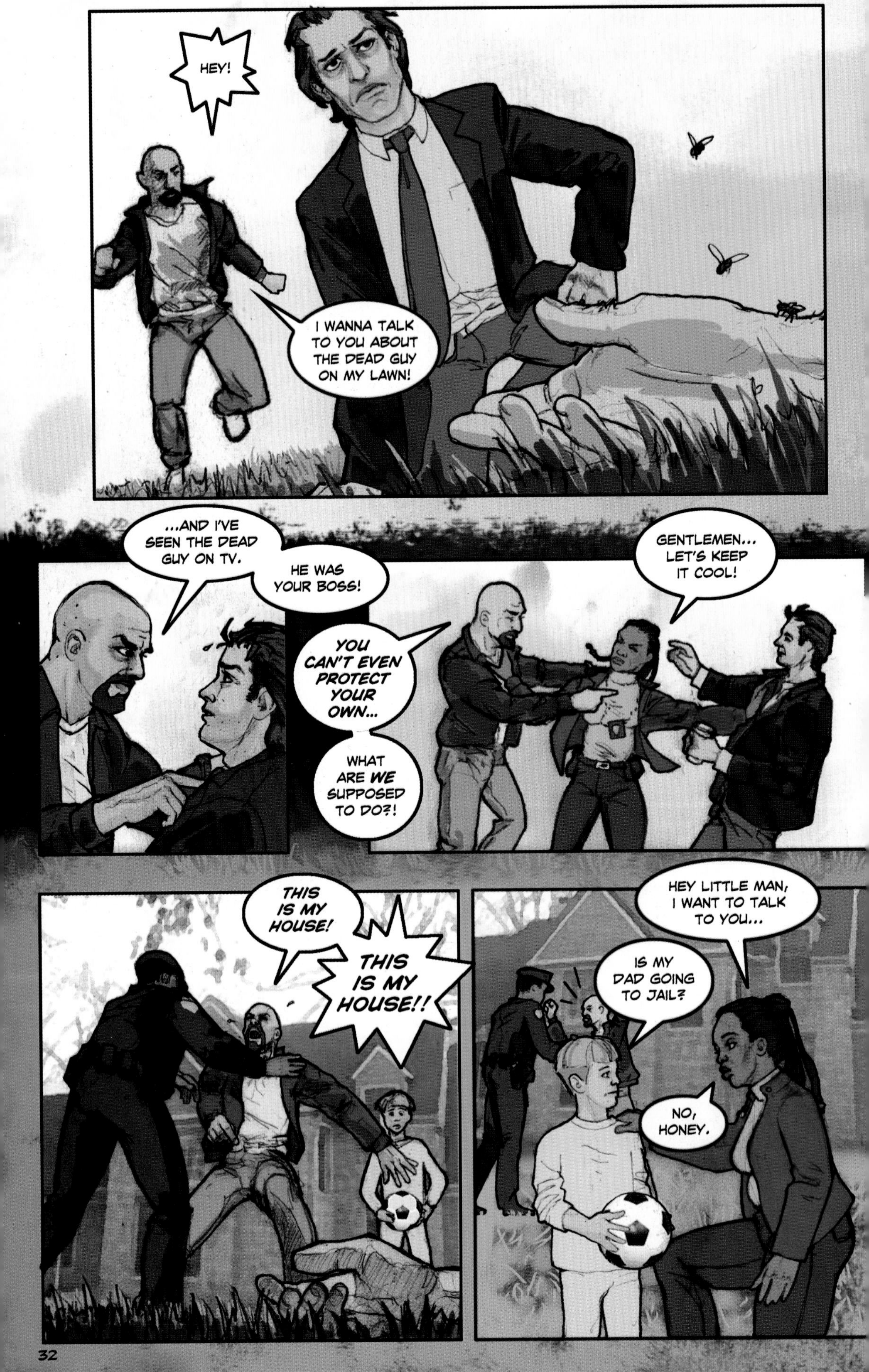

HEY!
I WANNA TALK TO YOU ABOUT THE DEAD GUY ON MY LAWN!
...AND I'VE SEEN THE DEAD GUY ON TV.
HE WAS YOUR BOSS!
YOU CAN'T EVEN PROTECT YOUR OWN...
WHAT ARE WE SUPPOSED TO DO?!
GENTLEMEN... LET'S KEEP IT COOL!
THIS IS MY HOUSE!
THIS IS MY HOUSE!!
HEY LITTLE MAN, I WANT TO TALK TO YOU...
IS MY DAD GOING TO JAIL?
NO, HONEY.

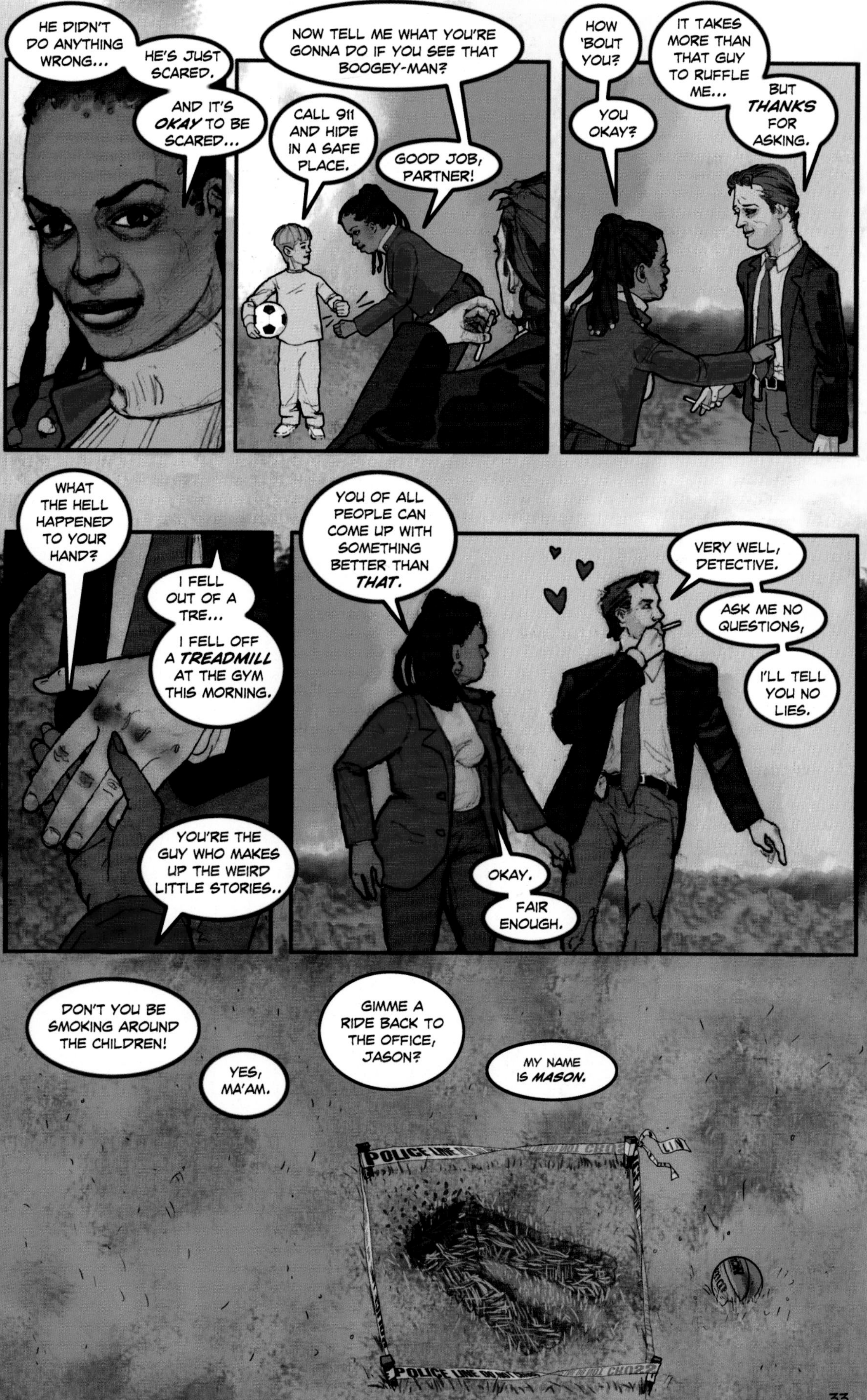
HE DIDN'T DO ANYTHING WRONG...
HE'S JUST SCARED.
AND IT'S *OKAY* TO BE SCARED...
NOW TELL ME WHAT YOU'RE GONNA DO IF YOU SEE THAT BOOGEY-MAN?
CALL 911 AND HIDE IN A SAFE PLACE.
GOOD JOB, PARTNER!
HOW 'BOUT YOU?
YOU OKAY?
IT TAKES MORE THAN THAT GUY TO RUFFLE ME...
BUT *THANKS* FOR ASKING.
WHAT THE HELL HAPPENED TO YOUR HAND?
I FELL OUT OF A TRE...
I FELL OFF A *TREADMILL* AT THE GYM THIS MORNING.
YOU'RE THE GUY WHO MAKES UP THE WEIRD LITTLE STORIES..
YOU OF ALL PEOPLE CAN COME UP WITH SOMETHING BETTER THAN *THAT*.
VERY WELL, DETECTIVE.
ASK ME NO QUESTIONS,
I'LL TELL YOU NO LIES.
OKAY.
FAIR ENOUGH.
DON'T YOU BE SMOKING AROUND THE CHILDREN!
YES, MA'AM.
GIMME A RIDE BACK TO THE OFFICE, JASON?
MY NAME IS *MASON.*
POLICE LINE

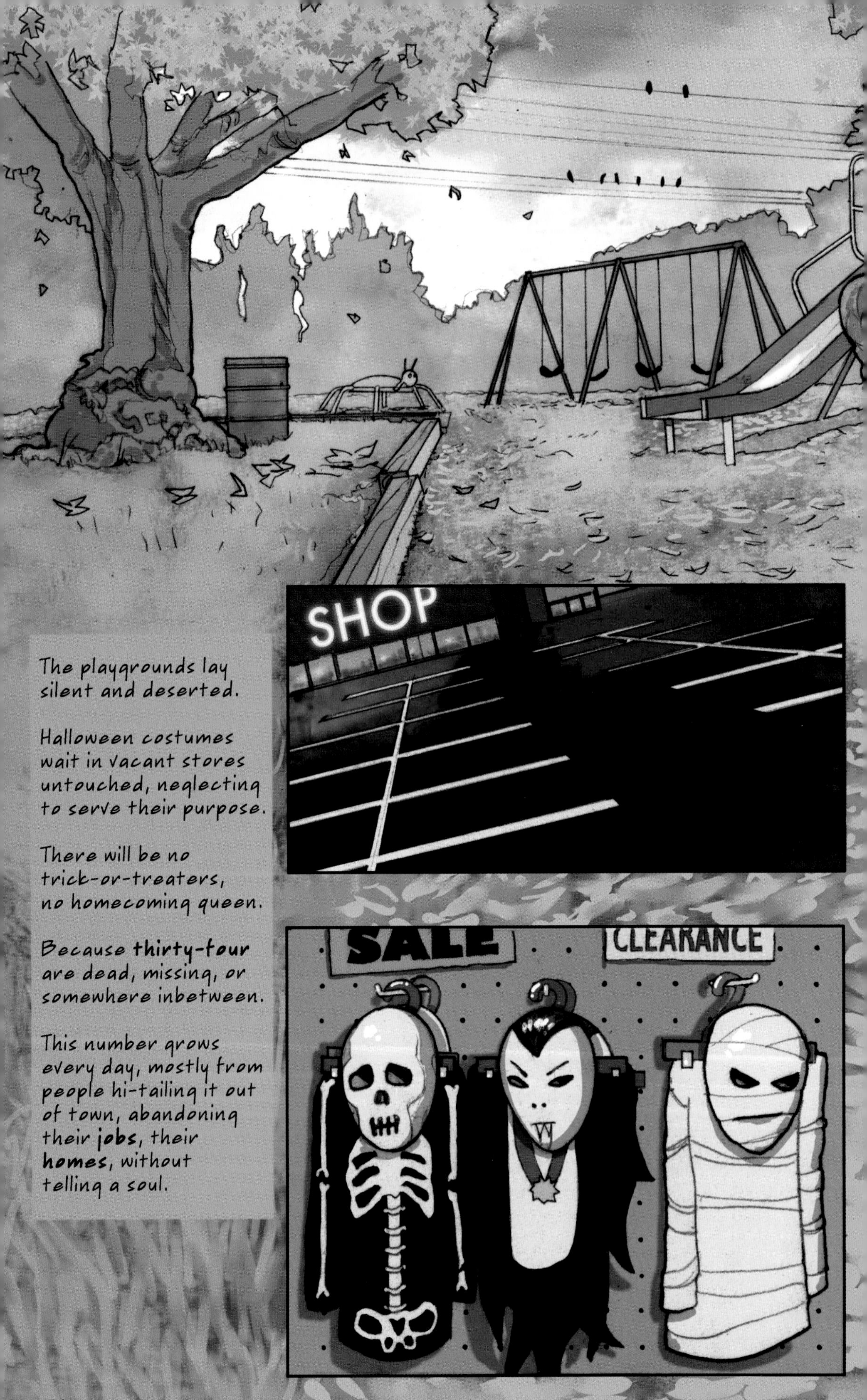
SHOP
The playgrounds lay silent and deserted.
Halloween costumes wait in vacant stores untouched, neglecting to serve their purpose.
There will be no trick-or-treaters, no homecoming queen.
Because **thirty-four** are dead, missing, or somewhere inbetween.
This number grows every day, mostly from people hi-tailing it out of town, abandoning their **jobs**, their **homes**, without telling a soul.
SALE
CLEARANCE

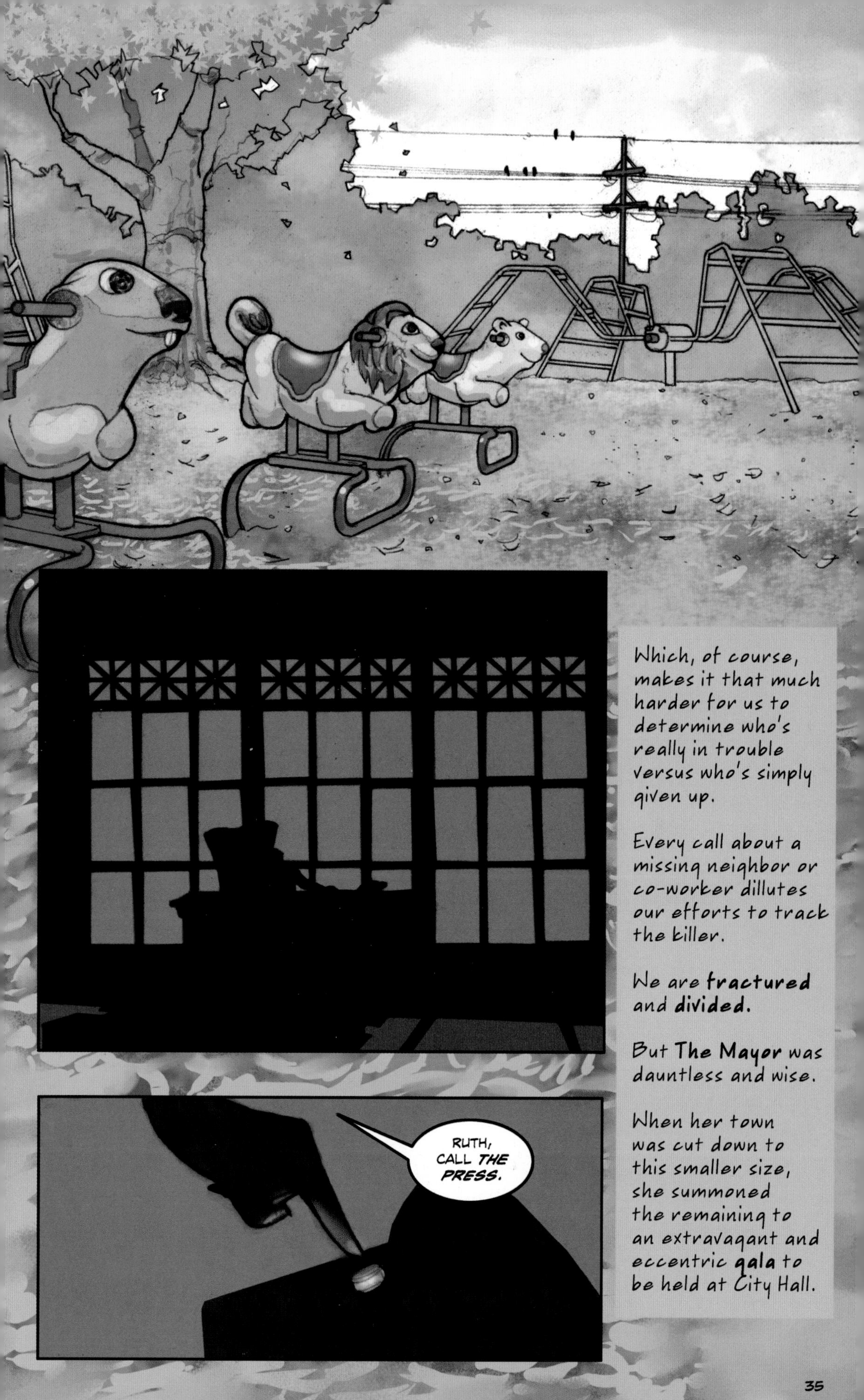
Which, of course, makes it that much harder for us to determine who's really in trouble versus who's simply given up.
Every call about a missing neighbor or co-worker dilutes our efforts to track the killer.
We are **fractured** and **divided.**
But **The Mayor** was dauntless and wise.
When her town was cut down to this smaller size, she summoned the remaining to an extravagant and eccentric **gala** to be held at City Hall.
RUTH, CALL *THE PRESS.*

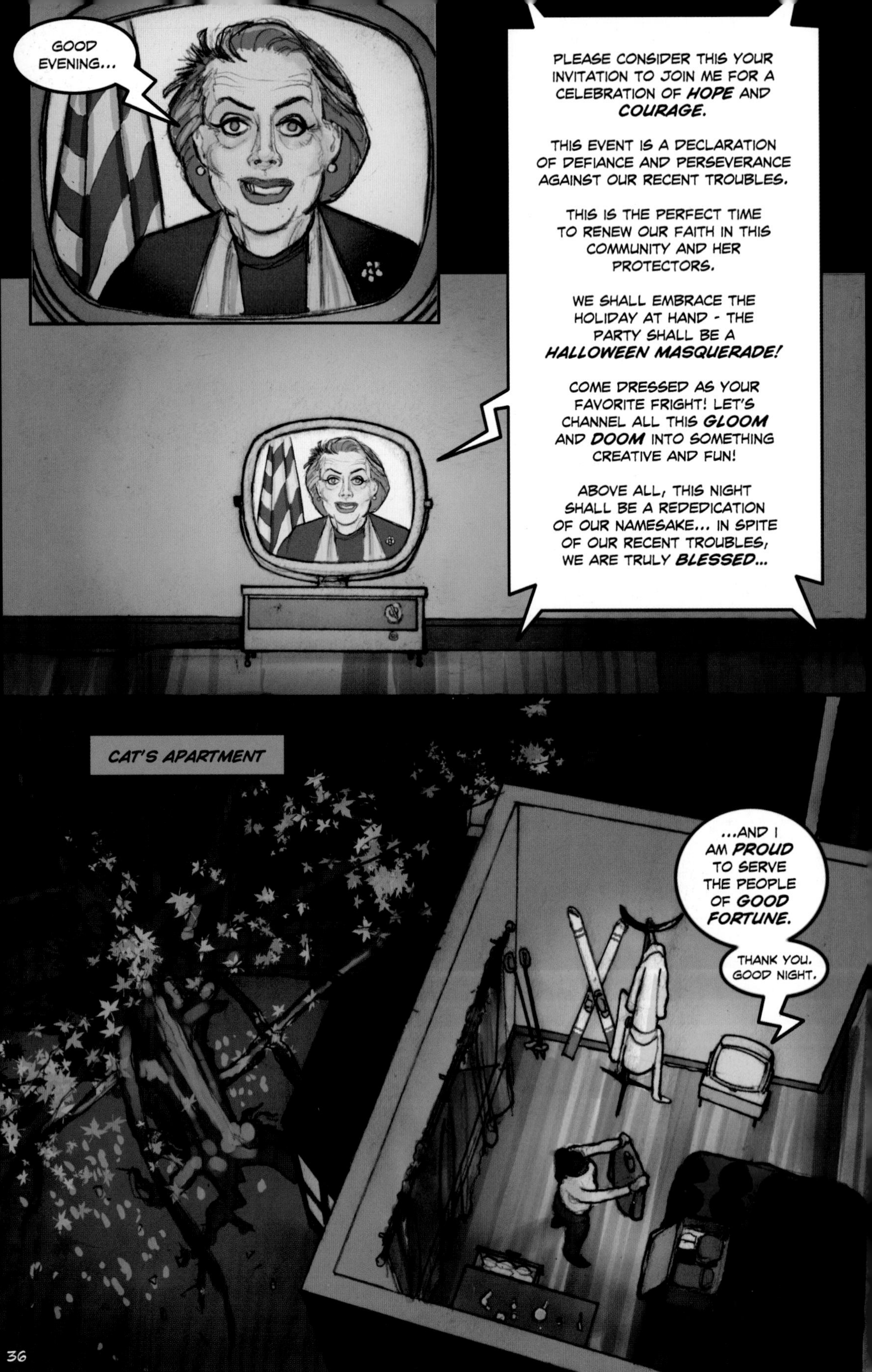
GOOD EVENING...
PLEASE CONSIDER THIS YOUR INVITATION TO JOIN ME FOR A CELEBRATION OF HOPE AND COURAGE.
THIS EVENT IS A DECLARATION OF DEFIANCE AND PERSEVERANCE AGAINST OUR RECENT TROUBLES.
THIS IS THE PERFECT TIME TO RENEW OUR FAITH IN THIS COMMUNITY AND HER PROTECTORS.
WE SHALL EMBRACE THE HOLIDAY AT HAND - THE PARTY SHALL BE A HALLOWEEN MASQUERADE!
COME DRESSED AS YOUR FAVORITE FRIGHT! LET'S CHANNEL ALL THIS GLOOM AND DOOM INTO SOMETHING CREATIVE AND FUN!
ABOVE ALL, THIS NIGHT SHALL BE A REDEDICATION OF OUR NAMESAKE... IN SPITE OF OUR RECENT TROUBLES, WE ARE TRULY BLESSED...
CAT'S APARTMENT
...AND I AM PROUD TO SERVE THE PEOPLE OF GOOD FORTUNE.
THANK YOU. GOOD NIGHT.

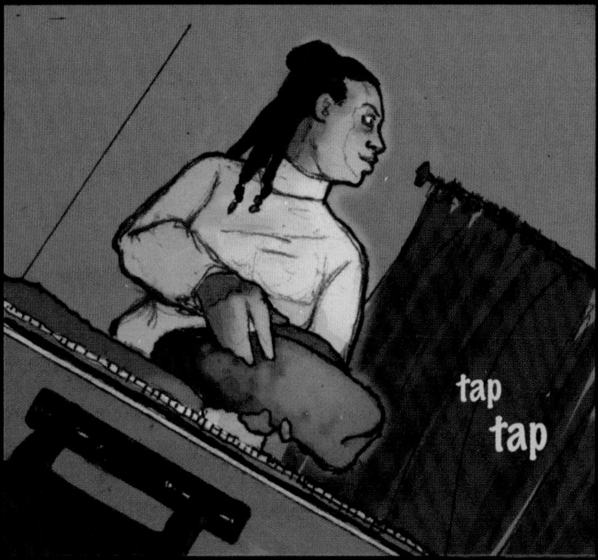
tap
tap

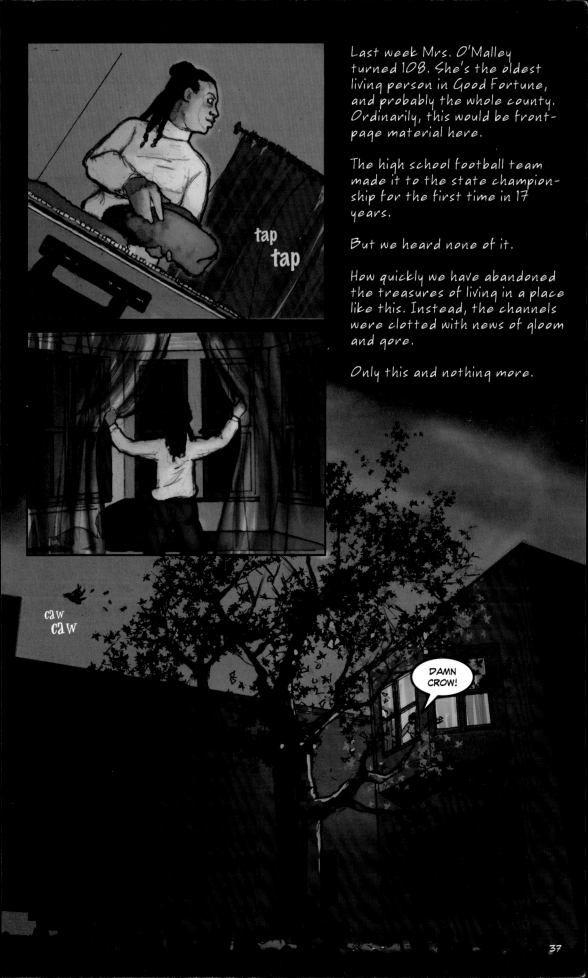

Last week Mrs. O'Malley turned 108. She's the oldest living person in Good Fortune, and probably the whole county. Ordinarily, this would be front-page material here.

The high school football team made it to the state championship for the first time in 17 years.

But we heard none of it.

How quickly we have abandoned the treasures of living in a place like this. Instead, the channels were clotted with news of gloom and gore.

Only this and nothing more.

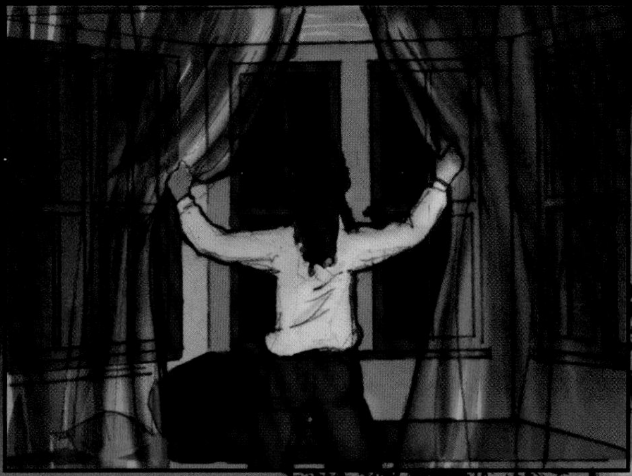

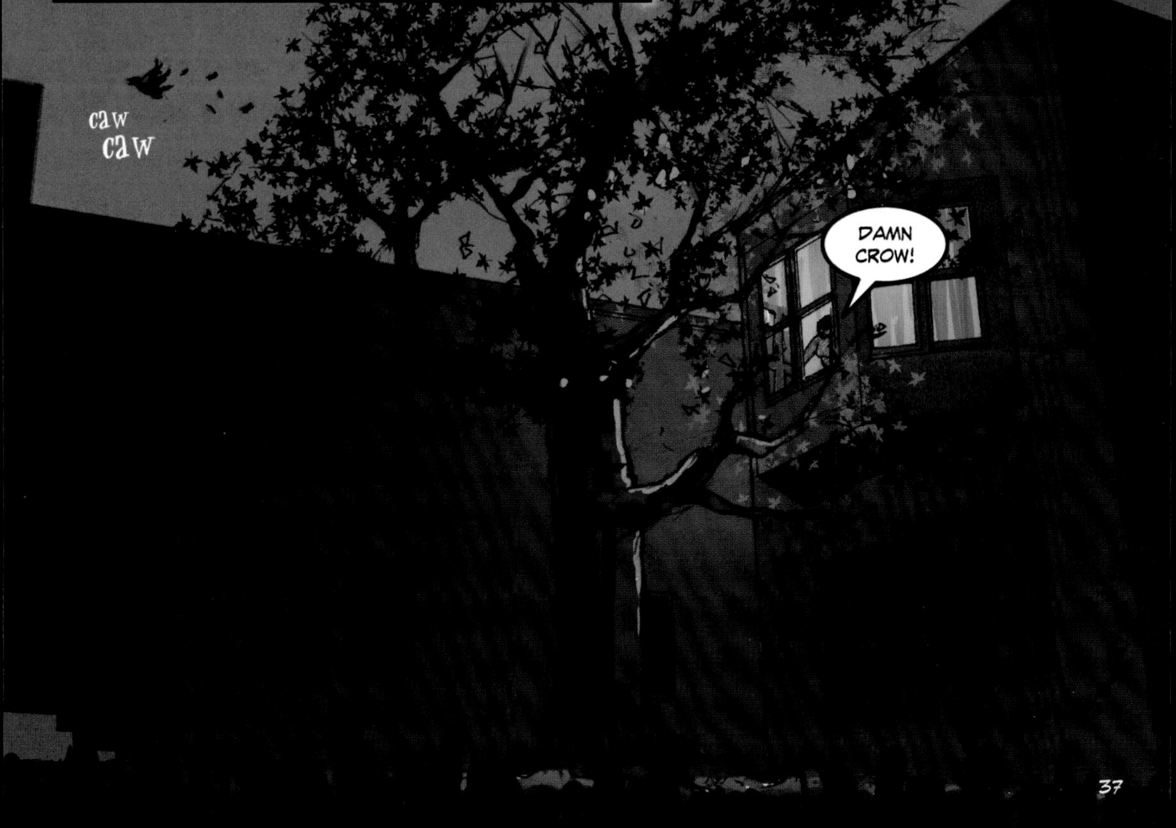
caw
caw
DAMN CROW!

I question how much **freedom** the monster has taken from us versus how much **power** we have willfully surrendered.

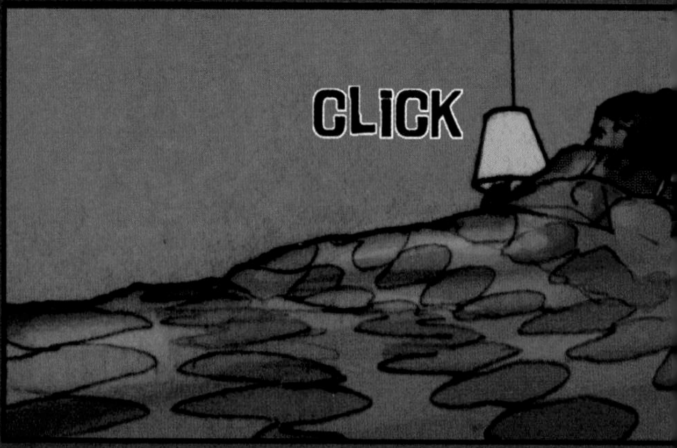
CLICK

I mean, is it our choice to live this way... paranoid, fearful, racist, selfish? I must believe that even in our darkest hour, we are capable of better.

From a very early age, I secured a romantic vision of fighting crime, and it has been an unexpected challenge to educate people about all their options - clearly and fairly.

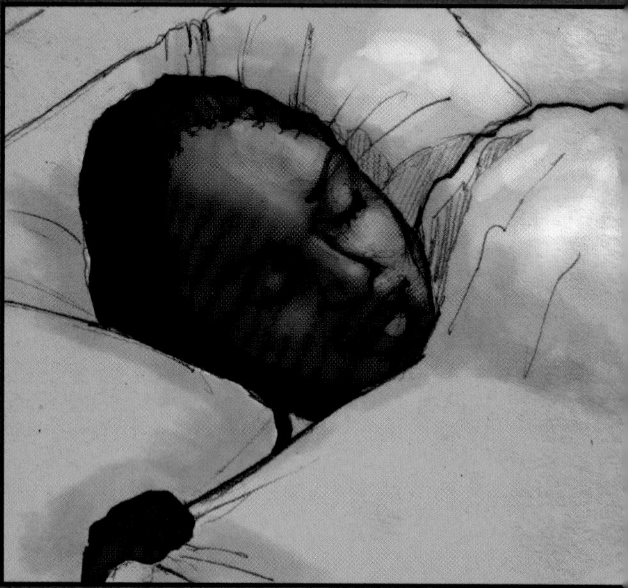

It is to my dismay, that in times of crisis, how unwilling people are **to listen**.

These things I have pondered in the inky black hours when all the world is sleeping. Maybe if I can at least manage to spare this one woman from the reaper's blade, I am, in effect, preserving that rare little bit that is right with the world.

Here lies someone who has a front-row ticket to the horror-show every day, yet still freely chooses to not let it invade her spirit or break her will.

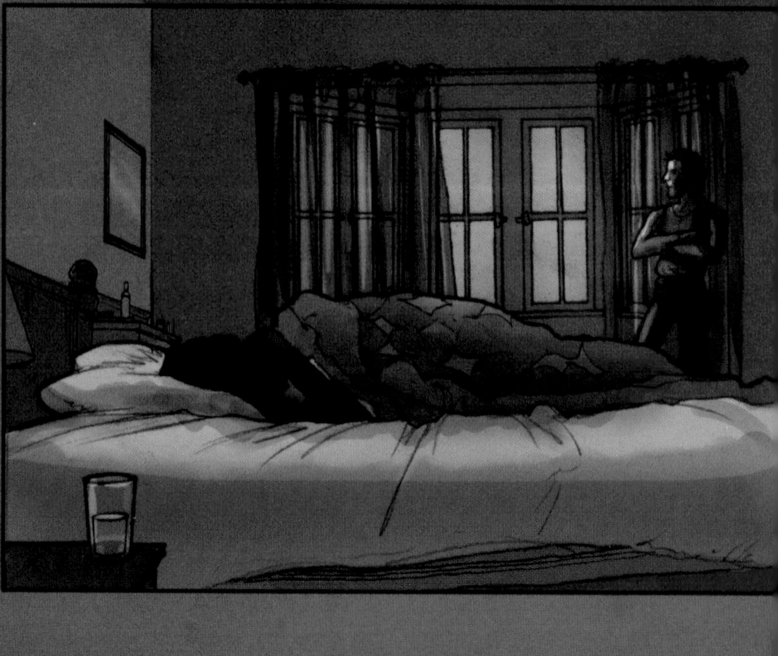

While the killer remains free to ravage the people of this town, I know if I can somehow manage to keep Cat safe - **everything is going to be okay.**

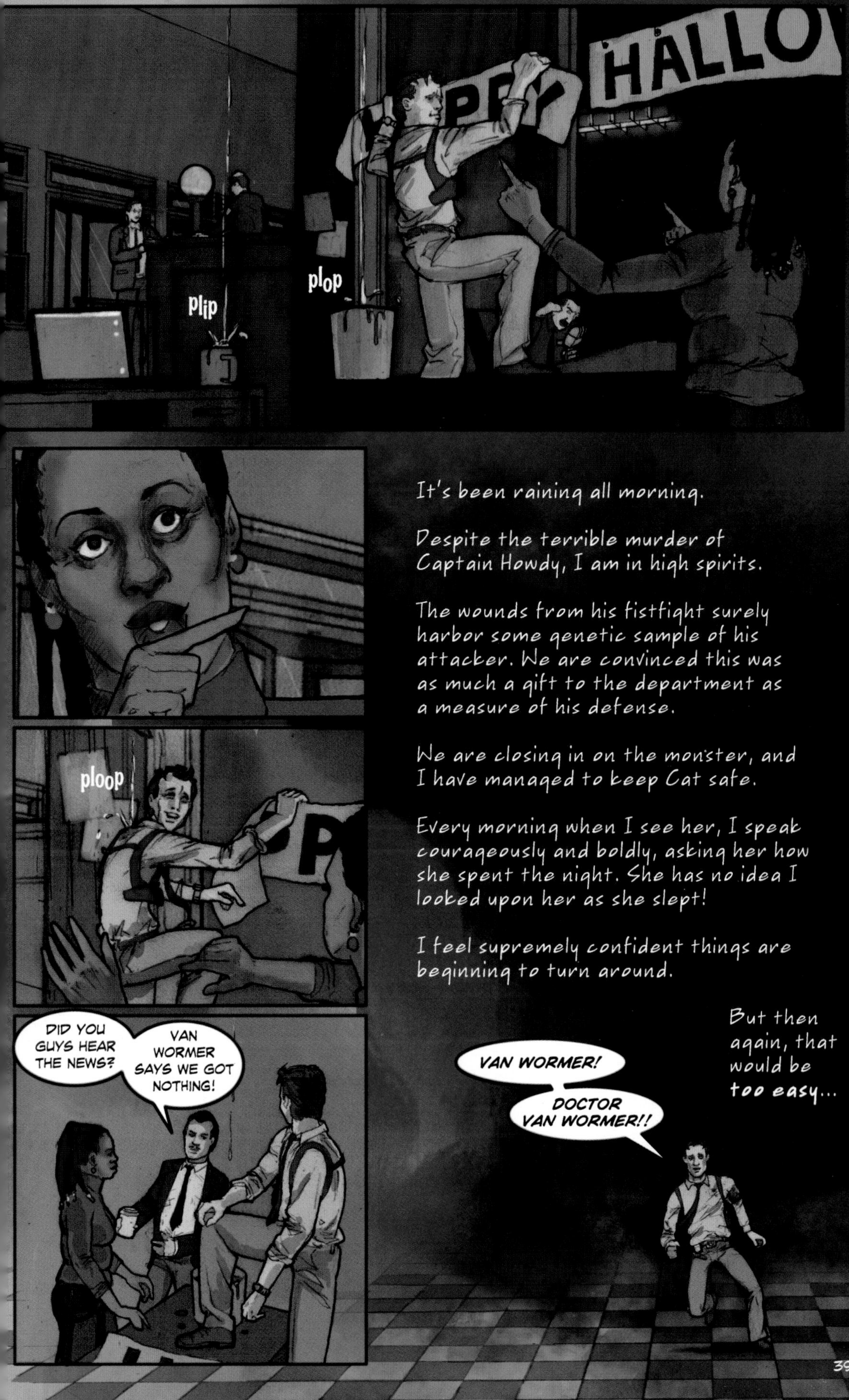
HALLO
plip
plop
It's been raining all morning.
Despite the terrible murder of Captain Howdy, I am in high spirits.
The wounds from his fistfight surely harbor some genetic sample of his attacker. We are convinced this was as much a gift to the department as a measure of his defense.
We are closing in on the monster, and I have managed to keep Cat safe.
ploop
Every morning when I see her, I speak courageously and boldly, asking her how she spent the night. She has no idea I looked upon her as she slept!
I feel supremely confident things are beginning to turn around.
DID YOU GUYS HEAR THE NEWS?
VAN WORMER SAYS WE GOT NOTHING!
But then again, that would be **too easy**...
VAN WORMER!
DOCTOR VAN WORMER!!

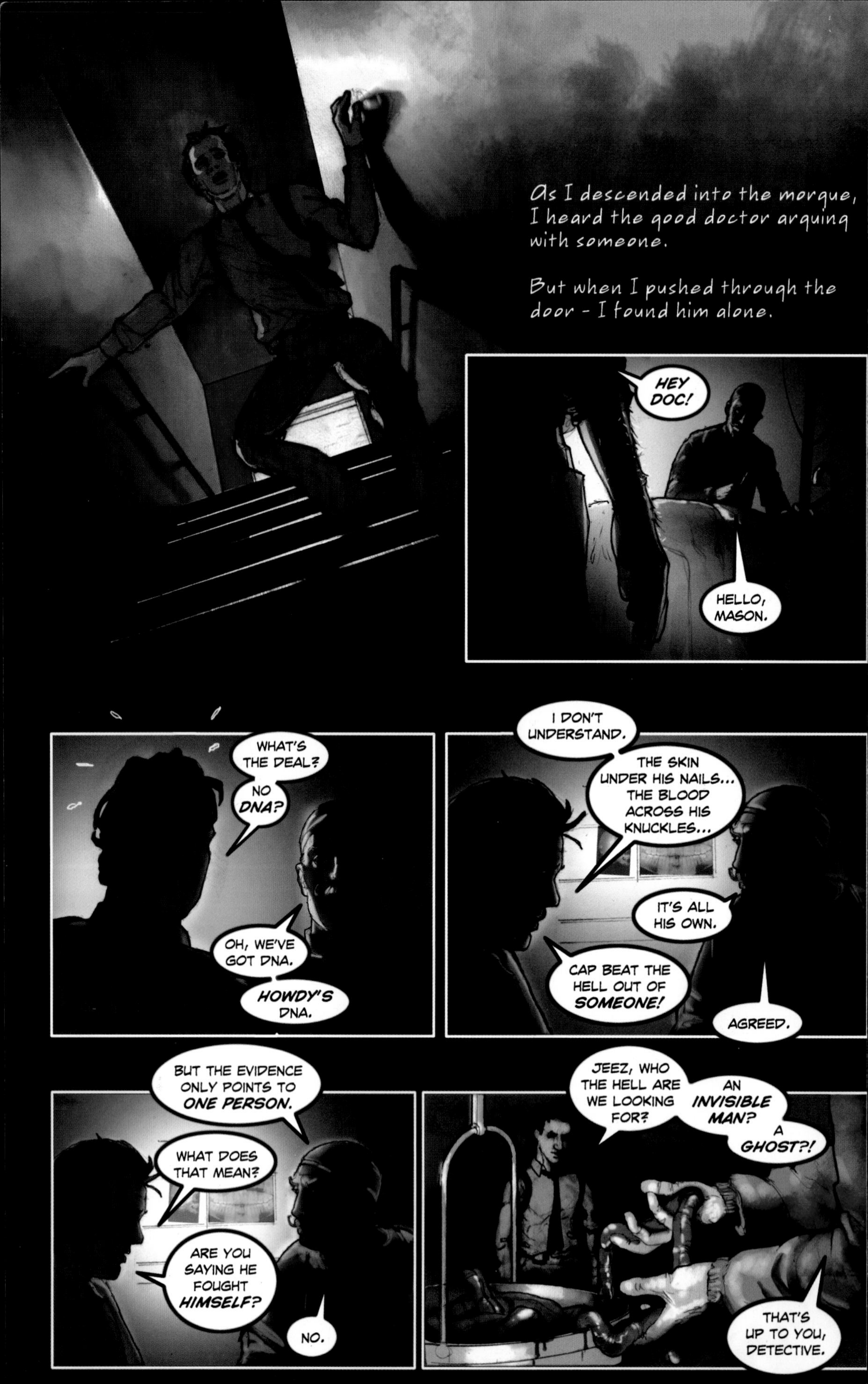
As I descended into the morgue, I heard the good doctor arguing with someone.
But when I pushed through the door - I found him alone.
HEY DOC!
HELLO, MASON.
WHAT'S THE DEAL?
NO DNA?
OH, WE'VE GOT DNA.
HOWDY'S DNA.
I DON'T UNDERSTAND.
THE SKIN UNDER HIS NAILS... THE BLOOD ACROSS HIS KNUCKLES...
IT'S ALL HIS OWN.
CAP BEAT THE HELL OUT OF SOMEONE!
AGREED.
BUT THE EVIDENCE ONLY POINTS TO ONE PERSON.
WHAT DOES THAT MEAN?
ARE YOU SAYING HE FOUGHT HIMSELF?
NO.
JEEZ, WHO THE HELL ARE WE LOOKING FOR?
AN INVISIBLE MAN?
A GHOST?!
THAT'S UP TO YOU, DETECTIVE.

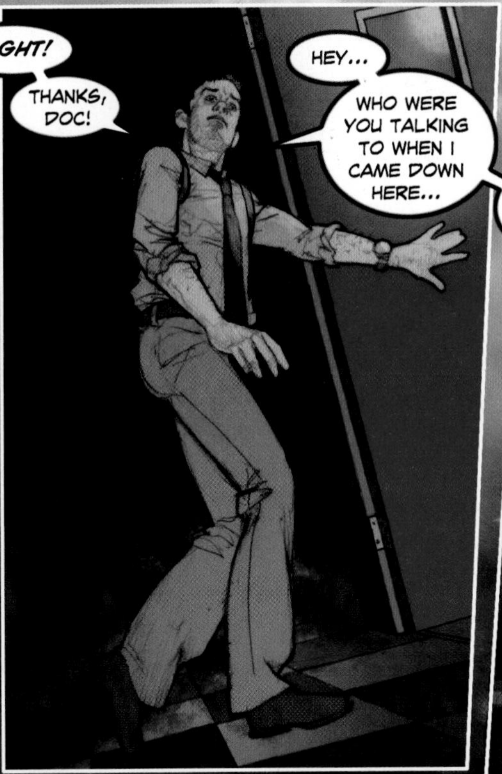
RIGHT!
THANKS, DOC!
HEY...
WHO WERE YOU TALKING TO WHEN I CAME DOWN HERE...
YOU'RE ALONE.

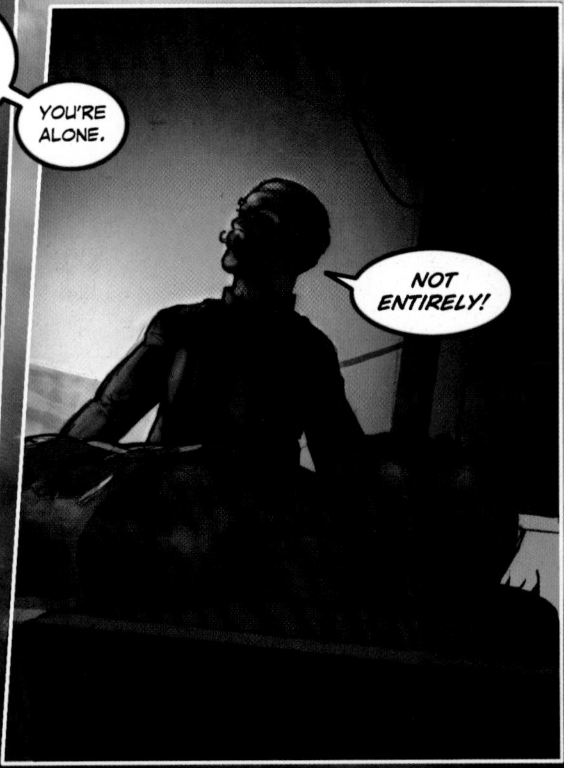
NOT ENTIRELY!

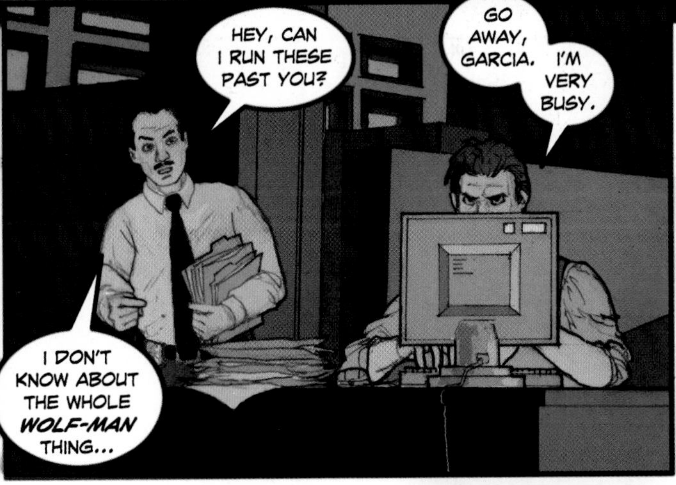
HEY, CAN I RUN THESE PAST YOU?
GO AWAY, GARCIA.
I'M VERY BUSY.
I DON'T KNOW ABOUT THE WHOLE WOLF-MAN THING...

So in the meantime, our investigation proceeded, if not always with good judgement.

Numerous individuals were examined with no purpose. Public anxiety continued to fester, mostly due to the continuous **absence** of **any** clues to this mystery.

Many of the most energetic on the case were relaxing their exertions and yielding to distraction.

More and more bitterly did I perceive the futility of our efforts.

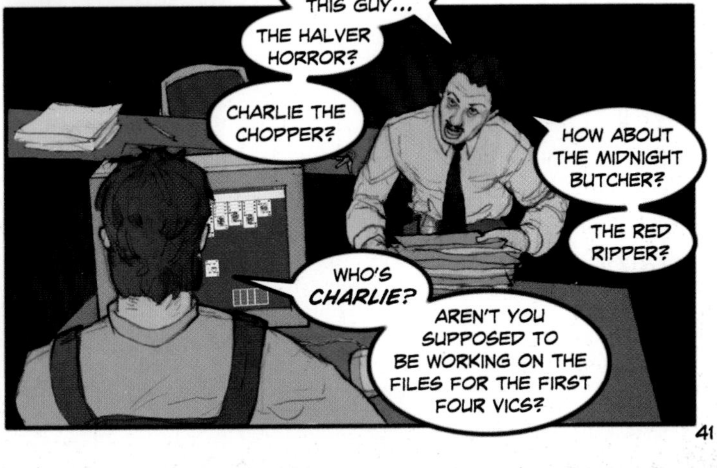
BUT WE NEED A NAME FOR THIS GUY...
THE HALVER HORROR?
CHARLIE THE CHOPPER?
HOW ABOUT THE MIDNIGHT BUTCHER?
THE RED RIPPER?
WHO'S CHARLIE?
AREN'T YOU SUPPOSED TO BE WORKING ON THE FILES FOR THE FIRST FOUR VICS?

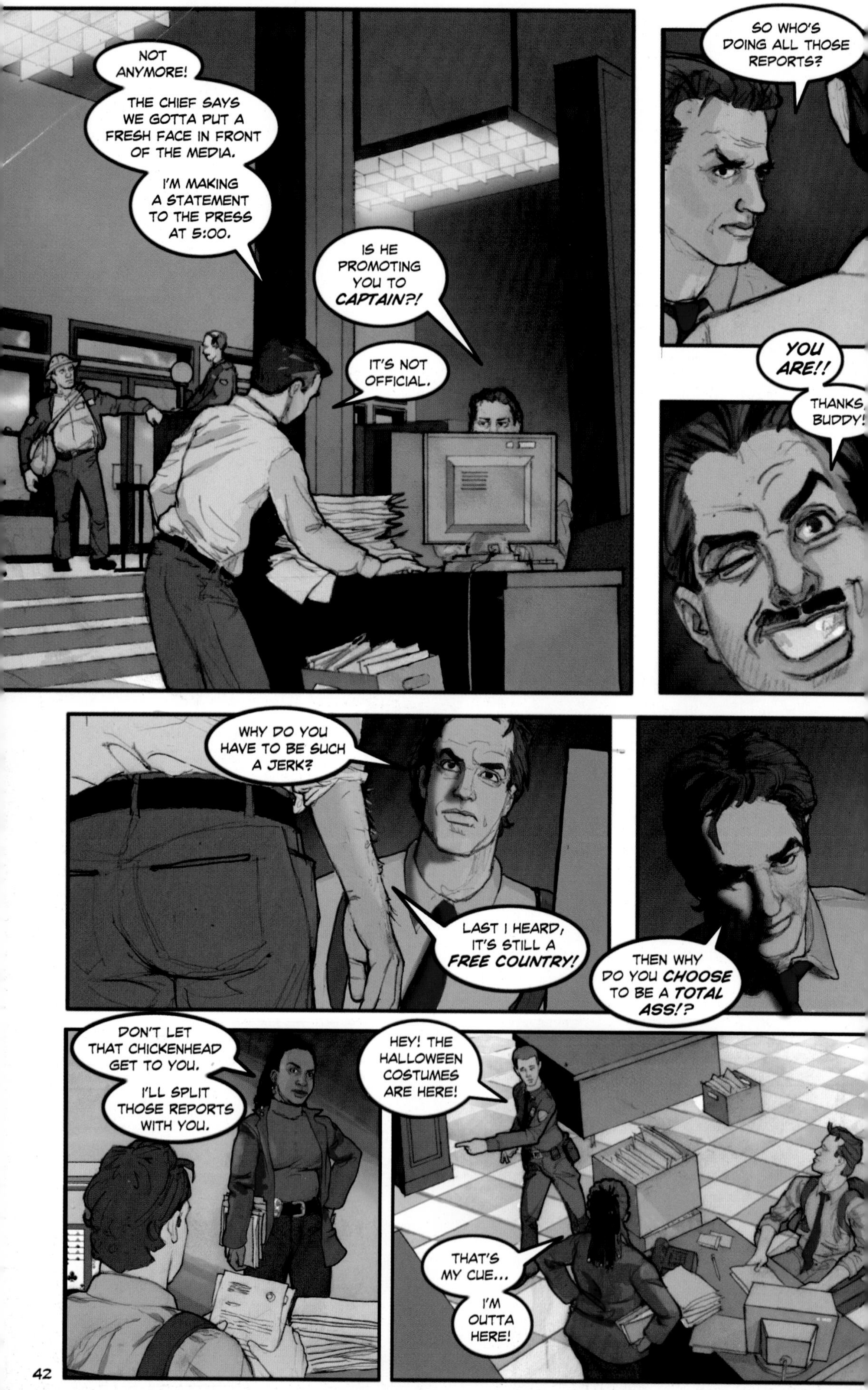
NOT ANYMORE!
THE CHIEF SAYS WE GOTTA PUT A FRESH FACE IN FRONT OF THE MEDIA.
I'M MAKING A STATEMENT TO THE PRESS AT 5:00.
IS HE PROMOTING YOU TO CAPTAIN?!
IT'S NOT OFFICIAL.
SO WHO'S DOING ALL THOSE REPORTS?
YOU ARE!!
THANKS, BUDDY!
WHY DO YOU HAVE TO BE SUCH A JERK?
LAST I HEARD, IT'S STILL A FREE COUNTRY!
THEN WHY DO YOU CHOOSE TO BE A TOTAL ASS!?
DON'T LET THAT CHICKENHEAD GET TO YOU.
I'LL SPLIT THOSE REPORTS WITH YOU.
HEY! THE HALLOWEEN COSTUMES ARE HERE!
THAT'S MY CUE...
I'M OUTTA HERE!

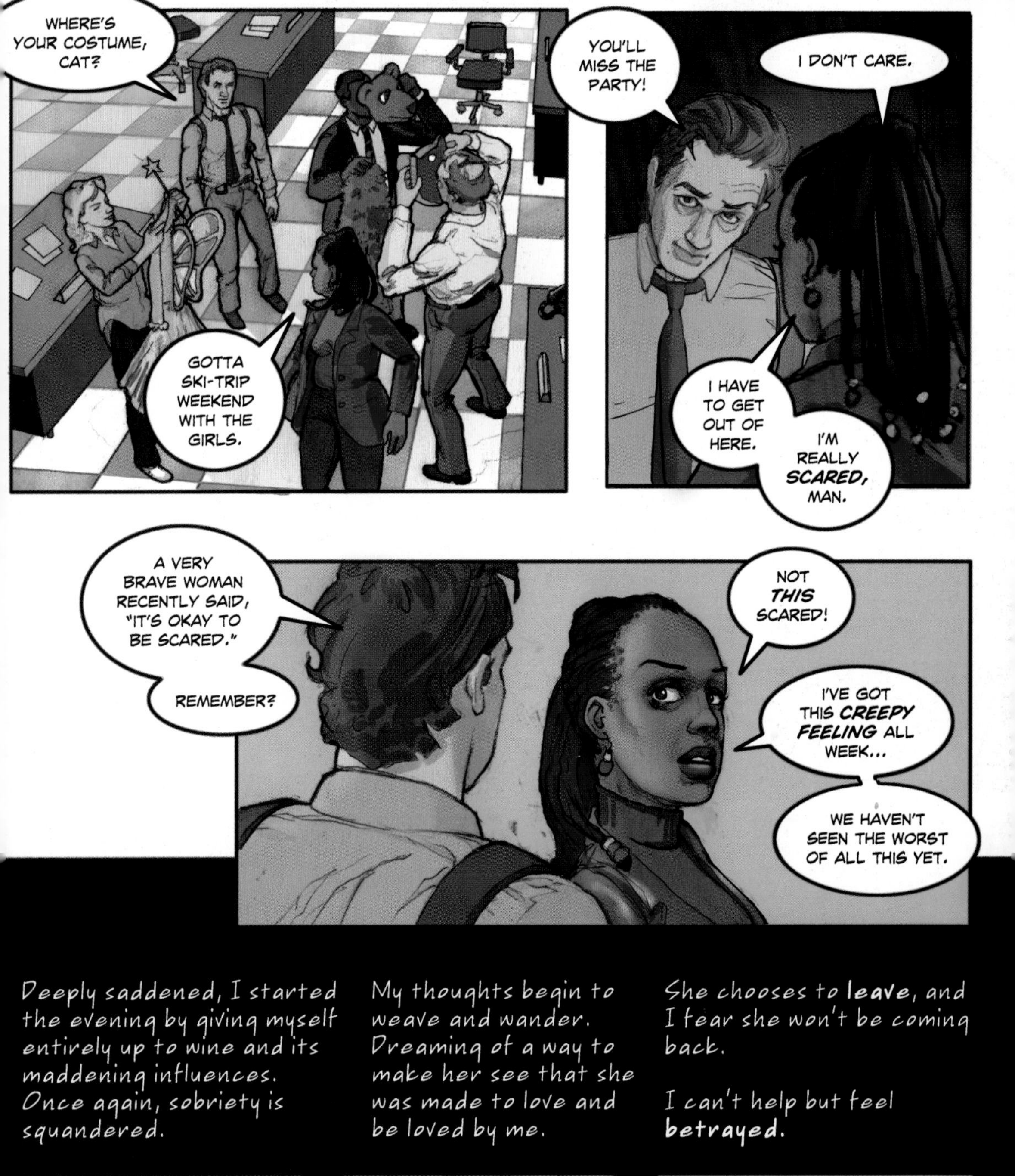
WHERE'S YOUR COSTUME, CAT?
GOTTA SKI-TRIP WEEKEND WITH THE GIRLS.
YOU'LL MISS THE PARTY!
I DON'T CARE.
I HAVE TO GET OUT OF HERE.
I'M REALLY **SCARED,** MAN.
A VERY BRAVE WOMAN RECENTLY SAID, "IT'S OKAY TO BE SCARED."
REMEMBER?
NOT ***THIS*** SCARED!
I'VE GOT THIS ***CREEPY FEELING*** ALL WEEK...
WE HAVEN'T SEEN THE WORST OF ALL THIS YET.

Deeply saddened, I started the evening by giving myself entirely up to wine and its maddening influences. Once again, sobriety is squandered.

My thoughts begin to weave and wander. Dreaming of a way to make her see that she was made to love and be loved by me.

She chooses to **leave**, and I fear she won't be coming back.

I can't help but feel **betrayed.**

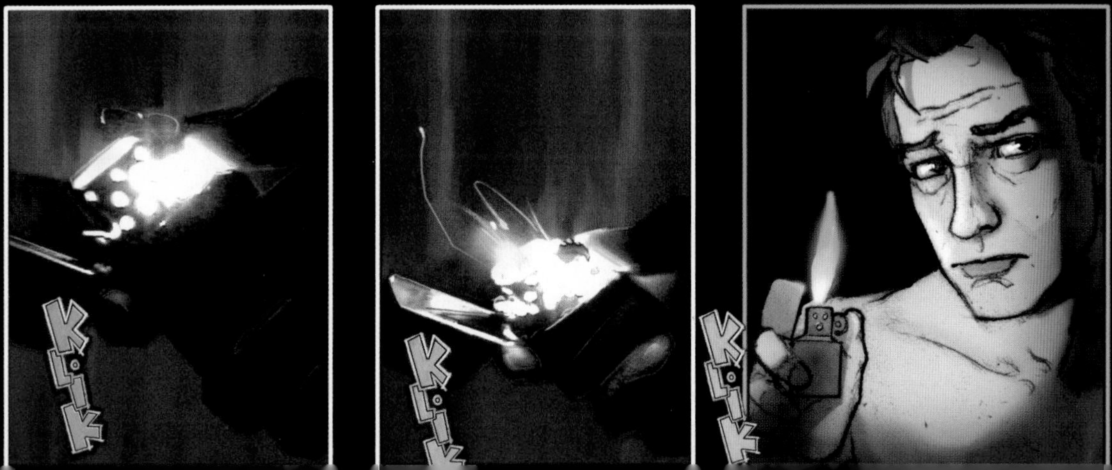
KLIK
KLIK
KLIK

Tonight is a good night for a story.

How 'bout one with **a witch**.

I pass many long and unwearied hours watching
my fitful flame throw shadows on the wall. Like
puppets performing as best they're able
to tell an old greek fable
or some dark tale of
forgotten lore.

Suddenly - I hear a noise
just outside the door.

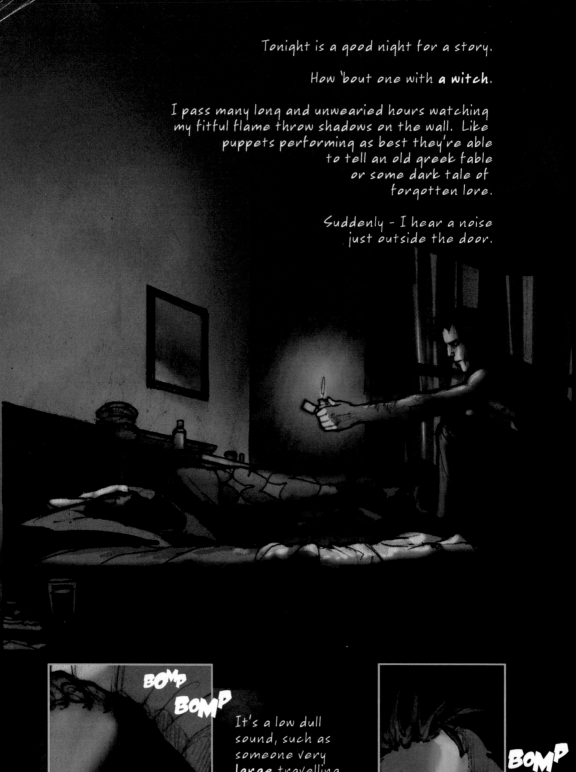

BOMP
BOMP

It's a low dull
sound, such as
someone very
large travelling
a staircase.

My pulse
quickens - for I
know **immediately**
who it is.

At last - the
hour has come!

BOMP
BOMP

BOMP

BOMP

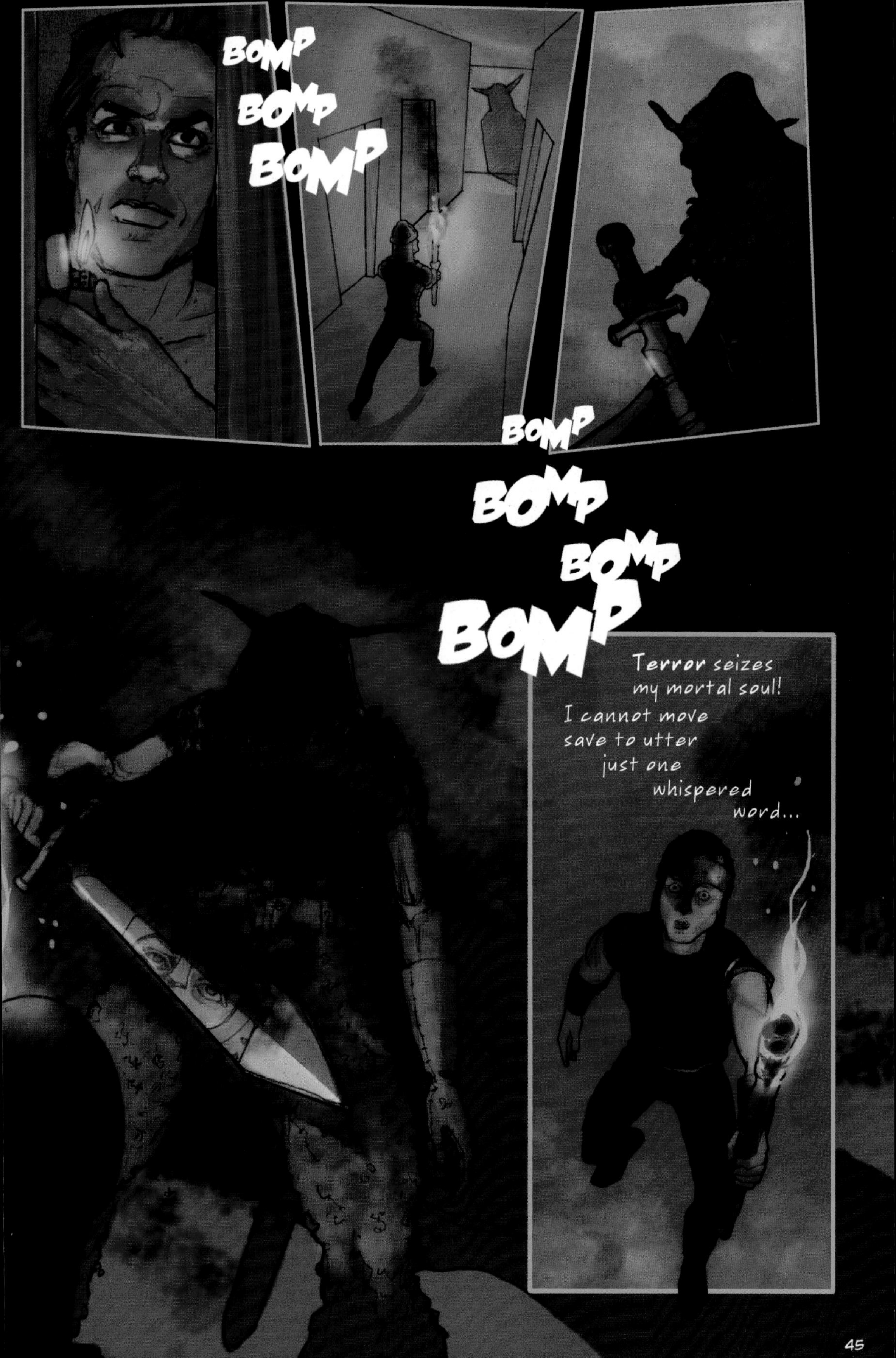
BOMP
BOMP
BOMP
BOMP
BOMP
BOMP
BOMP
Terror seizes my mortal soul! I cannot move save to utter just one whispered word...

AAAAAAHHHHH!

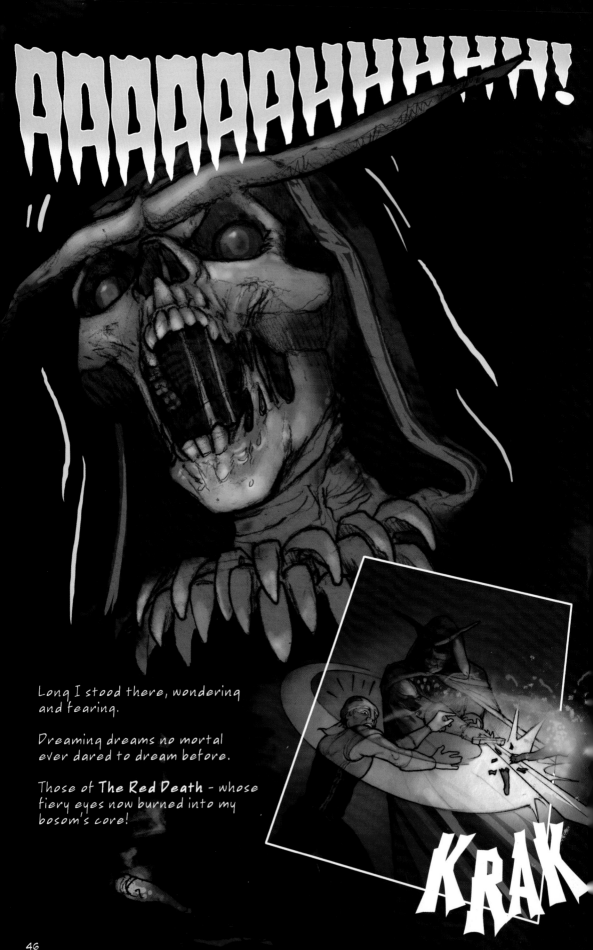

Long I stood there, wondering and fearing.

Dreaming dreams no mortal ever dared to dream before.

Those of **The Red Death** - whose fiery eyes now burned into my bosom's core!

KRAK

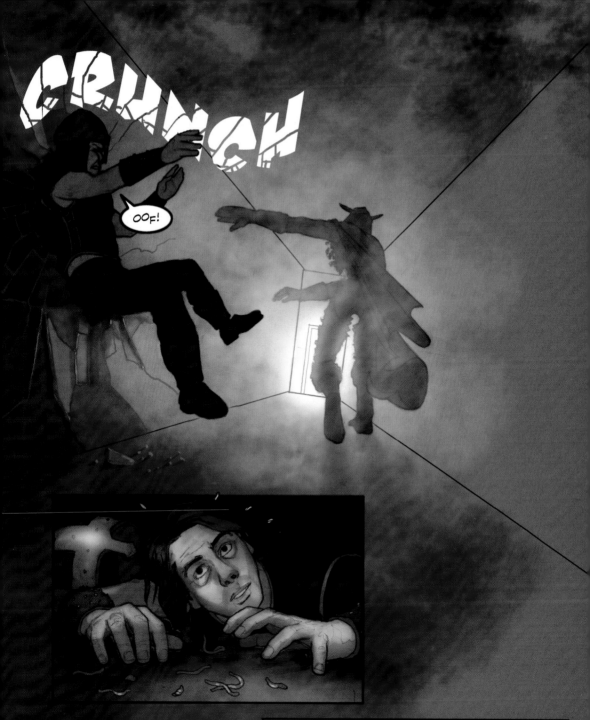

I was foolish to believe I was strong enough. He disarmed me effortlessly and immediately.

He continues down the hall in a deliberate cantor that runs in time with the beating of my own thunderous heart. He is clearly intending to cut her apart.

I must improvise a better defense!

BREAK GLASS IN CASE OF EMERGENCY

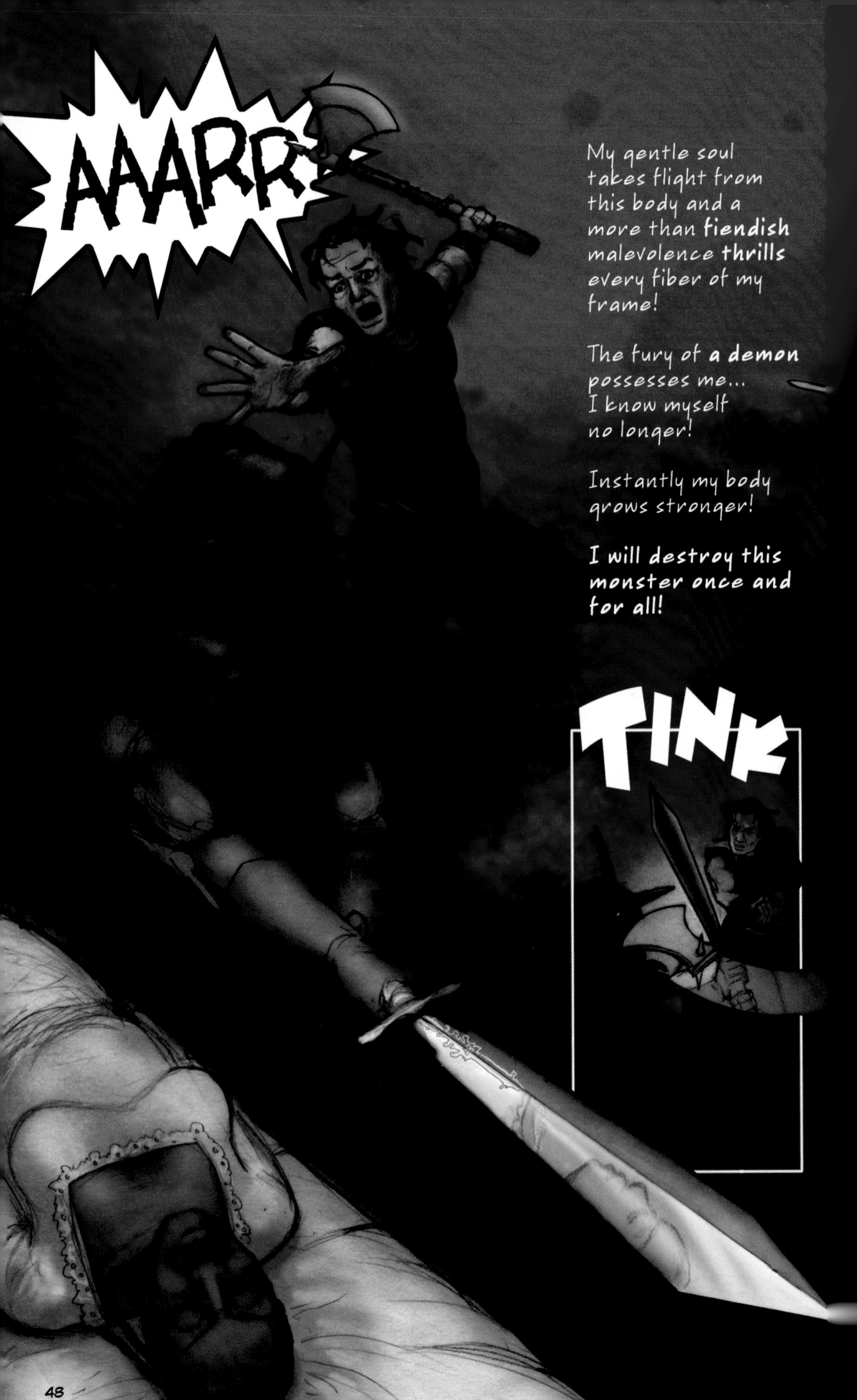
AAARR
My gentle soul takes flight from this body and a more than **fiendish** malevolence **thrills** every fiber of my frame!
The fury of **a demon** possesses me... I know myself no longer!
Instantly my body grows stronger!
I will destroy this monster once and for all!
TINK

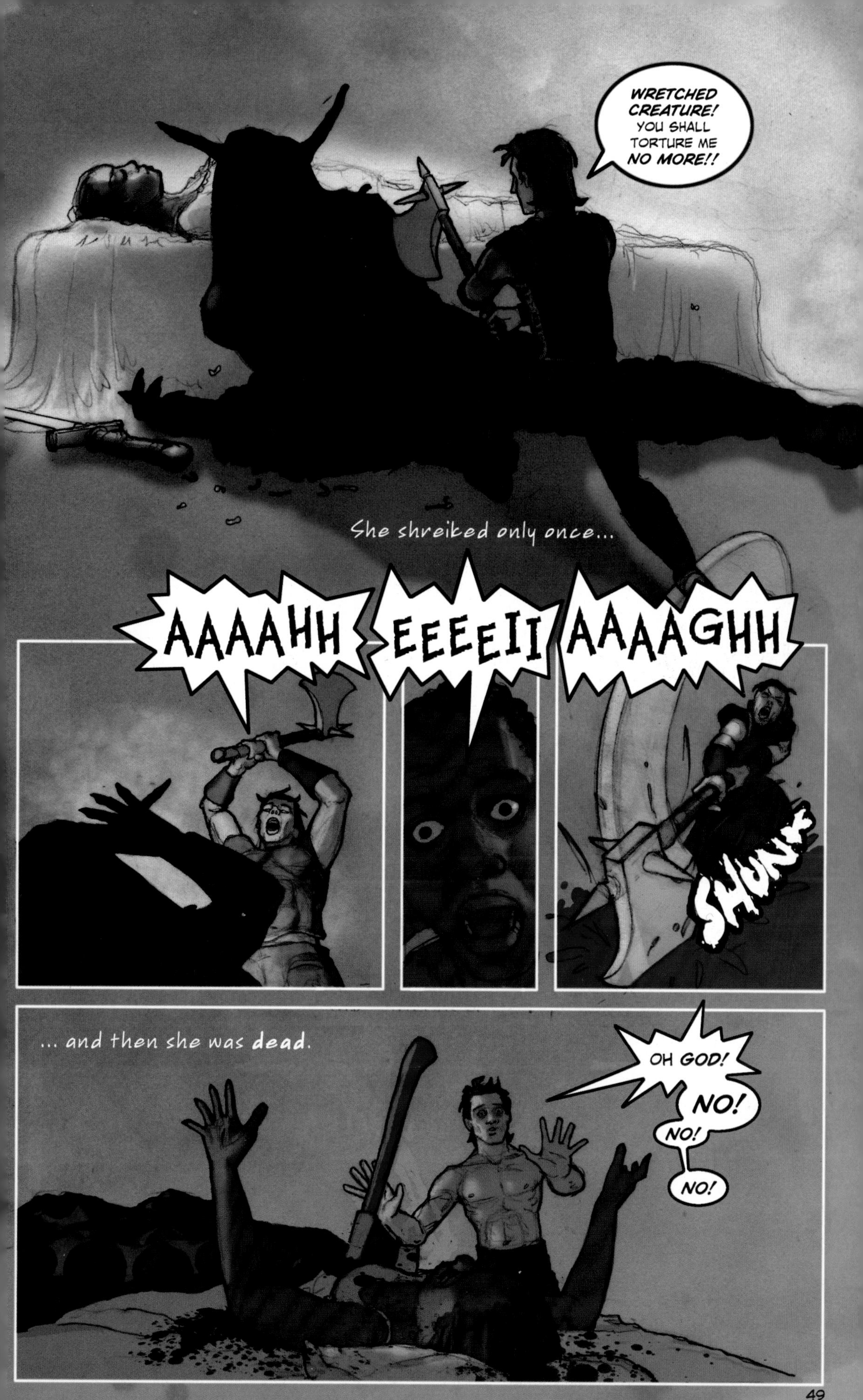
WRETCHED CREATURE! YOU SHALL TORTURE ME NO MORE!!
She shreiked only once...
AAAAHH
EEEEII
AAAAGHH
SHUNK
... and then she was dead.
OH GOD!
NO!
NO!
NO!

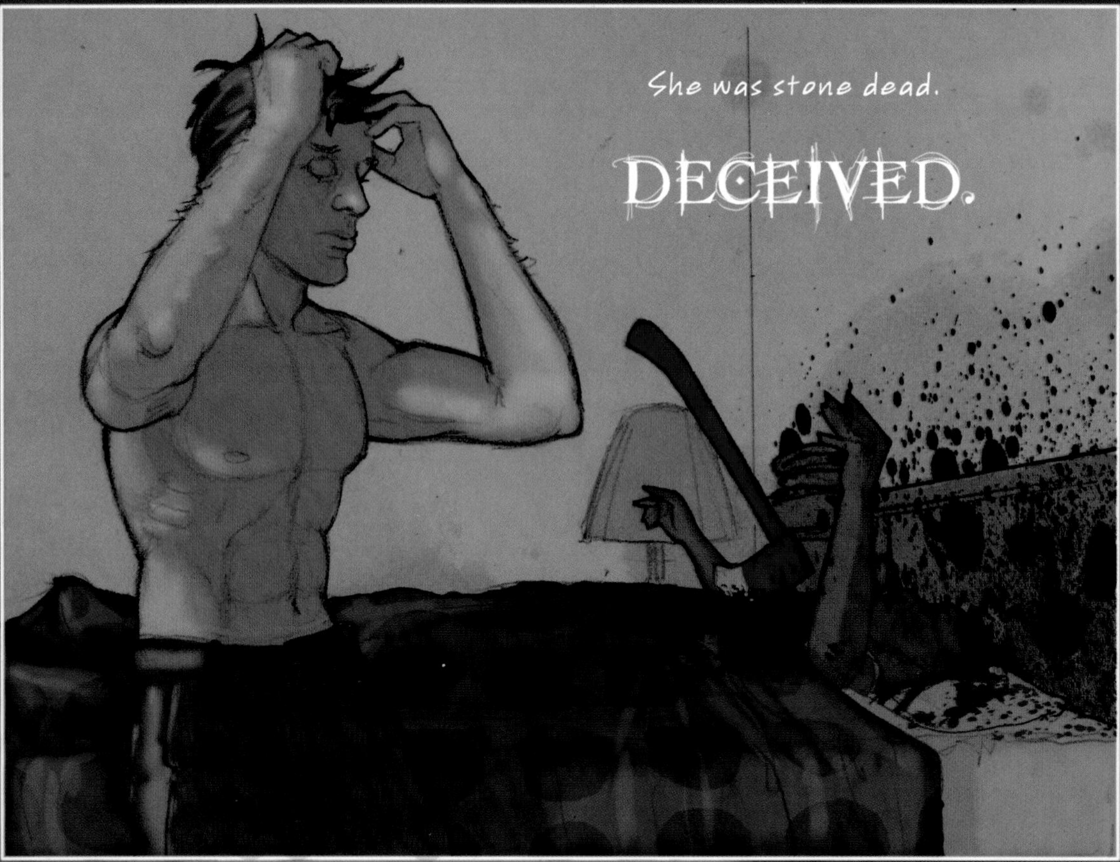
She was stone dead.
DECEIVED.

Fooled again.

Wild thoughts escape - not of chasing The Red Death, but of protecting my own self.

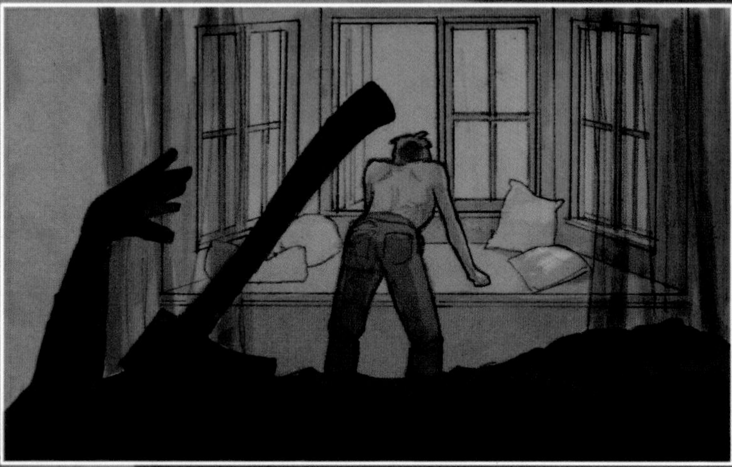

Because this mystery has taken a turn, and **the truth** is quite clear.

If I tried to tell **anyone** this story... it would be the **craziest** thing they've ever heard.

No one would believe The Red Death keeps flipping me the bird!

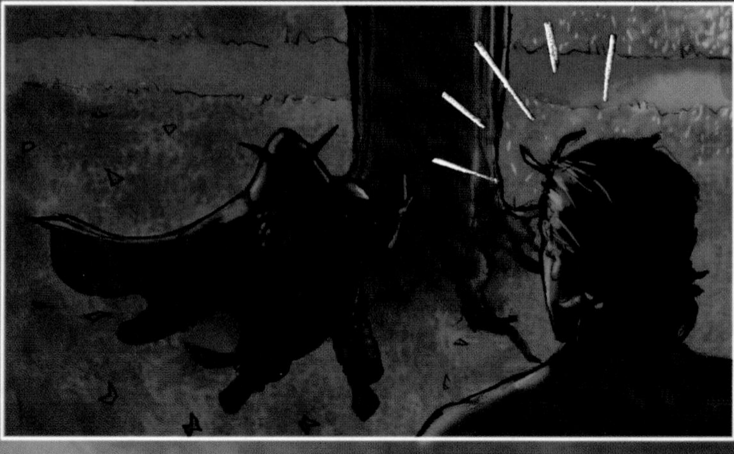

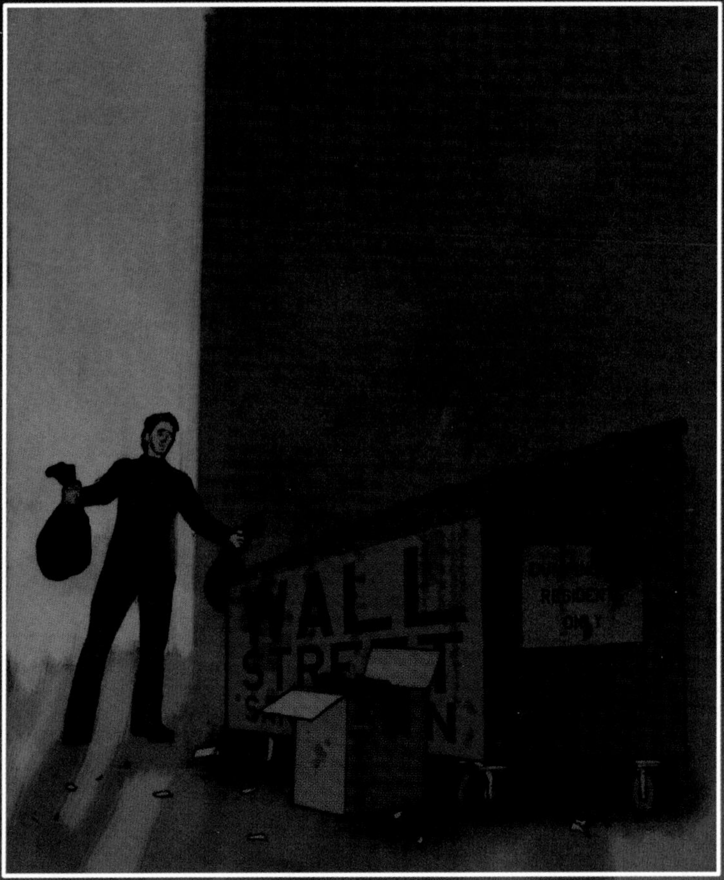

First, there is the matter of disposing **the corpse.** The hallways are teeming with the comings and goings of the other tenants, as tonight is the mayor's party.

I cannot remove it from the apartment without risk of being observed.

So I dismembered the body.

I cut off the head and the arms and the legs. Then I severed the torso in two.

Also, there was the matter of the bedroom. I replaced the bedding with fresh linens and used the soiled sheets to wrap her remains.

I scrubbed and washed the rest of the room so there was no stain of any kind. When I finished, there were no blood spots whatsoever!

The dumpster would soon enough be retreived and hauled far away. It would be a long while - if ever- she would be discovered.

She is believed to be skiing, it would be **days** before she is even missed.

May God forgive me.

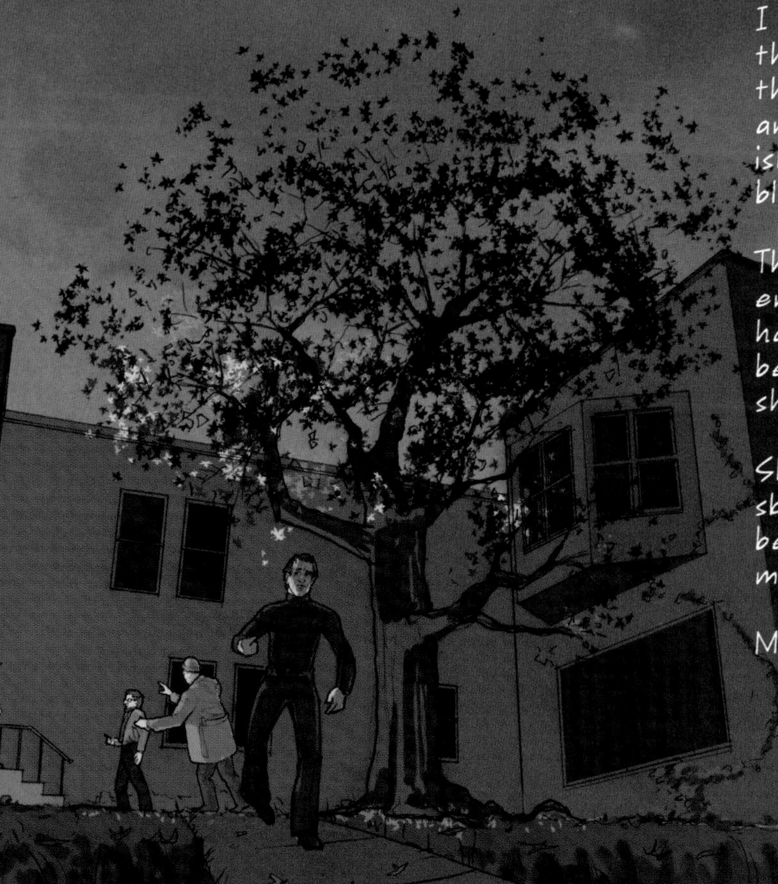

chapter three

A grand affair.

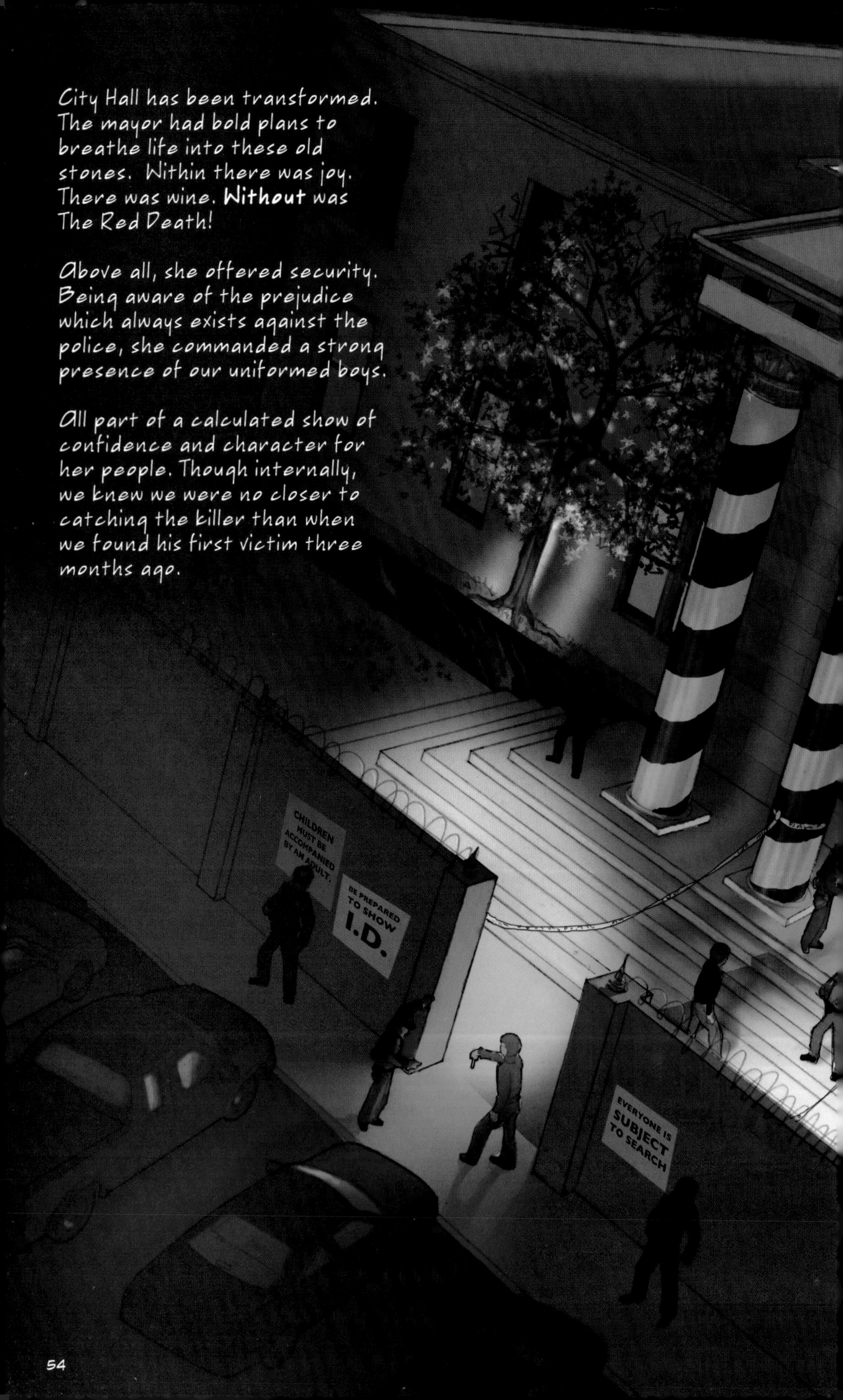
City Hall has been transformed. The mayor had bold plans to breathe life into these old stones. Within there was joy. There was wine. **Without** was The Red Death!
Above all, she offered security. Being aware of the prejudice which always exists against the police, she commanded a strong presence of our uniformed boys.
All part of a calculated show of confidence and character for her people. Though internally, we knew we were no closer to catching the killer than when we found his first victim three months ago.
CHILDREN MUST BE ACCOMPANIED BY AN ADULT.
BE PREPARED TO SHOW I.D.
EVERYONE IS SUBJECT TO SEARCH

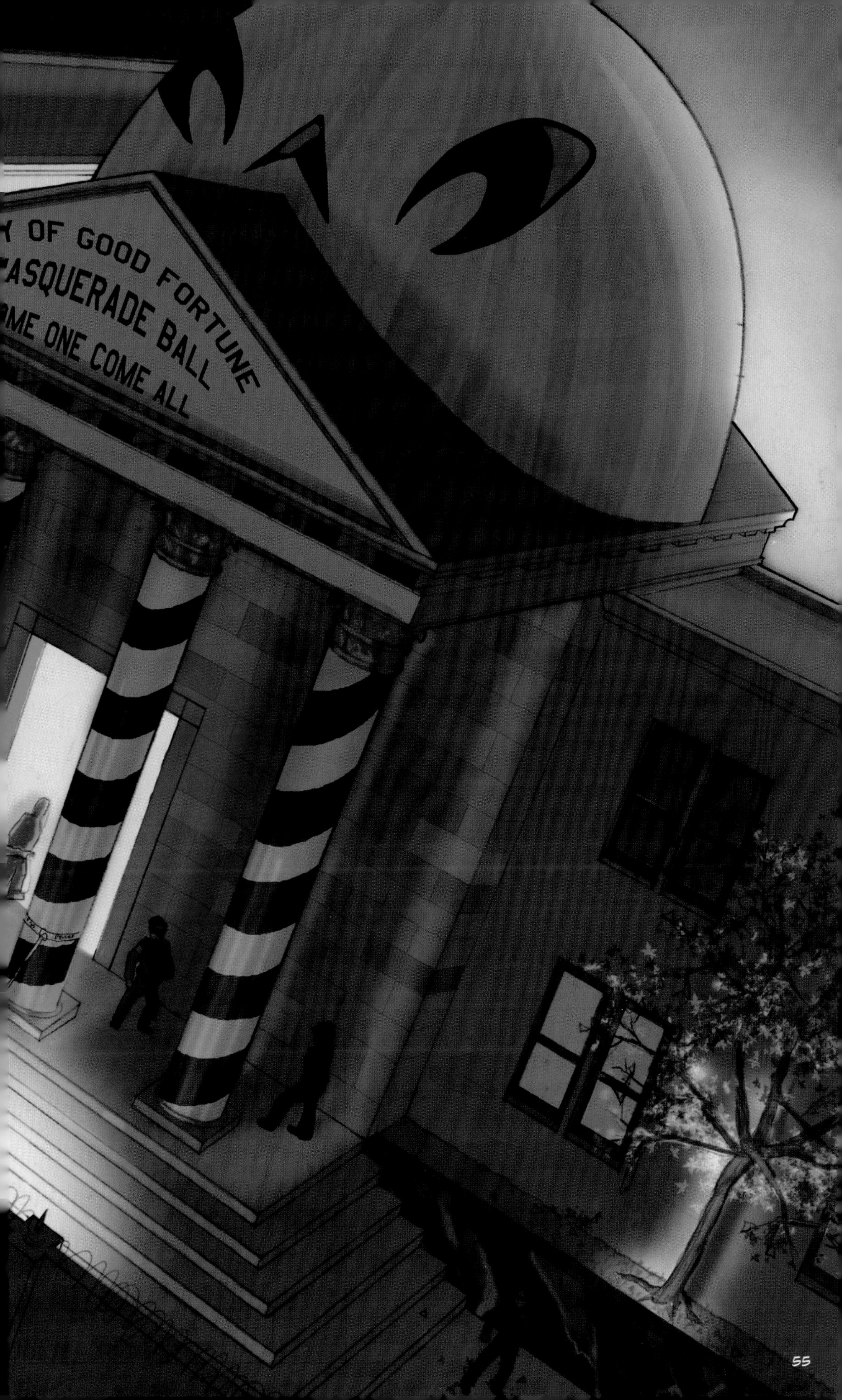

Y OF GOOD FORTUNE
ASQUERADE BALL
ME ONE COME ALL

Within the safety of this impenetrable womb beats the heart of human life. My pulse quickens and soon runs in time with the thundering drums. I can already feel myself reviving by sure degrees. Amazing!

True to her word, the mayor has provided all the vices of **pleasure**...

Above all, **spirits** were in no short supply. There were busty beer maidens and exotic fire-eaters. The young ones transformed into trick-or-treaters.

There were games that measured skill and luck. They dined on tender angus and roasted duck.

There were homemade pies and lemon tarts. Songs by the Junior League Performing Arts.

The occassion seems to have been embraced whole-heartedly by the community.

Above all, there was an **energy** - a ravenous desire to **live** and be **free**.

This is the Good Fortune that is so dear to me.

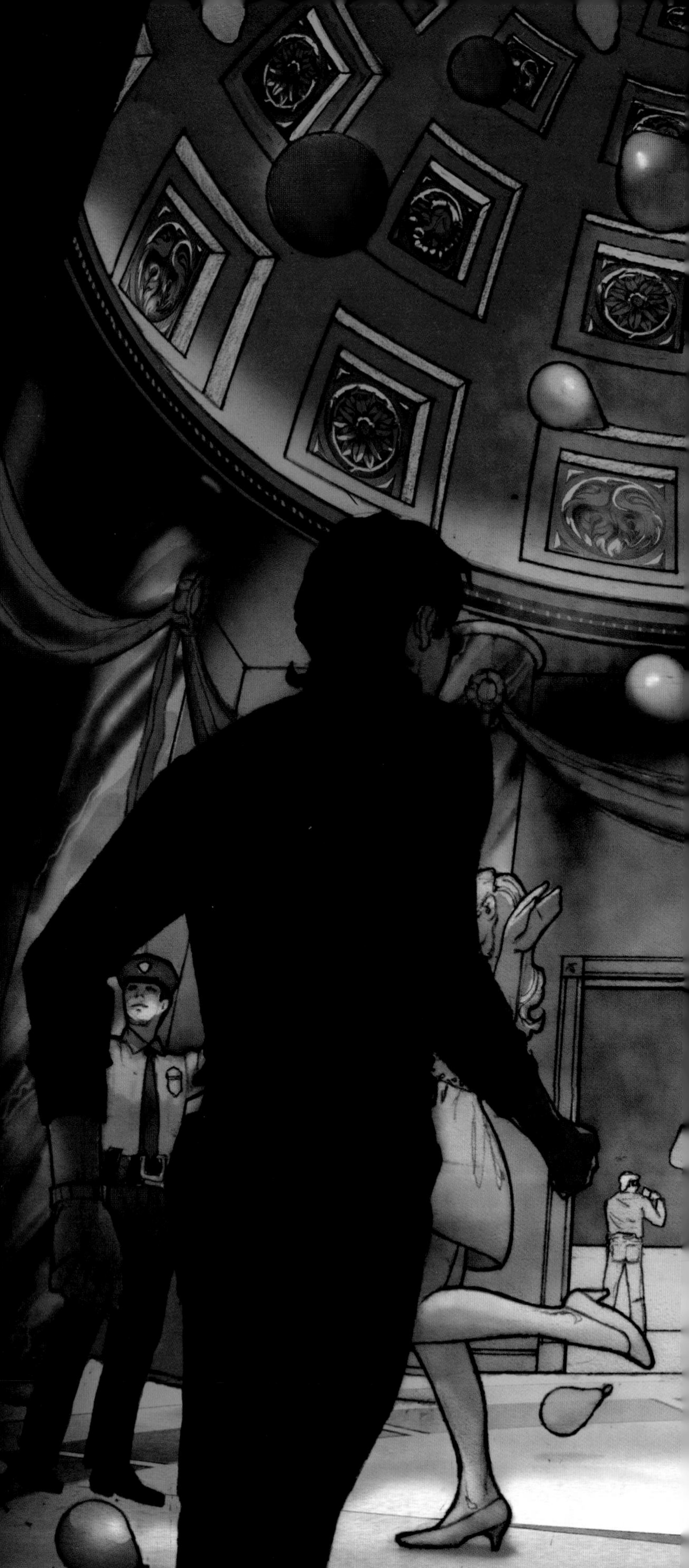

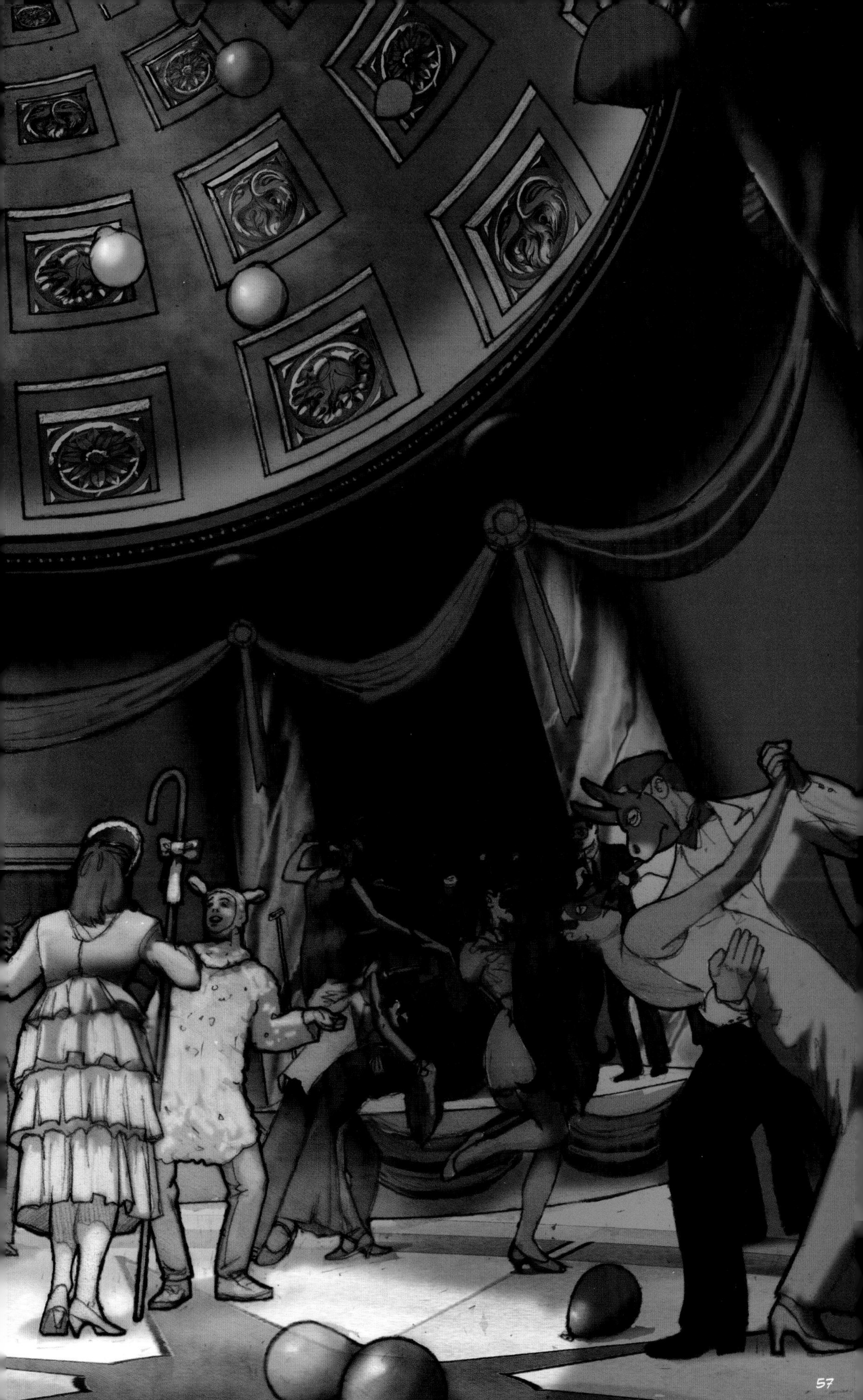

Yes, I am experiencing a sentiment of sorrow, and horror - for my unforgivable deed, but I think my soul remains **largely untouched**.

After all, I **was tricked**!

And it would be folly to grieve now! Everything will be put on hold for the rest of the night, and I set out to enjoy the pleasures of the party.

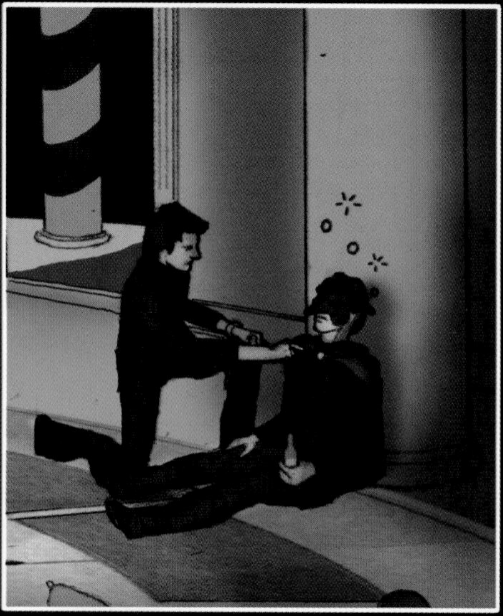

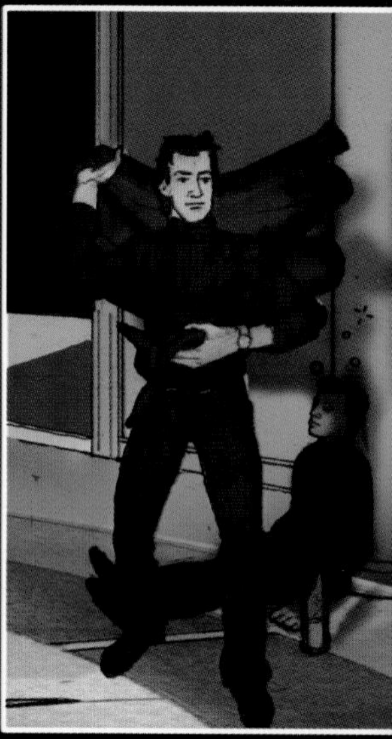

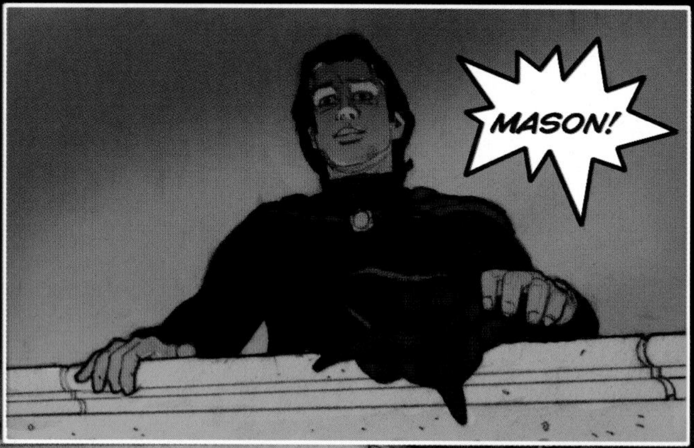
MASON!

It is at this point a familiar voice rings in my ears. I can feel his vulture eyes on my body and the tiny hairs on the back of my neck erect themselves on end....

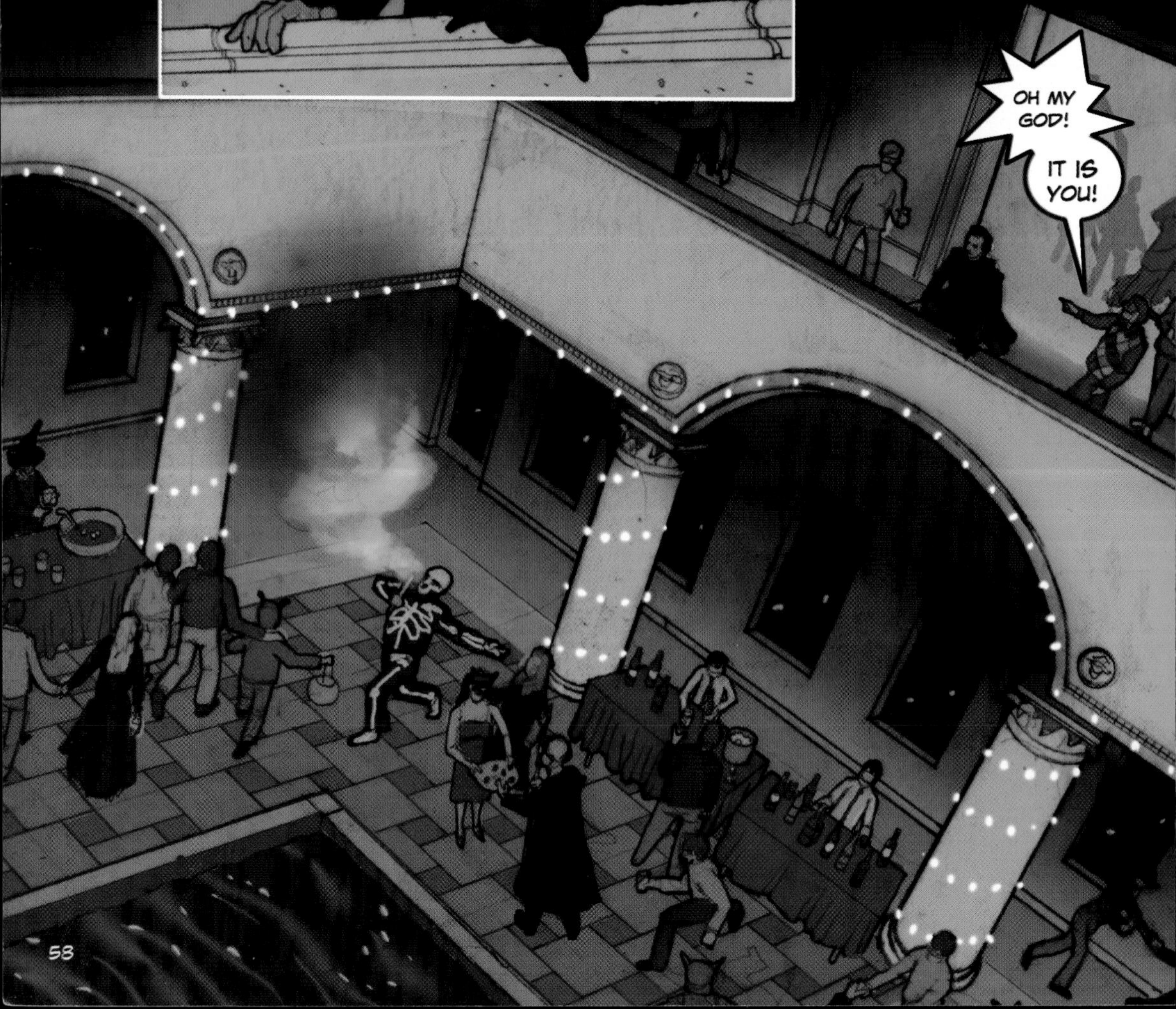
OH MY GOD!
IT IS YOU!

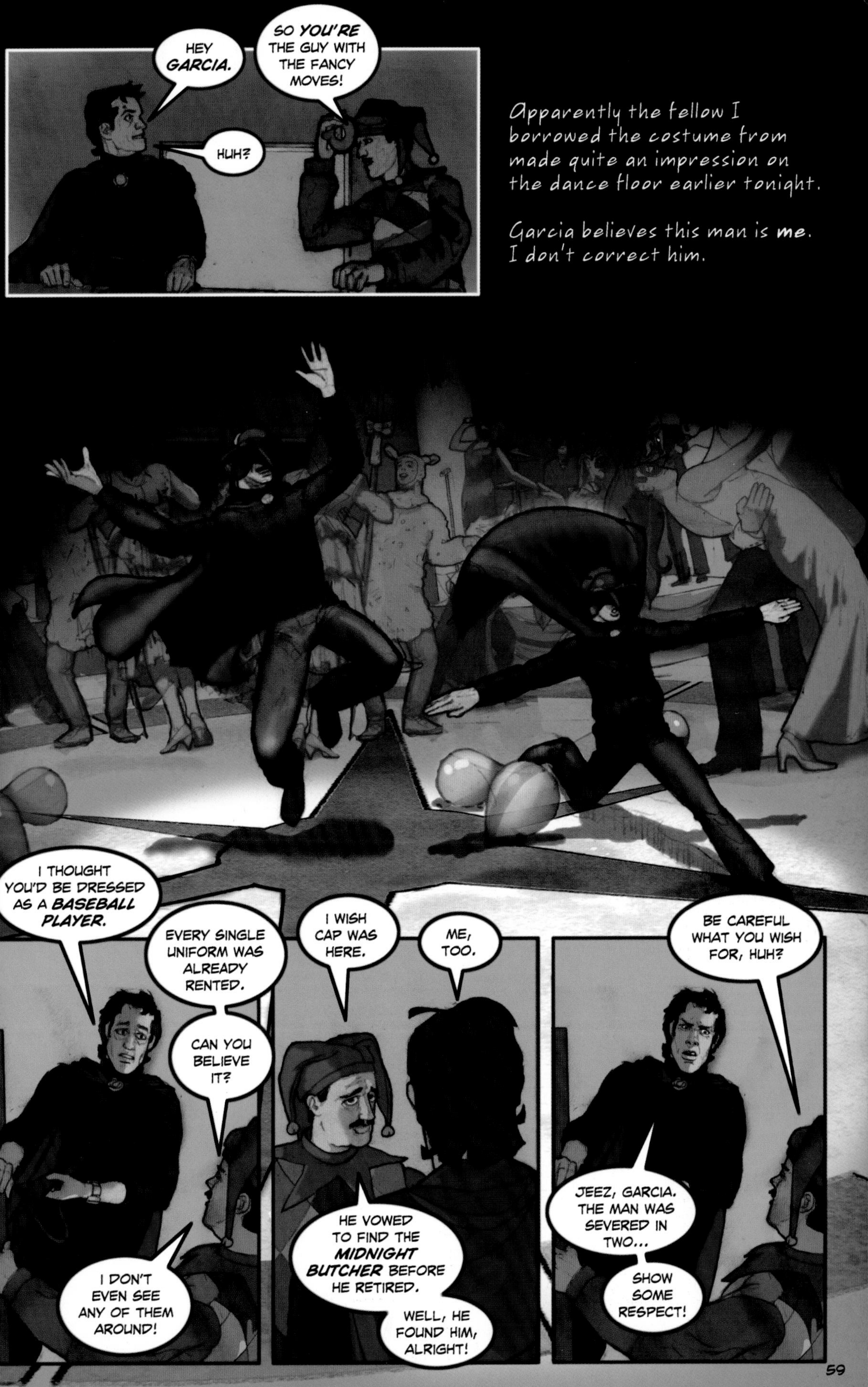
HEY GARCIA.
SO YOU'RE THE GUY WITH THE FANCY MOVES!
HUH?
Apparently the fellow I borrowed the costume from made quite an impression on the dance floor earlier tonight.
Garcia believes this man is me. I don't correct him.
I THOUGHT YOU'D BE DRESSED AS A BASEBALL PLAYER.
EVERY SINGLE UNIFORM WAS ALREADY RENTED.
CAN YOU BELIEVE IT?
I DON'T EVEN SEE ANY OF THEM AROUND!
I WISH CAP WAS HERE.
ME, TOO.
HE VOWED TO FIND THE MIDNIGHT BUTCHER BEFORE HE RETIRED.
WELL, HE FOUND HIM, ALRIGHT!
BE CAREFUL WHAT YOU WISH FOR, HUH?
JEEZ, GARCIA. THE MAN WAS SEVERED IN TWO...
SHOW SOME RESPECT!

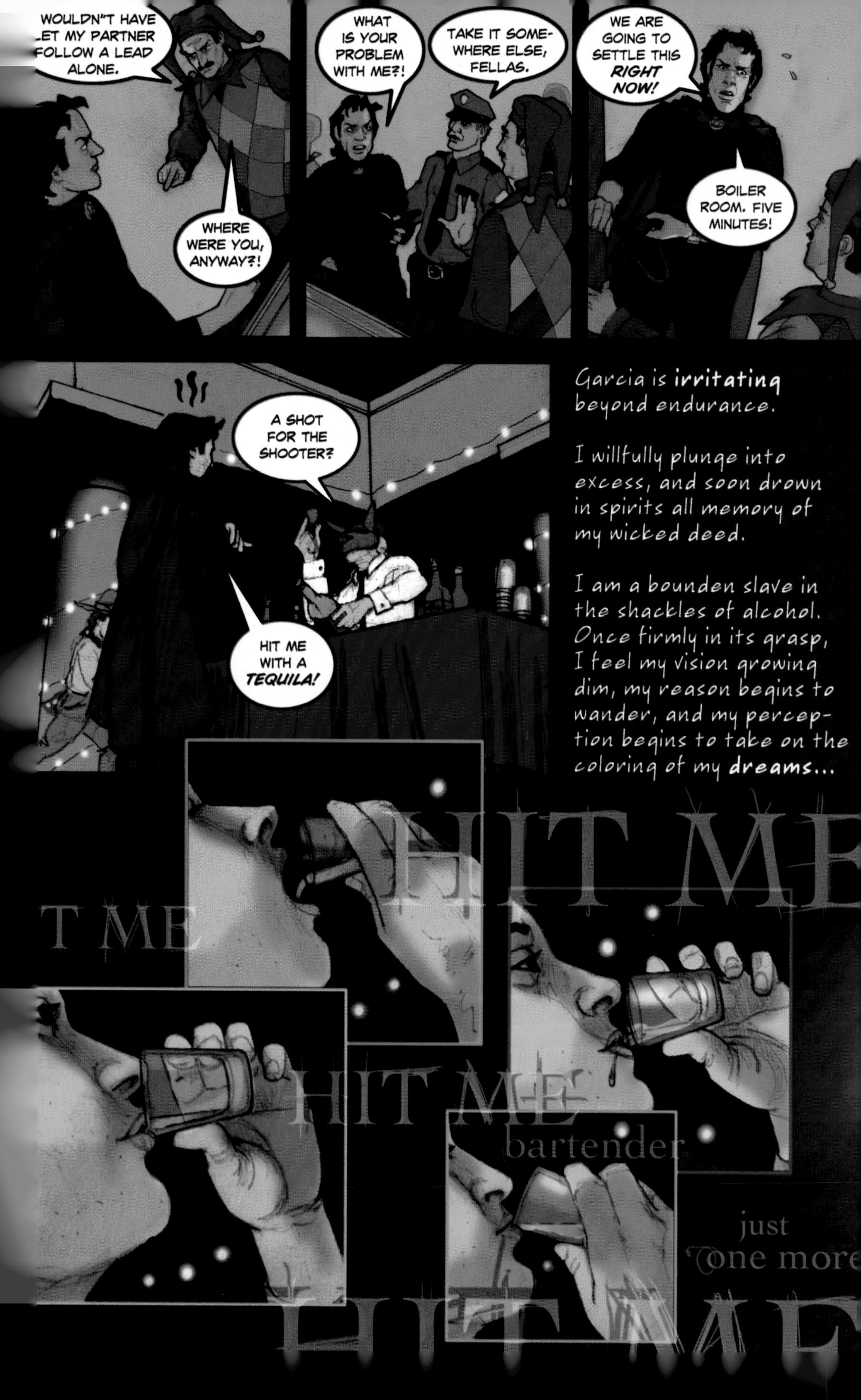
WOULDN'T HAVE LET MY PARTNER FOLLOW A LEAD ALONE.
WHERE WERE YOU, ANYWAY?!
WHAT IS YOUR PROBLEM WITH ME?!
TAKE IT SOME-WHERE ELSE, FELLAS.
WE ARE GOING TO SETTLE THIS RIGHT NOW!
BOILER ROOM. FIVE MINUTES!
A SHOT FOR THE SHOOTER?
HIT ME WITH A TEQUILA!
Garcia is irritating beyond endurance.
I willfully plunge into excess, and soon drown in spirits all memory of my wicked deed.
I am a bounden slave in the shackles of alcohol. Once firmly in its grasp, I feel my vision growing dim, my reason begins to wander, and my perception begins to take on the coloring of my dreams...
HIT ME
T ME
HIT ME
bartender
just one more

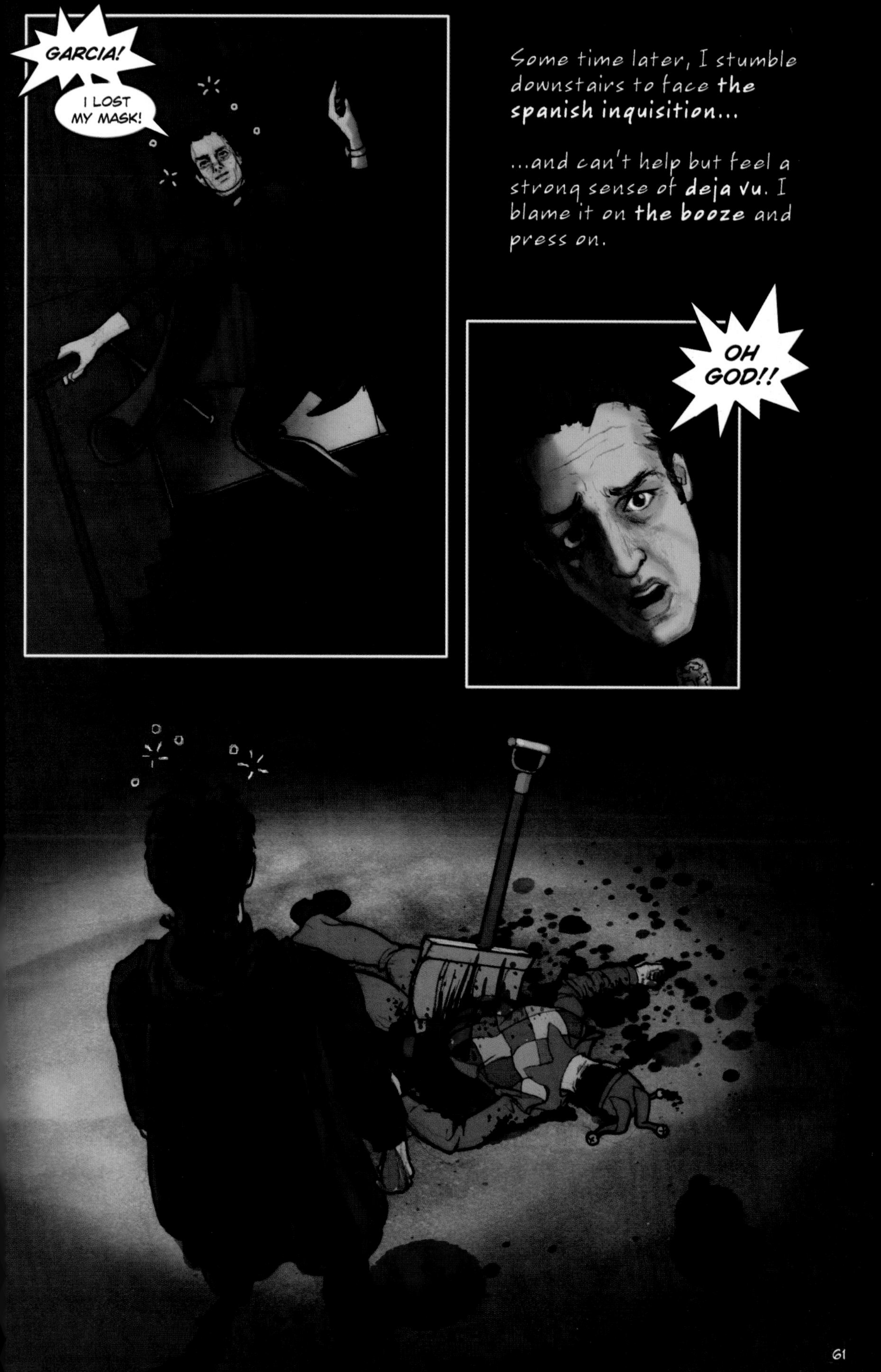
GARCIA!
I LOST MY MASK!
Some time later, I stumble downstairs to face the spanish inquisition...
...and can't help but feel a strong sense of deja vu. I blame it on the booze and press on.
OH GOD!!

Though I have spent countless hours dreaming of Garcia's demise - I took only a **small delight** in ending his life.

In the interest of protecting myself, I severed his body in two, maintaining the appearance of the Red Death's other victims.

I consider leaving his body to be discovered like the rest, that would be best - for me - but I cannot bear to have anyone else witness this carnage.

I have just killed two people.

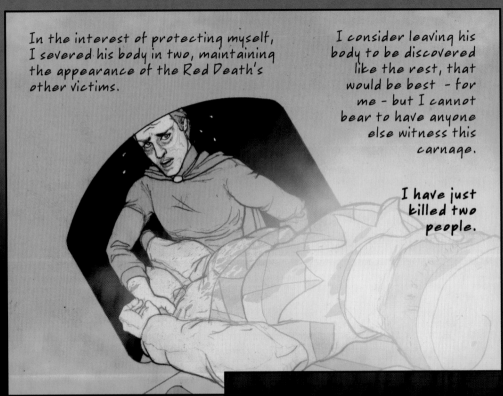

Sanity is fleeting.

I can no longer dismiss what has come to pass in these few hours.

The Red Death does **not** exist outside my head. The only monster terrorizing Good Fortune... **is me.**

I killed those eleven other people! I killed Captain Howdy!

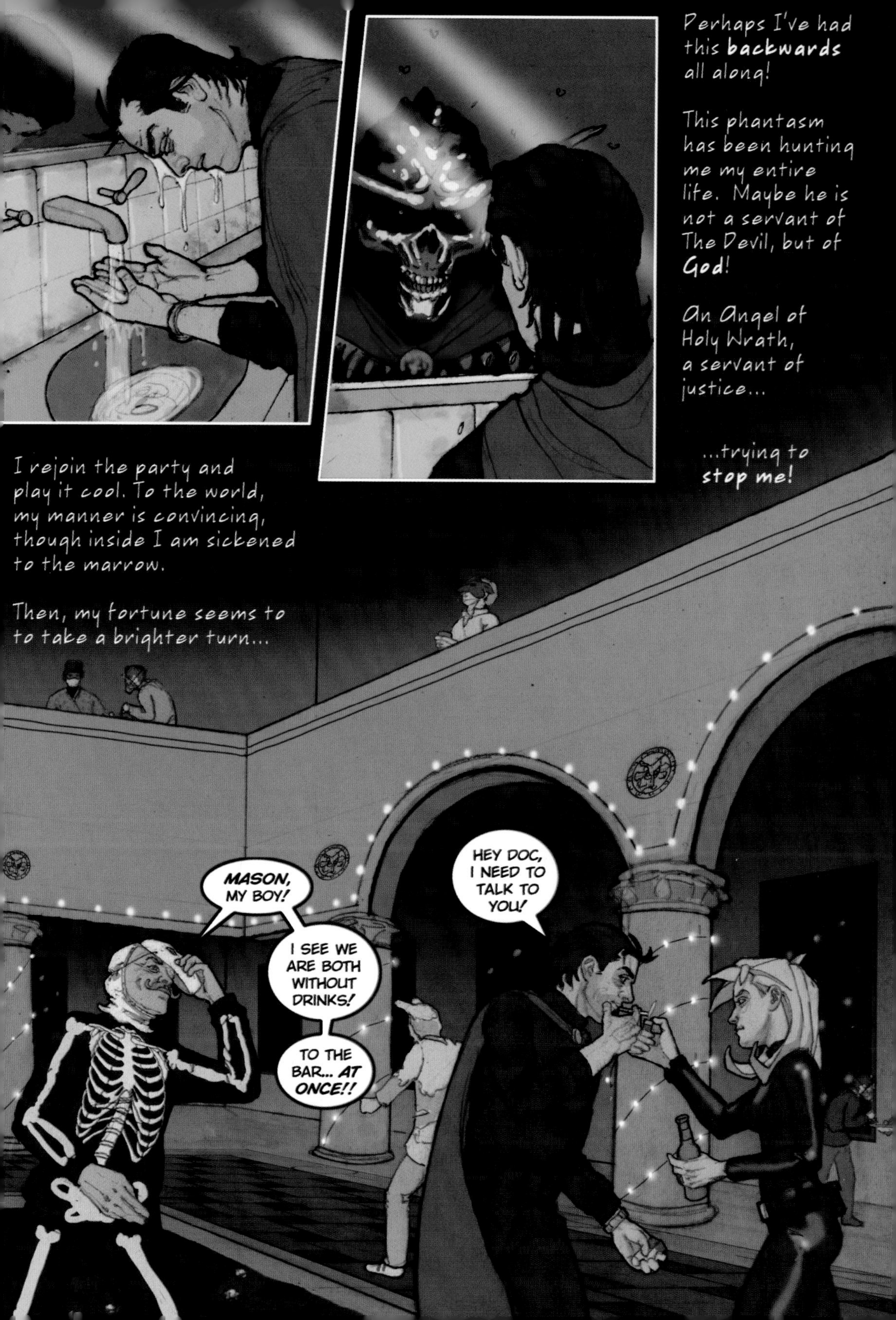

Perhaps I've had this **backwards** all along!
This phantasm has been hunting me my entire life. Maybe he is not a servant of The Devil, but of **God**!
An Angel of Holy Wrath, a servant of justice...
...trying to **stop me!**
I rejoin the party and play it cool. To the world, my manner is convincing, though inside I am sickened to the marrow.
Then, my fortune seems to to take a brighter turn...
MASON, MY BOY!
I SEE WE ARE BOTH WITHOUT DRINKS!
TO THE BAR... *AT ONCE!!*
HEY DOC, I NEED TO TALK TO YOU!

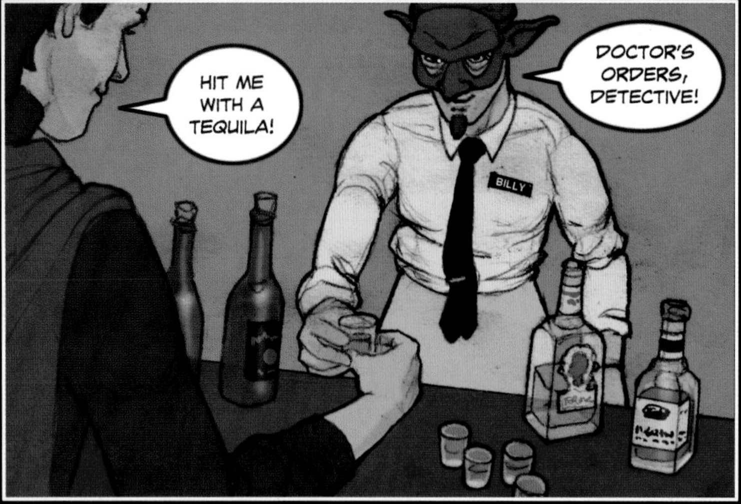
HIT ME WITH A TEQUILA!
DOCTOR'S ORDERS, DETECTIVE!
BILLY

I was hoping the good doctor might know what to do, but he wouldn't hear of it.

Together we plunge into excess and again I aspire to drown the memory of my bloody deeds.

I am all but **consumed** by the **utter hopelessness** of hope.

Then, something truly remarkable happened...

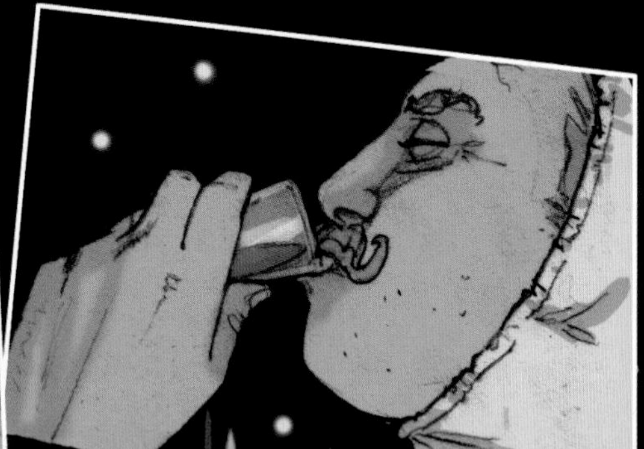

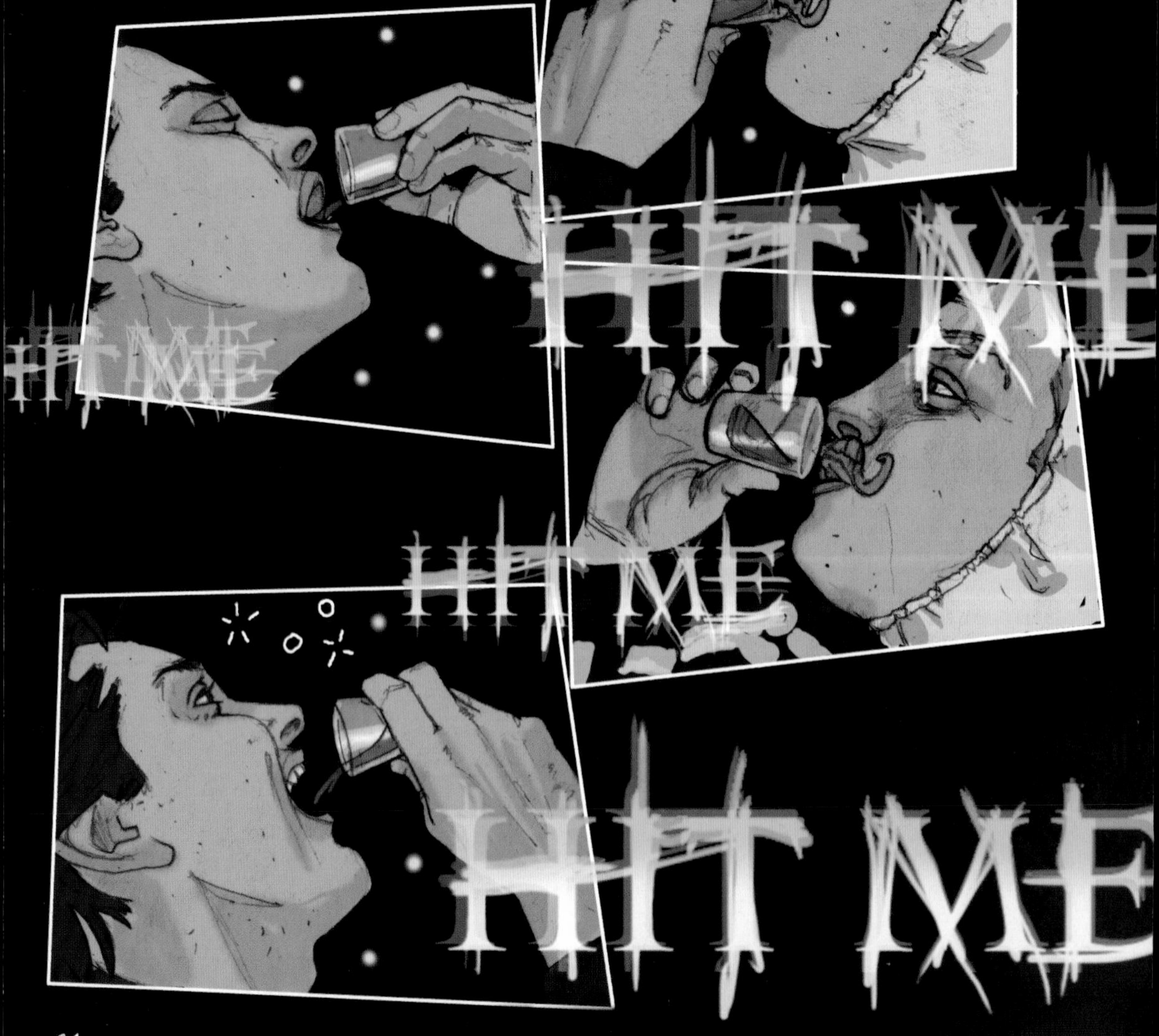
HIT ME
HIT ME
HIT ME
HIT ME

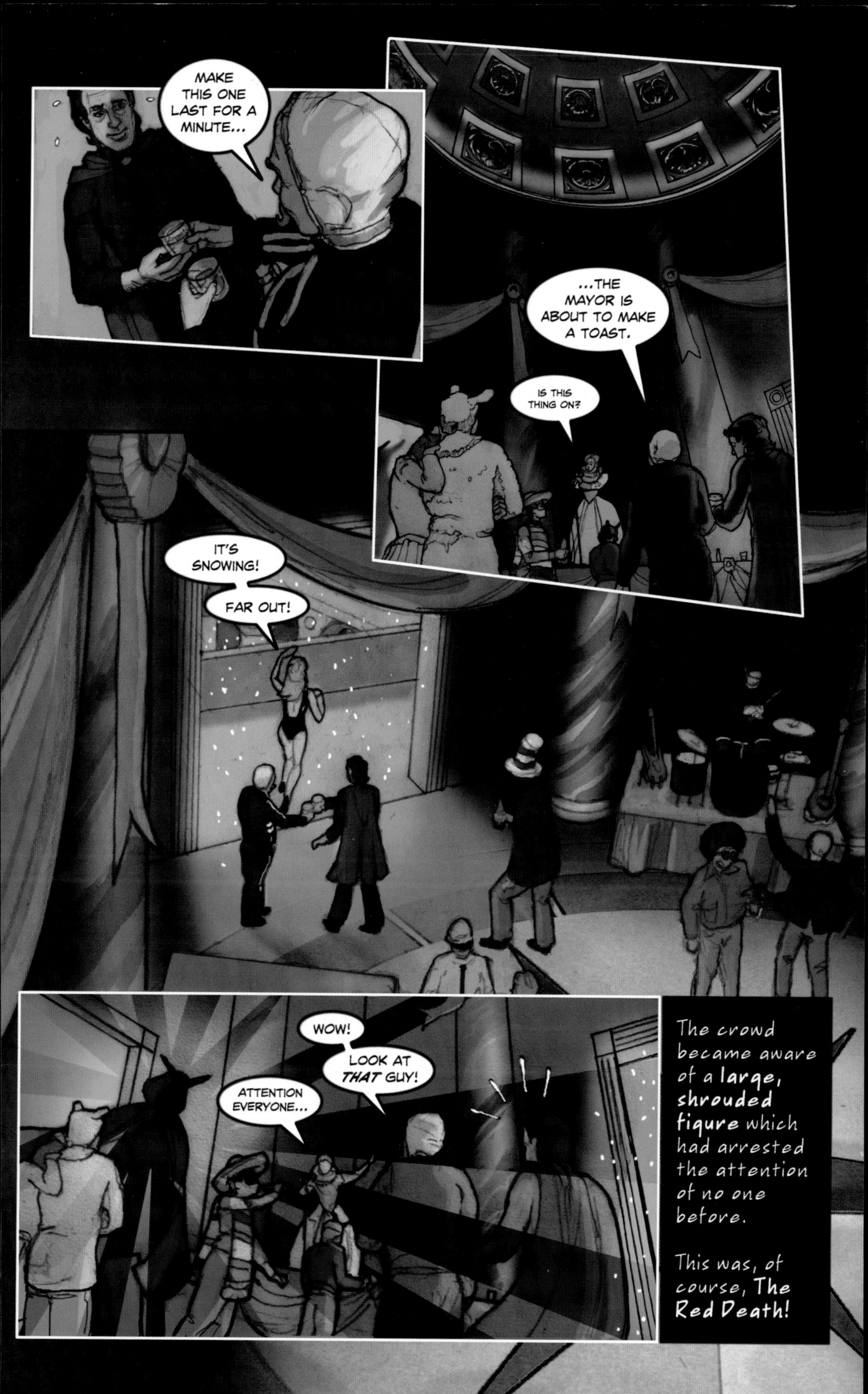
MAKE THIS ONE LAST FOR A MINUTE...
...THE MAYOR IS ABOUT TO MAKE A TOAST.
IS THIS THING ON?
IT'S SNOWING!
FAR OUT!
WOW!
LOOK AT THAT GUY!
ATTENTION EVERYONE...
The crowd became aware of a large, shrouded figure which had arrested the attention of no one before.
This was, of course, The Red Death!

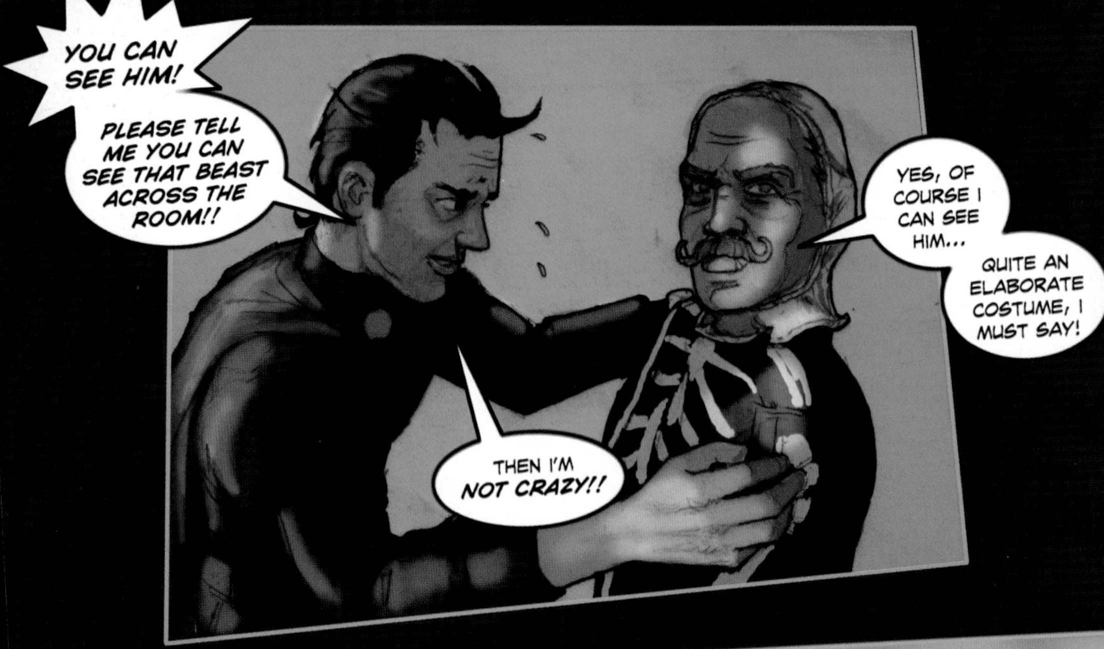
YOU CAN SEE HIM!
PLEASE TELL ME YOU CAN SEE THAT BEAST ACROSS THE ROOM!!
YES, OF COURSE I CAN SEE HIM...
QUITE AN ELABORATE COSTUME, I MUST SAY!
THEN I'M NOT CRAZY!!

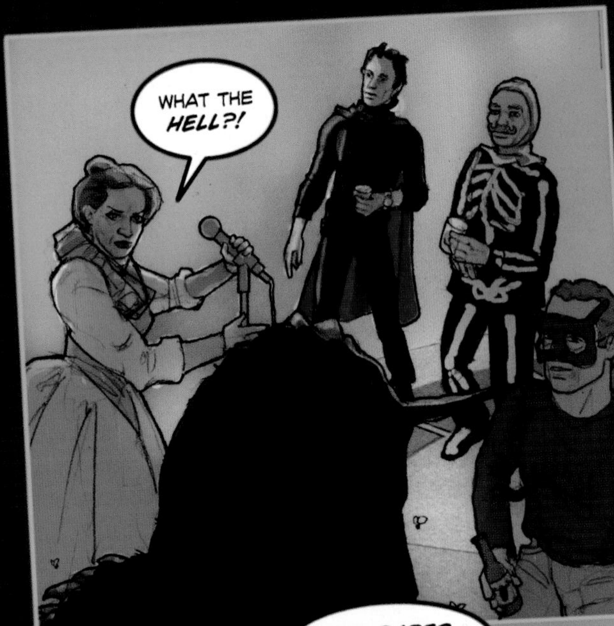
WHAT THE HELL?!

He brought with him a stench of death and rot **so strong** - forcing its way up my nostrils. This was a smell with which I was already acquainted, and tonight it has never smelled **so sweet!**

A Frankenstein **convulsed.** A pair of cowgirls **fainted.**

Van Wormer, seemingly unaffected by the rank odor, took extreme interest in the details of the stranger's costume.

The monster's cloak was sprinkled with **blood.** Garcia's **blood.** Cat's **blood.** The chinks in his armor were clotted with gore.

When the Mayor laid eyes on the stranger, I swear I noticed a strong shudder pass through her tiny frame - either of terror or distaste. Her face reddened with rage. She could tolerate no more.

True, she did extend an unlimited masquerade license for the night, but this stranger had clearly gone beyond the bounds of even indefinite decorum.

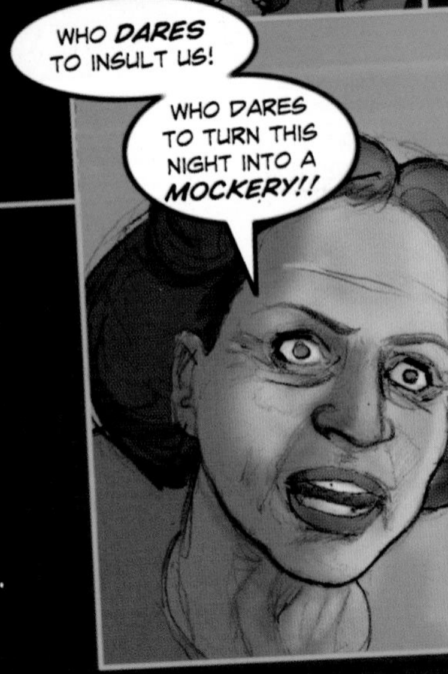
WHO DARES TO INSULT US!
WHO DARES TO TURN THIS NIGHT INTO A MOCKERY!!

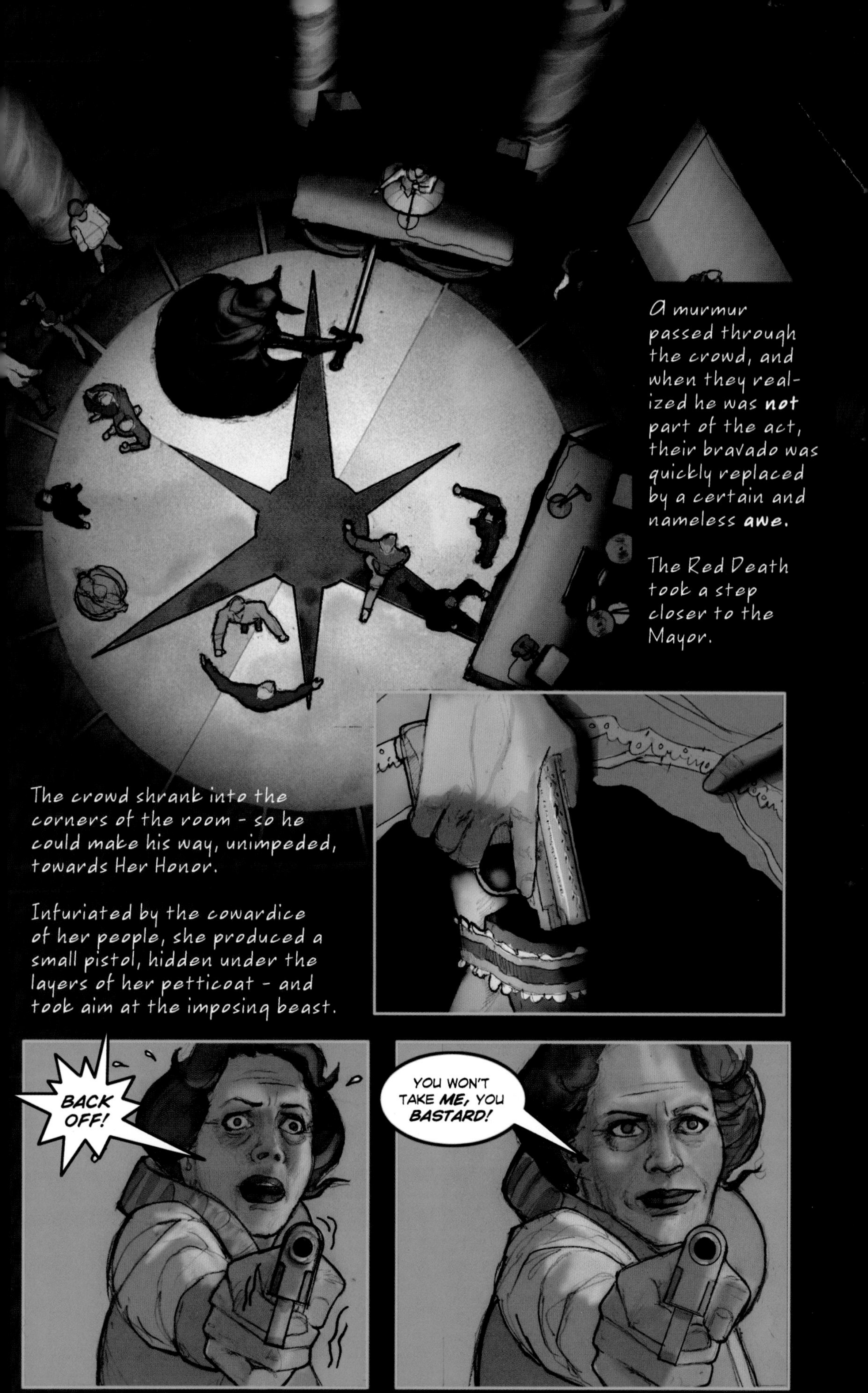
A murmur passed through the crowd, and when they realized he was **not** part of the act, their bravado was quickly replaced by a certain and nameless **awe.**
The Red Death took a step closer to the Mayor.
The crowd shrank into the corners of the room - so he could make his way, unimpeded, towards Her Honor.
Infuriated by the cowardice of her people, she produced a small pistol, hidden under the layers of her petticoat - and took aim at the imposing beast.
BACK OFF!
YOU WON'T TAKE *ME,* YOU *BASTARD!*

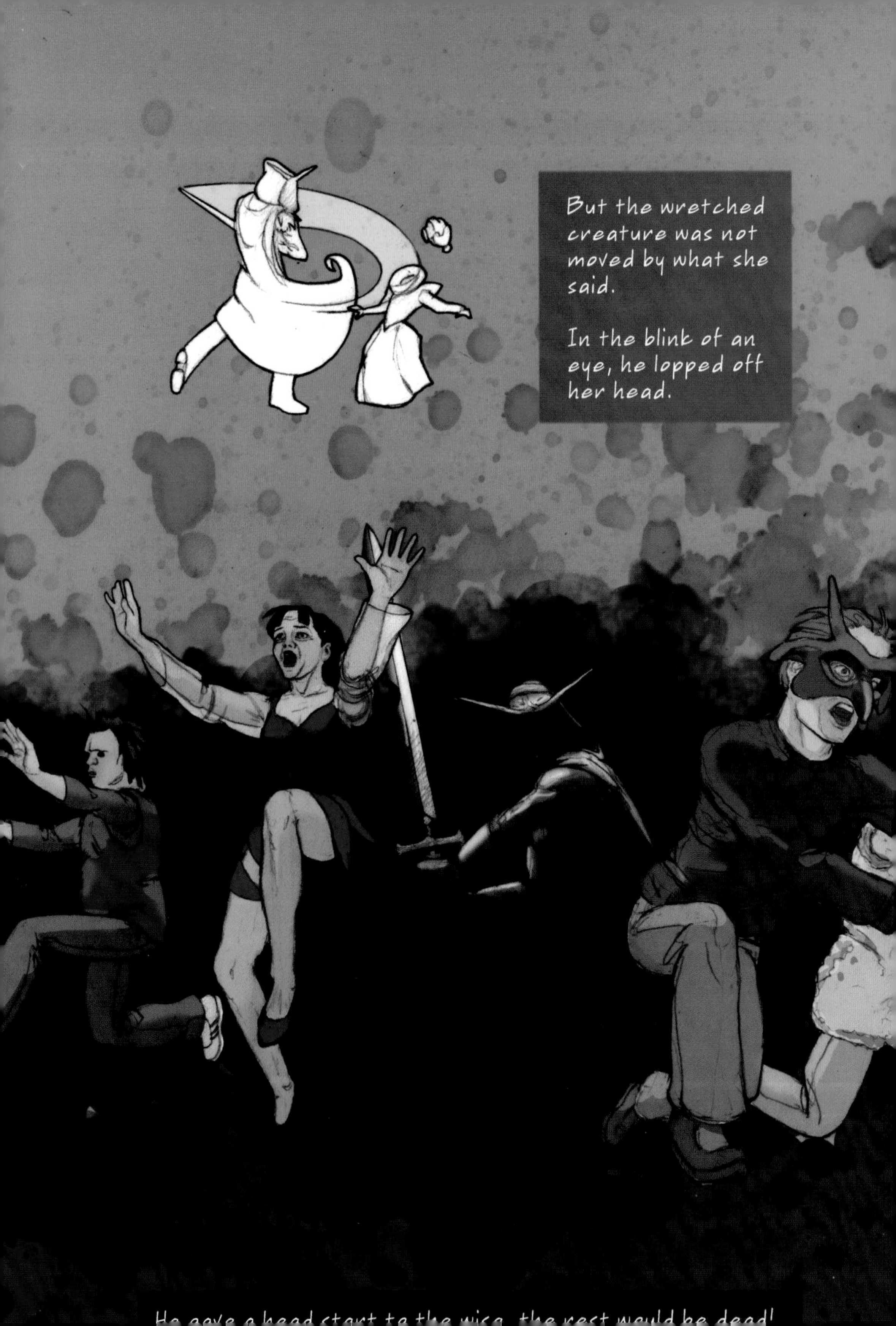

But the wretched creature was not moved by what she said.
In the blink of an eye, he lopped off her head.
He gave a head start to the wise, the rest would be dead!

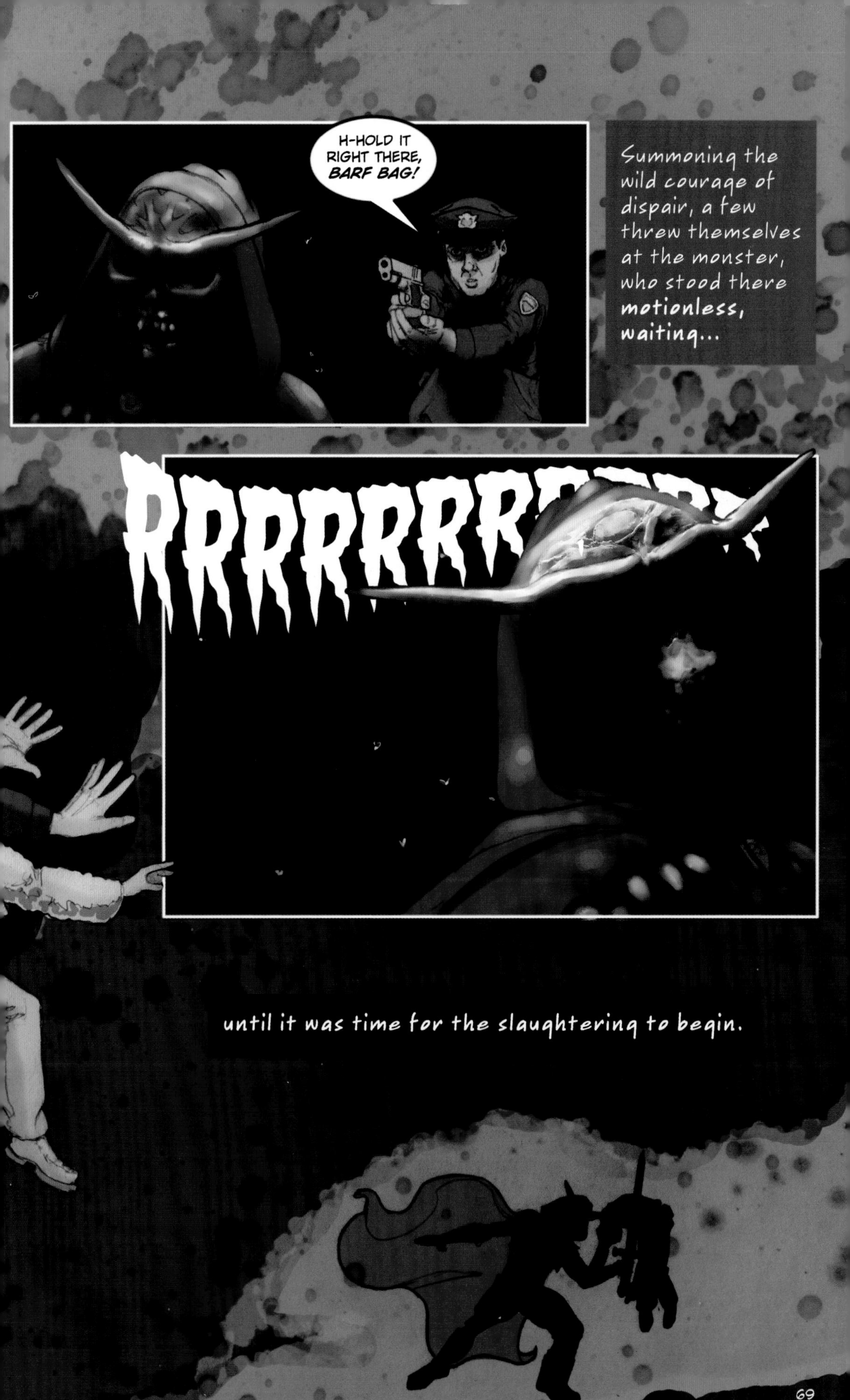
H-HOLD IT RIGHT THERE, BARF BAG!
Summoning the wild courage of dispair, a few threw themselves at the monster, who stood there motionless, waiting...
RRRRRRRRRRRR
until it was time for the slaughtering to begin.

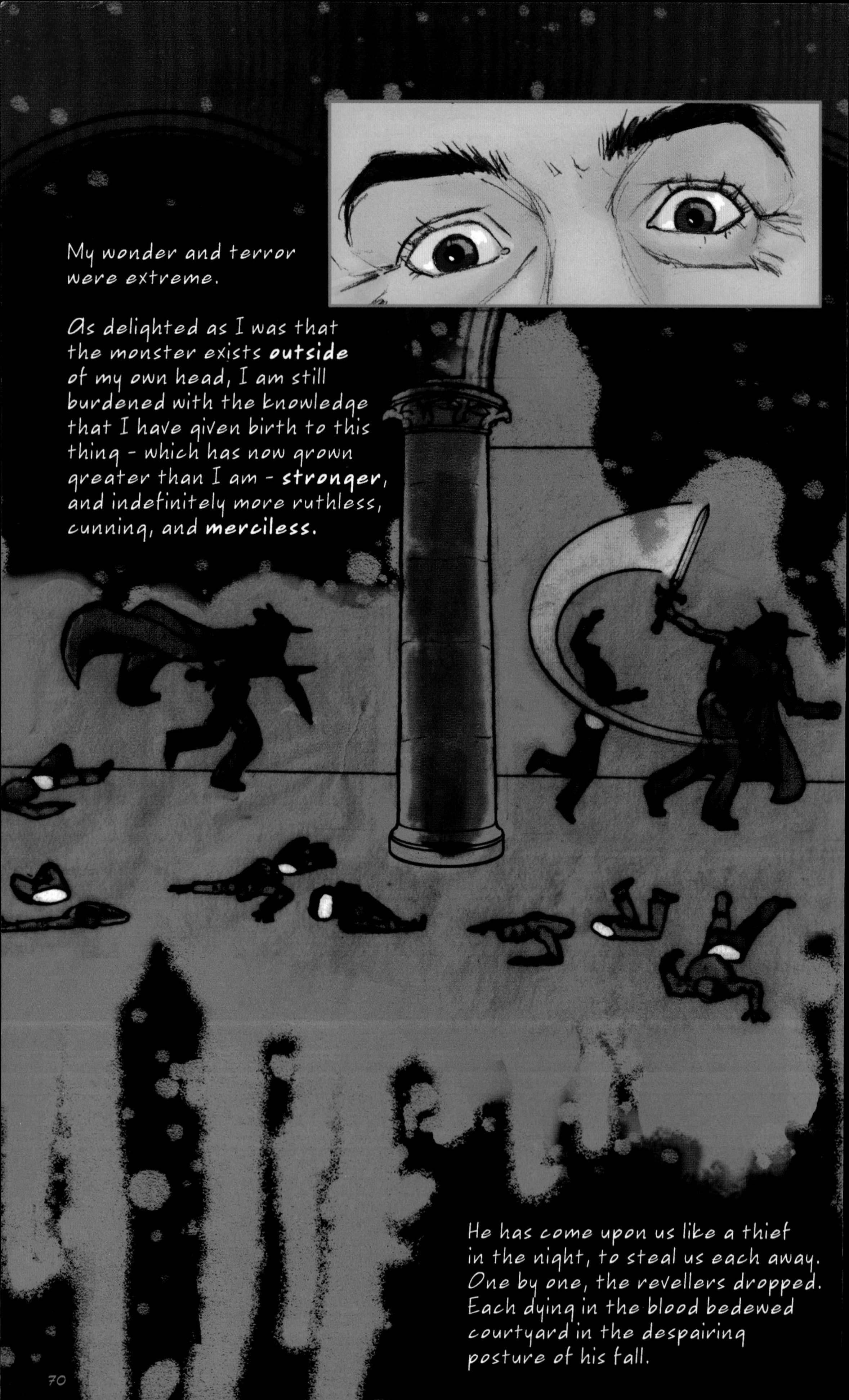
My wonder and terror were extreme.
As delighted as I was that the monster exists **outside** of my own head, I am still burdened with the knowledge that I have given birth to this thing - which has now grown greater than I am - **stronger**, and indefinitely more ruthless, cunning, and **merciless.**
He has come upon us like a thief in the night, to steal us each away. One by one, the revellers dropped. Each dying in the blood bedewed courtyard in the despairing posture of his fall.

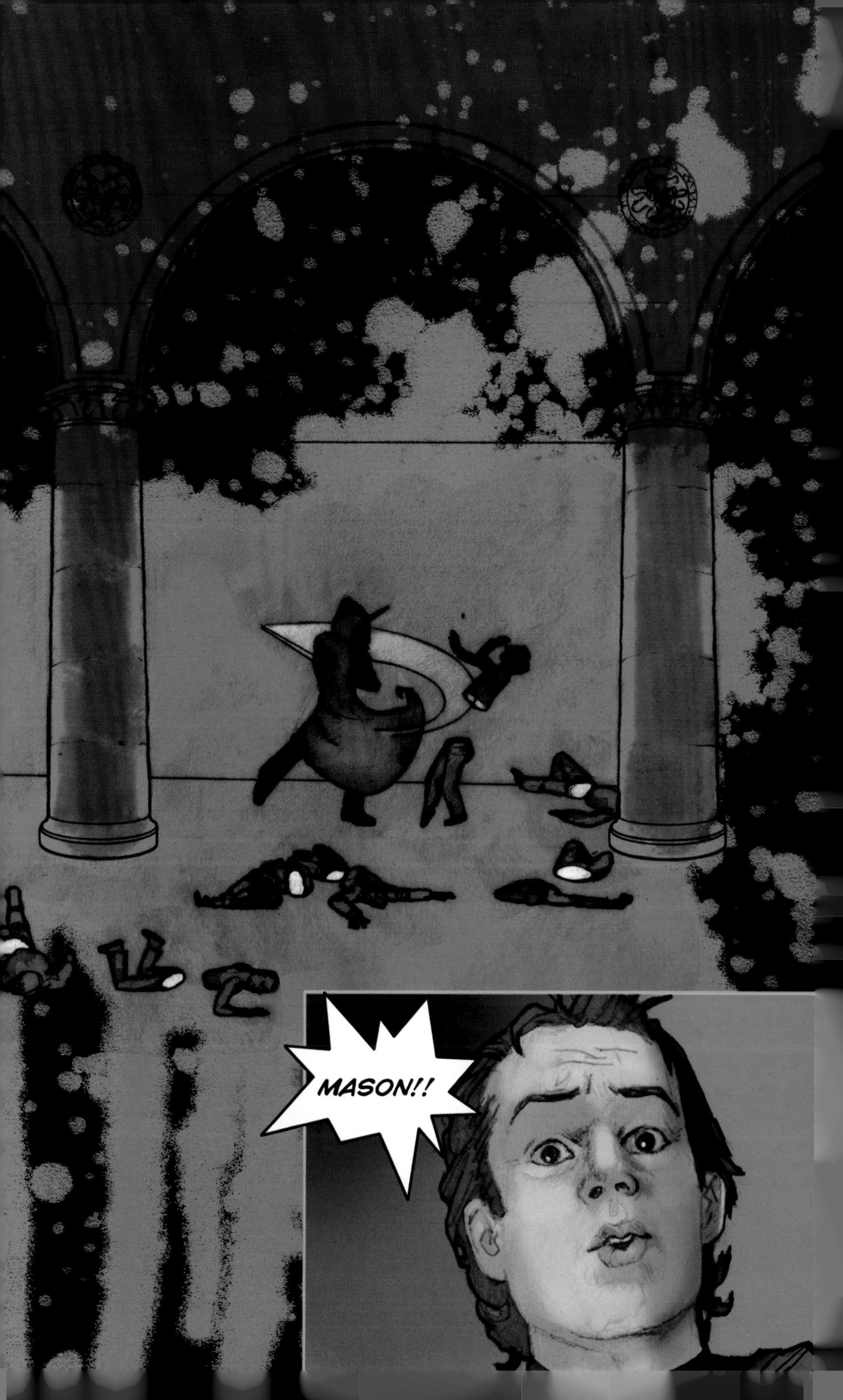
MASON!!

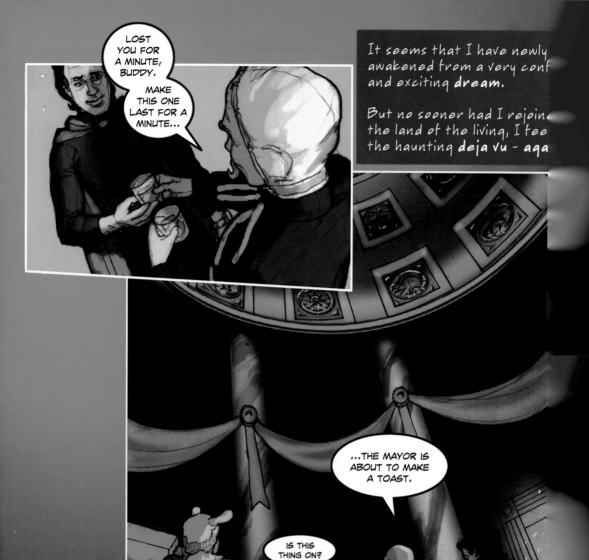

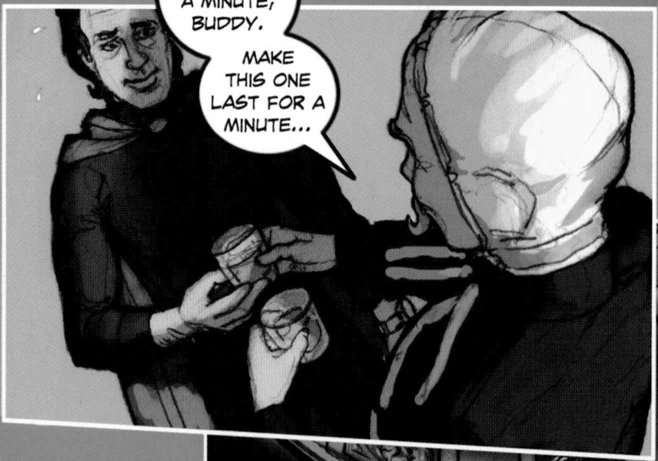
LOST YOU FOR A MINUTE, BUDDY.
MAKE THIS ONE LAST FOR A MINUTE...

It seems that I have newly awakened from a very conf
and exciting **dream.**

But no sooner had I rejoin
the land of the living, I fee
the haunting **deja vu - aga**

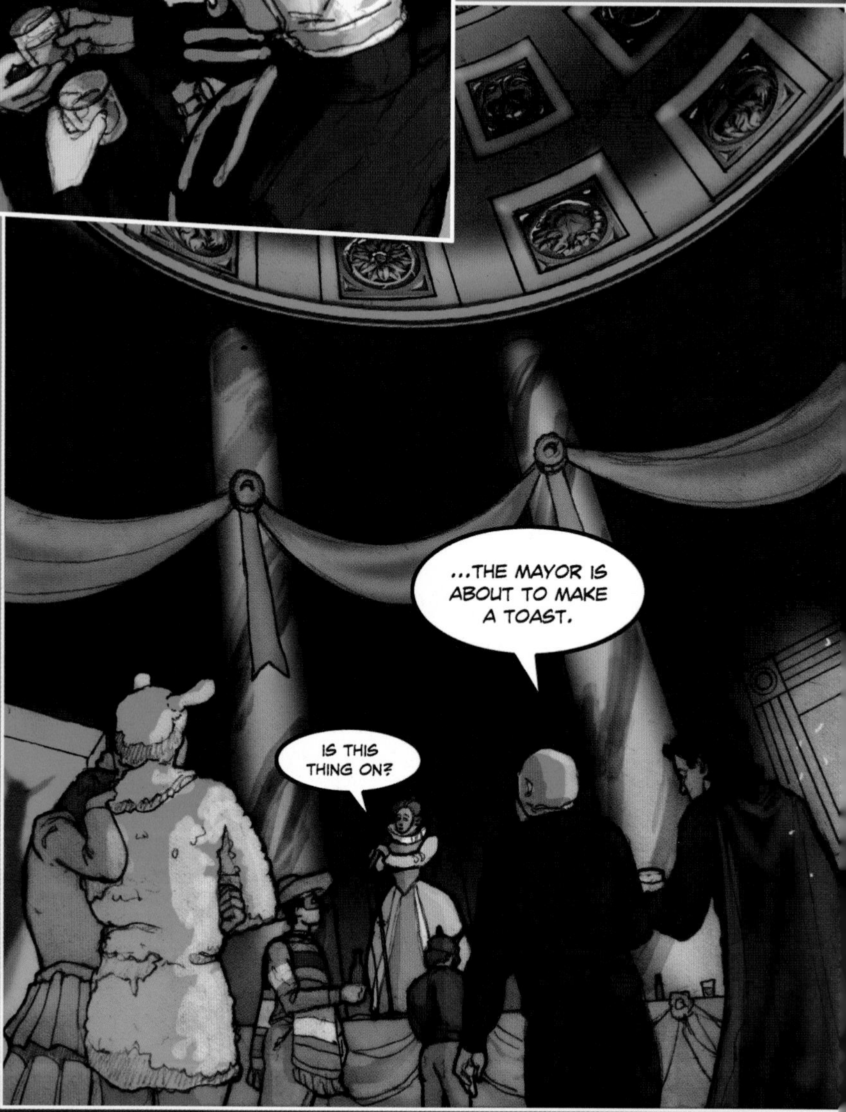
...THE MAYOR IS ABOUT TO MAKE A TOAST.
IS THIS THING ON?

It is the same, yet **different.**

As the events unfold for the **second** time - I feel myself empowered by the following revelation...

This is an incubus of **my design.** As simply as it all **started**, I can **stop** this nonsense.

It is simply a matter of **will.**

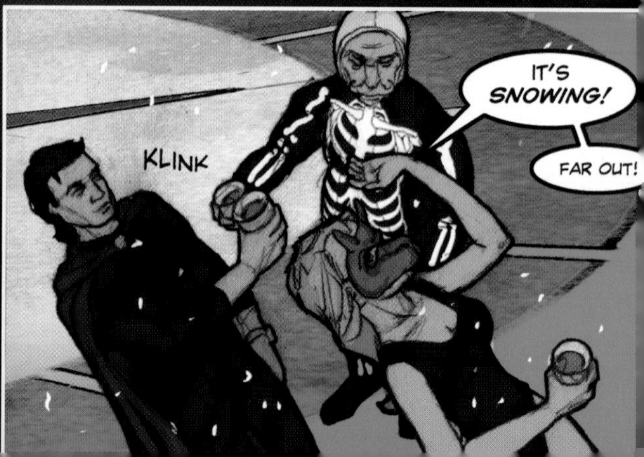
KLINK
IT'S SNOWING!
FAR OUT!

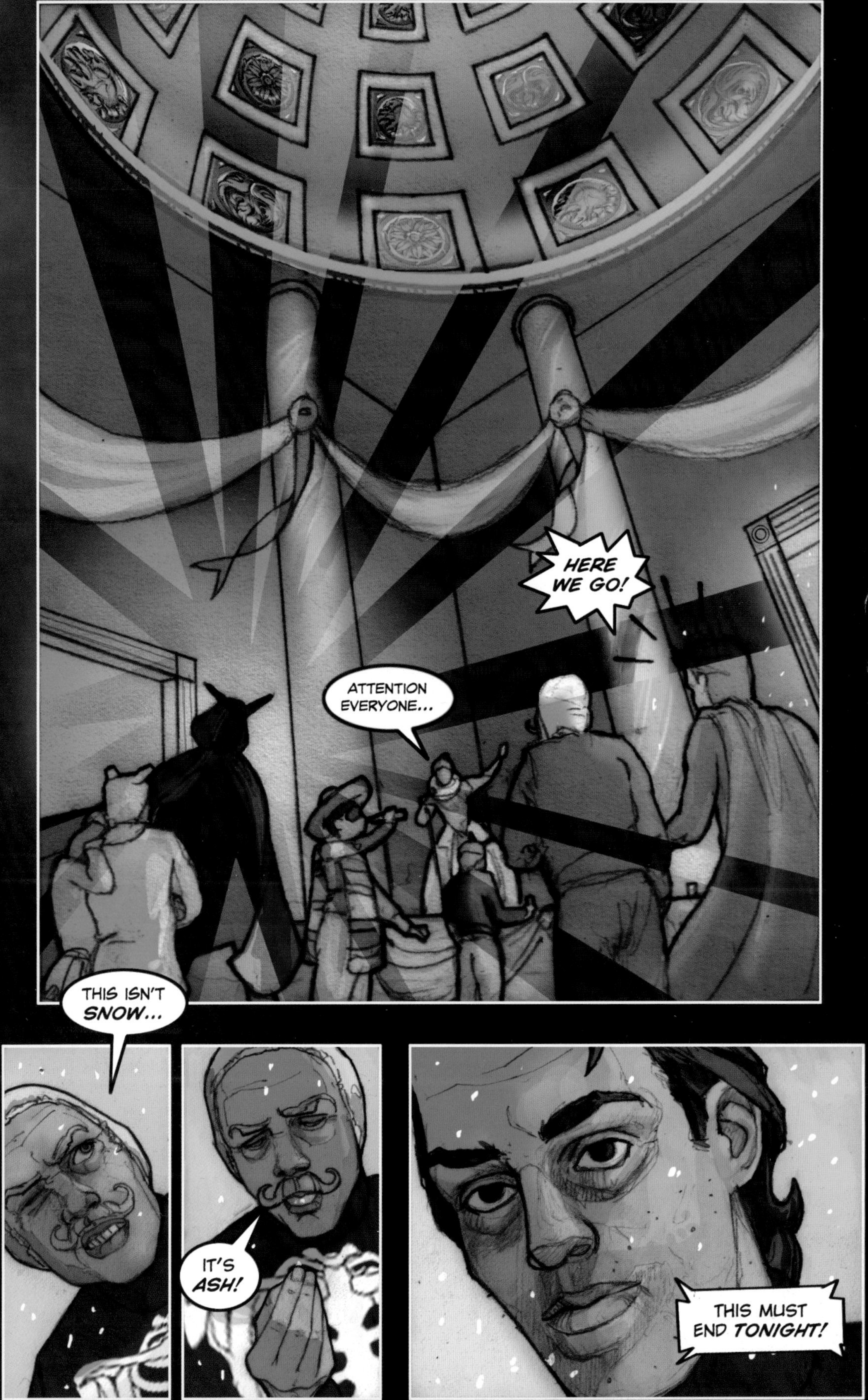
HERE WE GO!
ATTENTION EVERYONE...
THIS ISN'T SNOW...
IT'S ASH!
THIS MUST END TONIGHT!

chapter four

He is me.

The rays of my destiny are gathering to a focus.

It's time to take the battlefield – summon all my strength,
and become something more savage than ever.

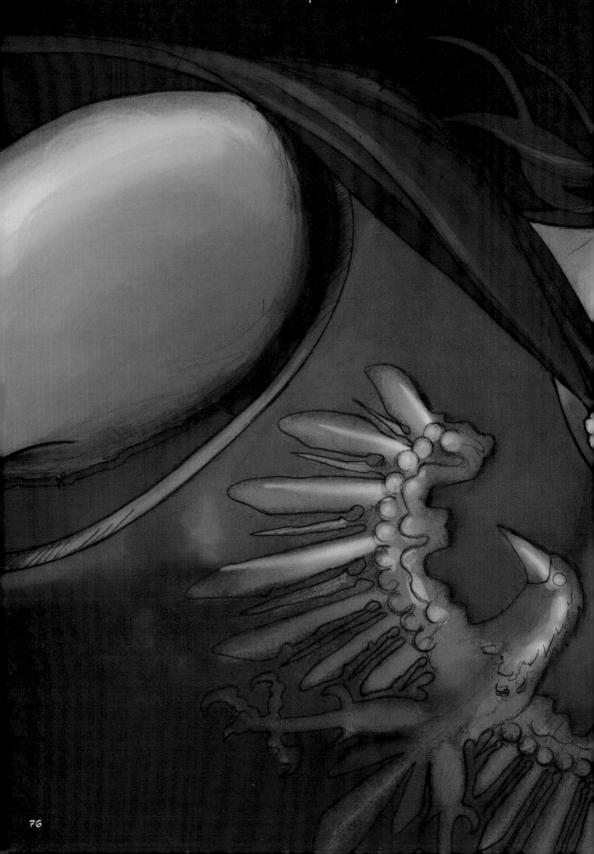

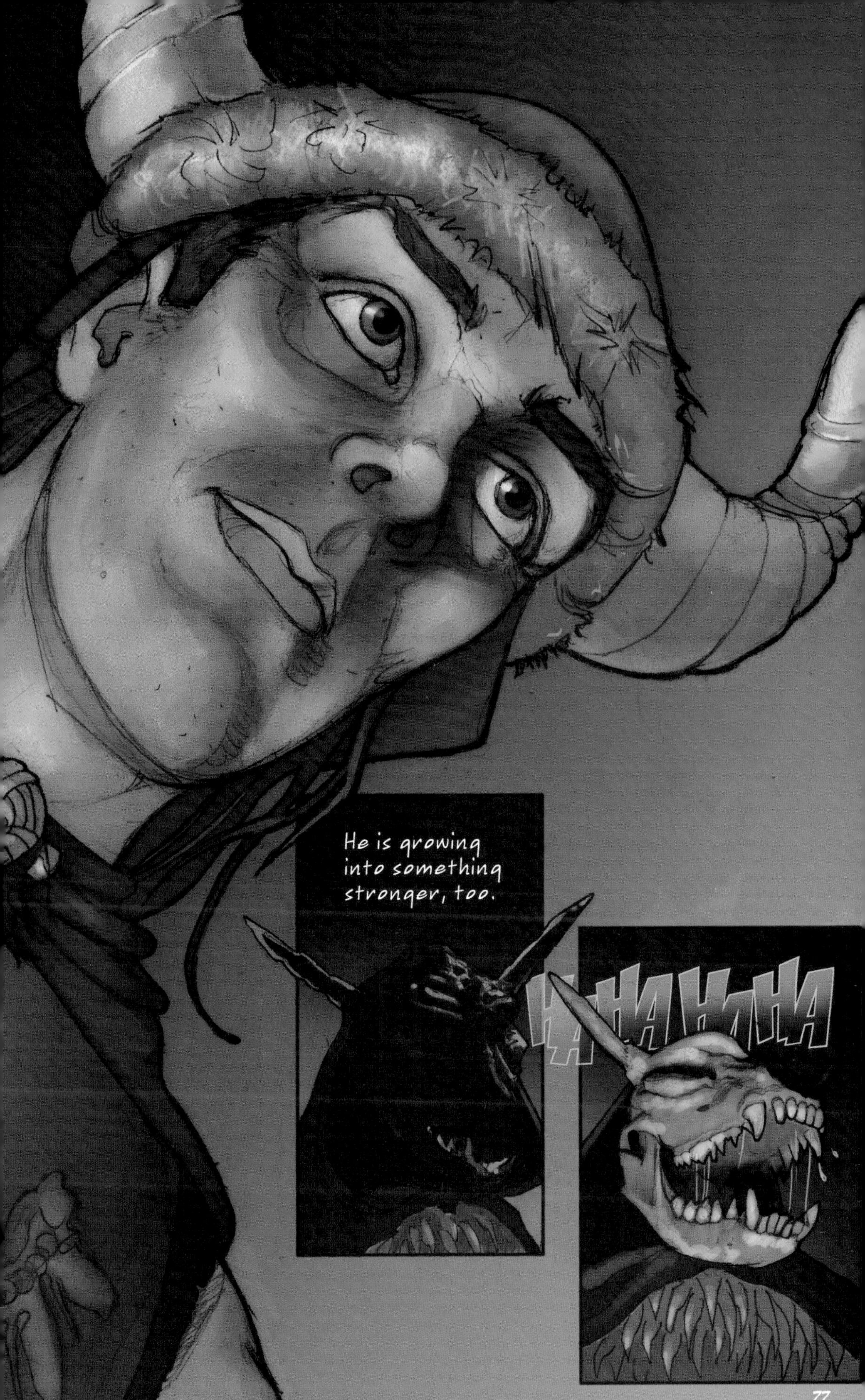
He is growing into something stronger, too.
HAHAHAHAHA

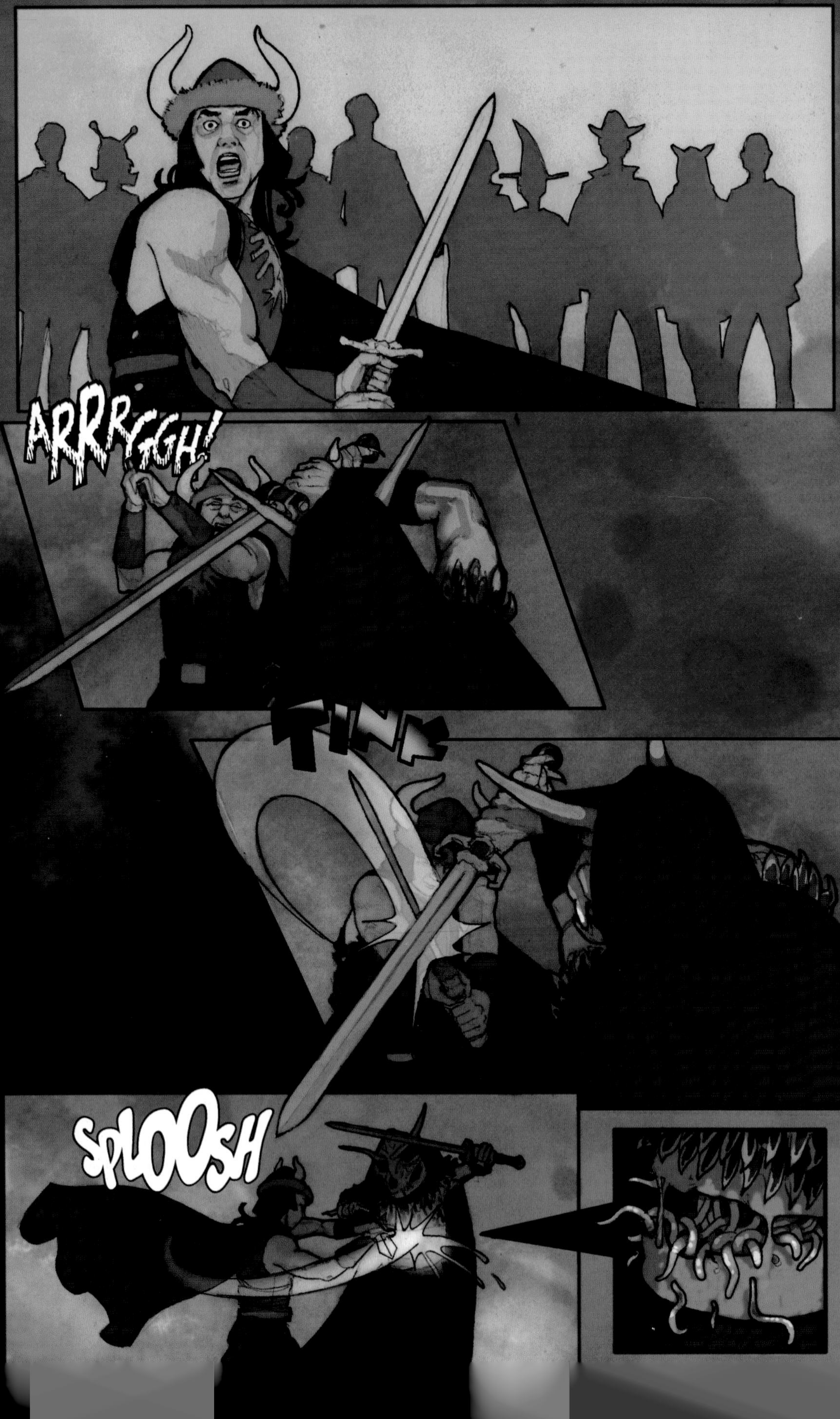
ARRRGGH!
TINK
SPLOOSH

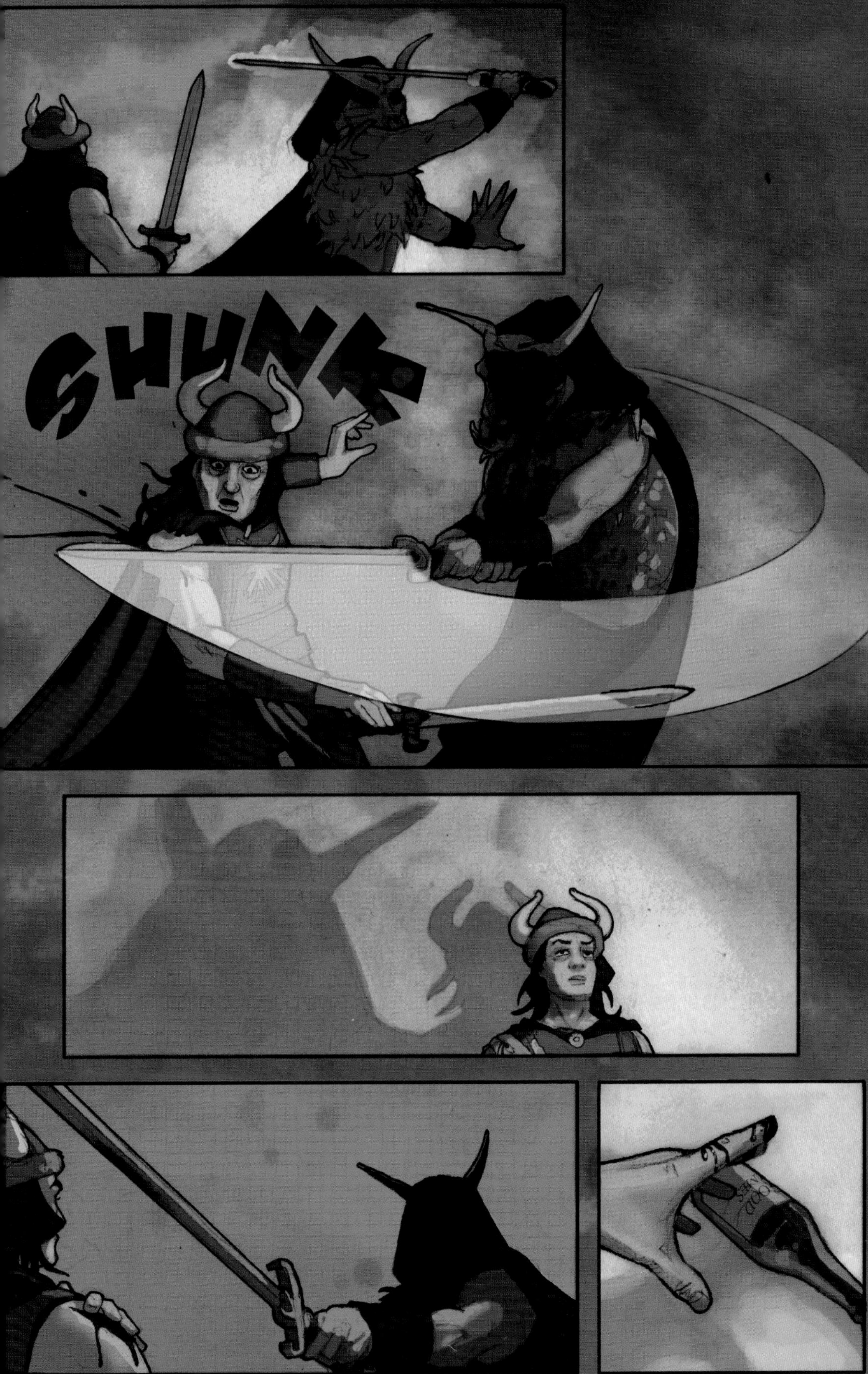
SHUNK

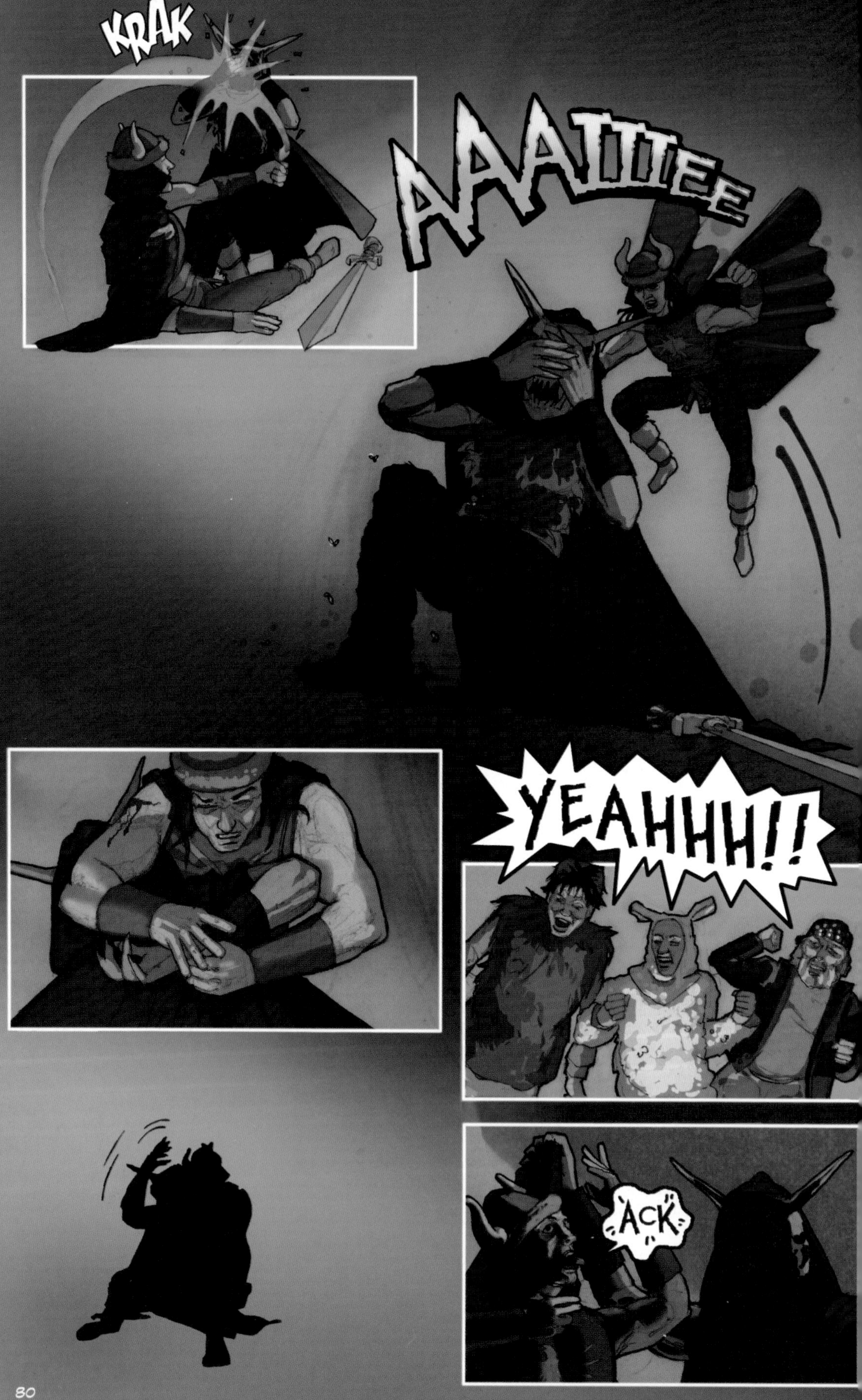
KRAK
AAATTTEE
YEAHHH!!
ACK

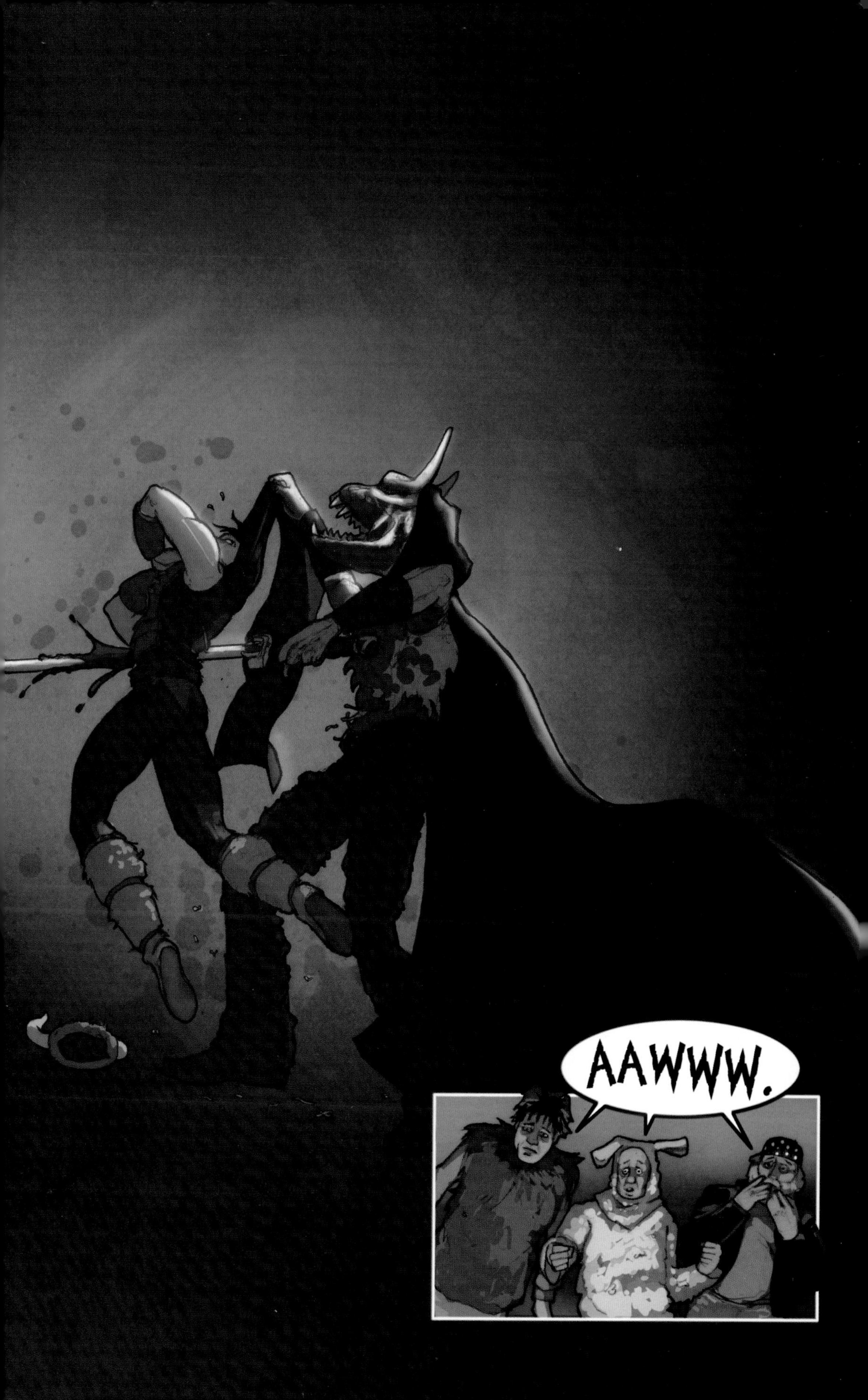
AAWWW.

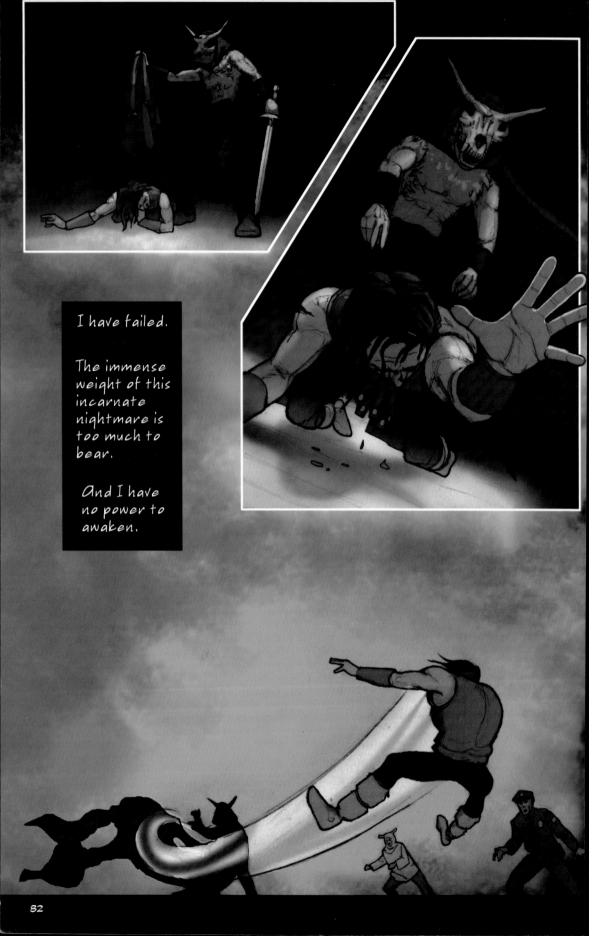

I have failed.

The immense weight of this incarnate nightmare is too much to bear.

And I have no power to awaken.

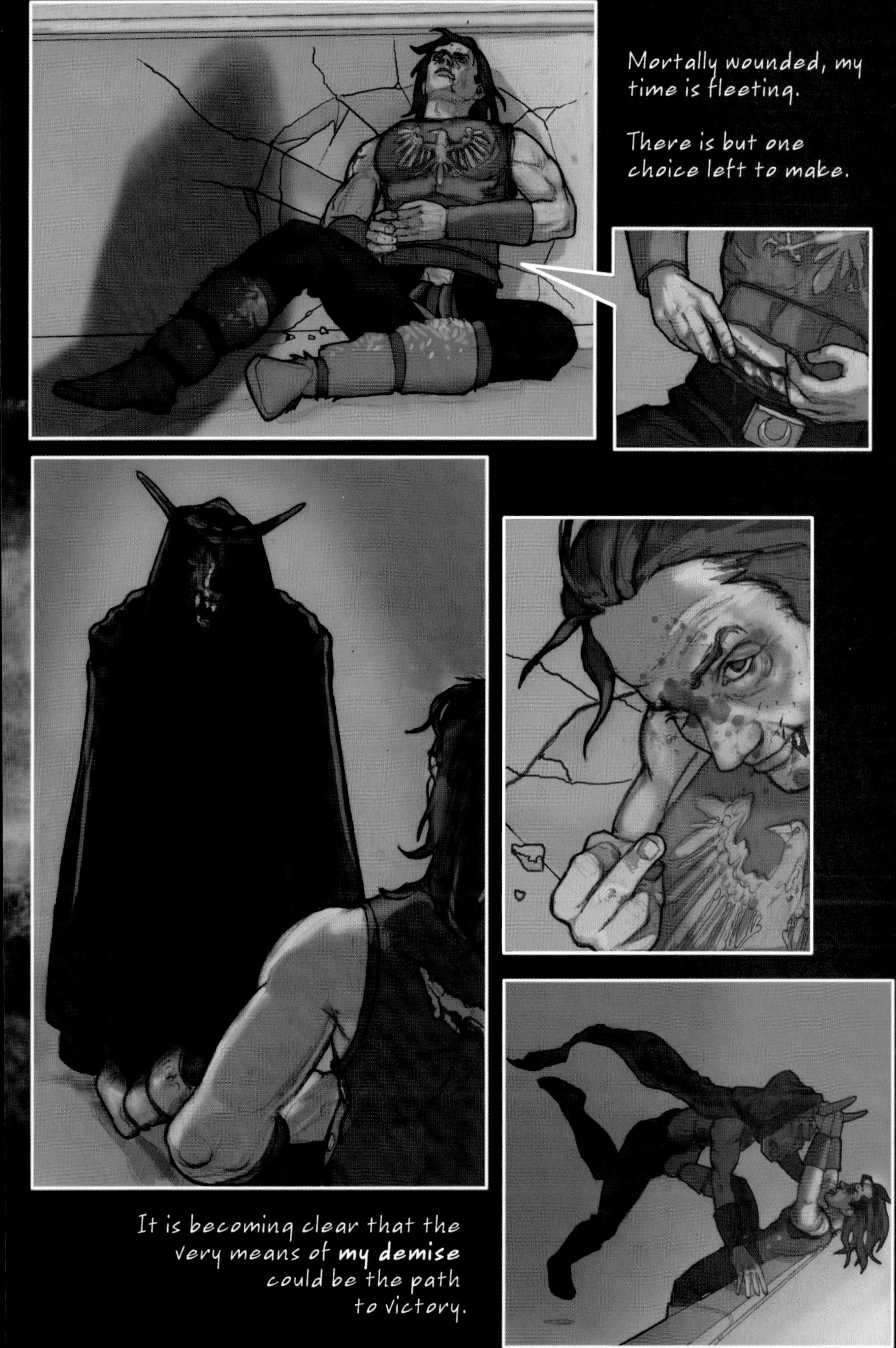
Mortally wounded, my time is fleeting.
There is but one choice left to make.
It is becoming clear that the very means of **my demise** could be the path to victory.

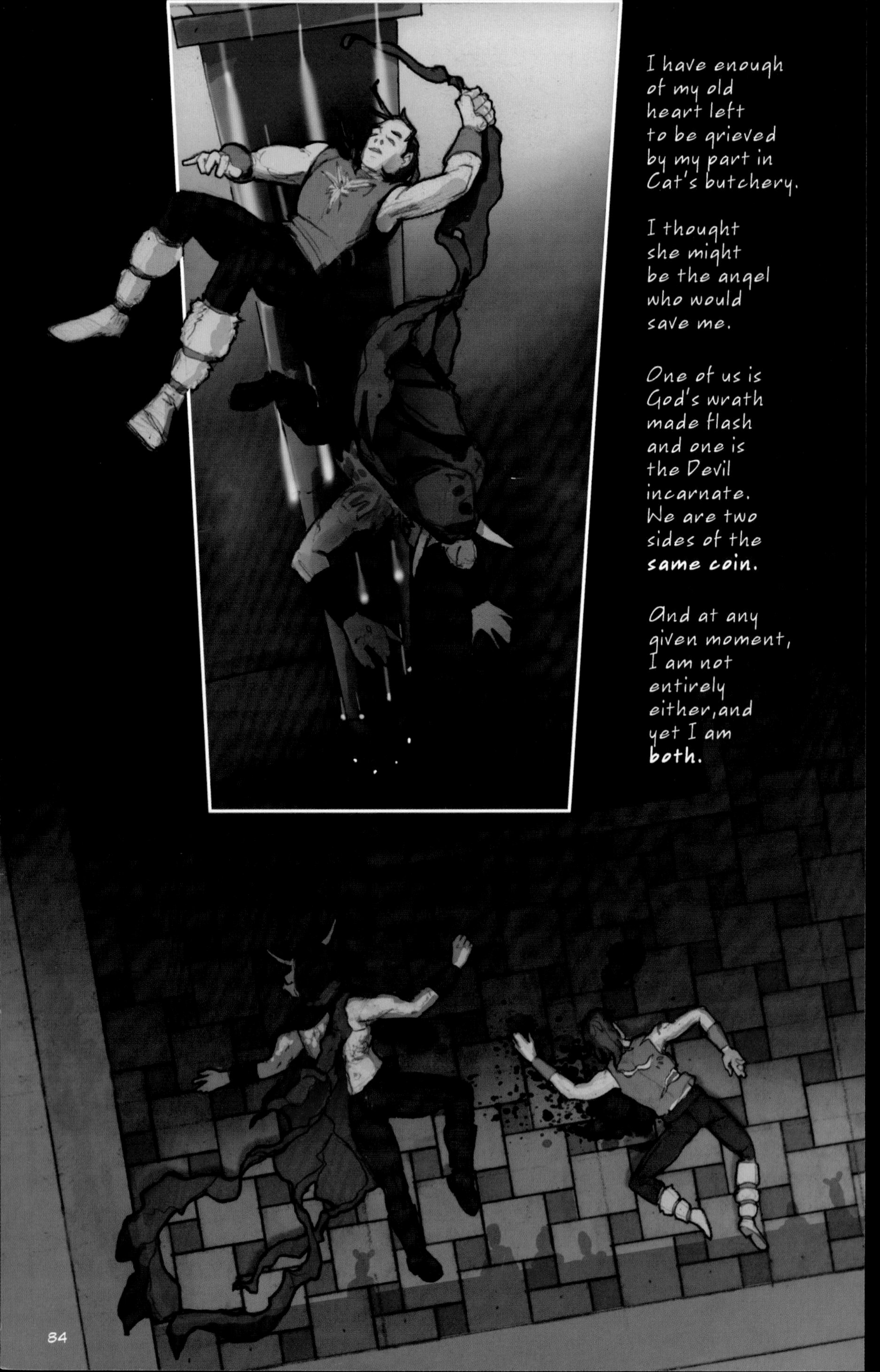
I have enough of my old heart left to be grieved by my part in Cat's butchery.
I thought she might be the angel who would save me.
One of us is God's wrath made flash and one is the Devil incarnate. We are two sides of the **same coin.**
And at any given moment, I am not entirely either, and yet I am **both.**

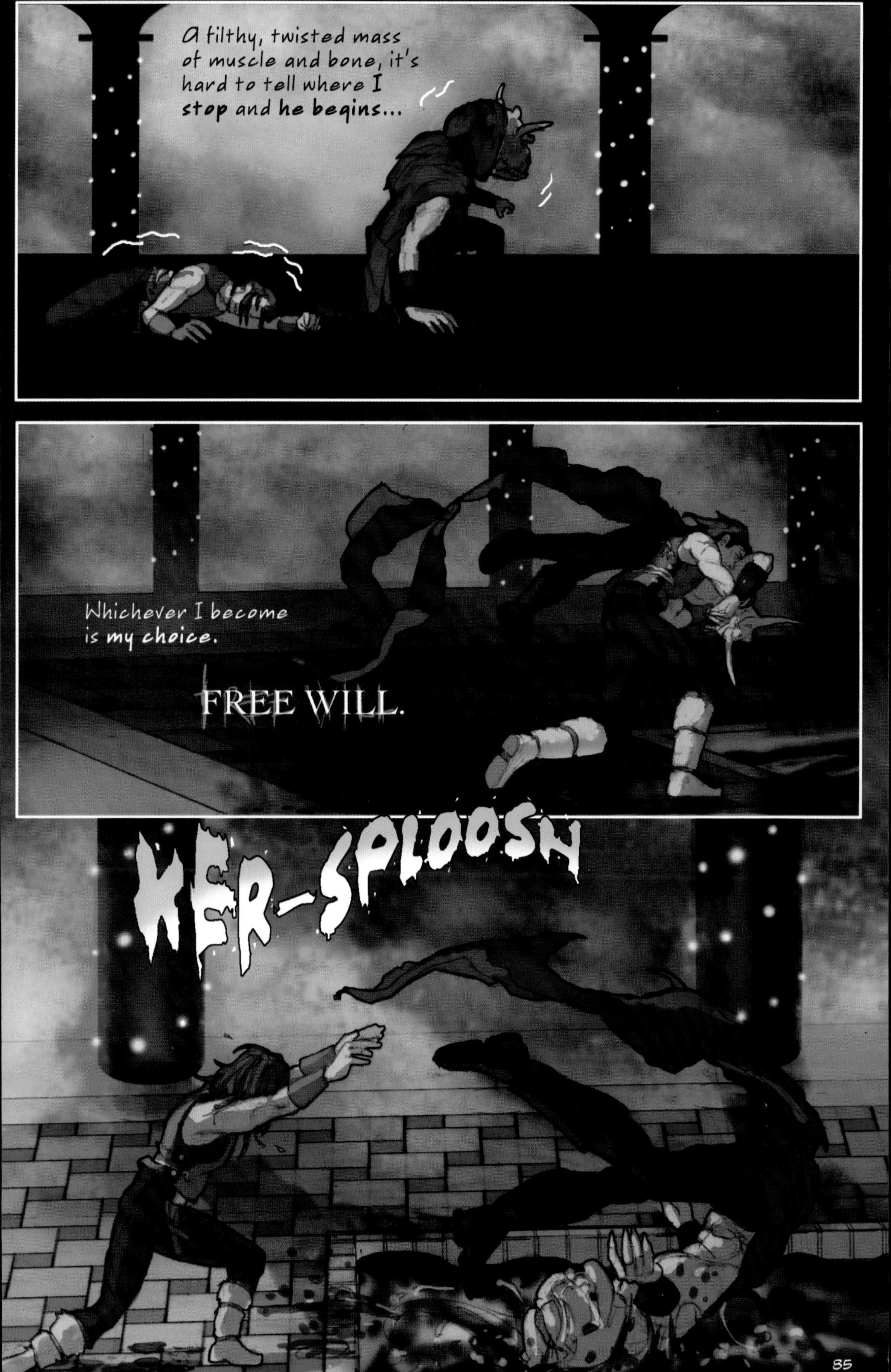

A filthy, twisted mass of muscle and bone, it's hard to tell where I stop and he begins...
Whichever I become is my choice.
FREE WILL.
HER-SPLOOSH

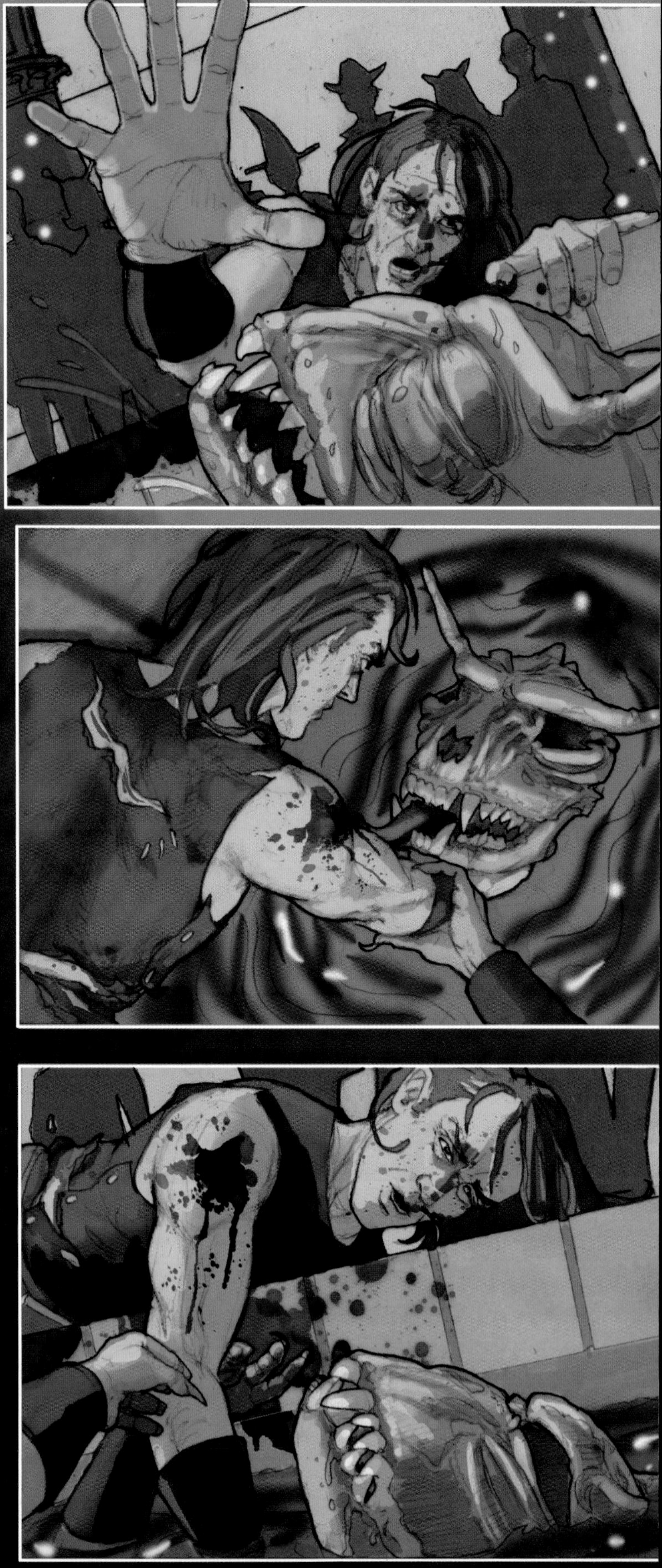

There is a line between good and evil that exists in all of us. A duality built into our nature. You see, we all exist without any real certainty that given the **right** to **choose**, we will **choose** what is **right**.

We have a perpetual inclination, in spite of our best judgement, to **violate** the law.

Who hasn't found himself committing a vile or silly act for no other reason than because he knows he should not?

In the spirit of this perverseness, I come to my final overthrow. It is the unfathomable longing of my soul to infect itself - to offer violence to its own nature.

I am urged to continue and finally consumate the maliciousness I intend to inflict upon this brute.

My fingers wrap around his throat and squeeze so tightly, his head could very well pop off and float away.

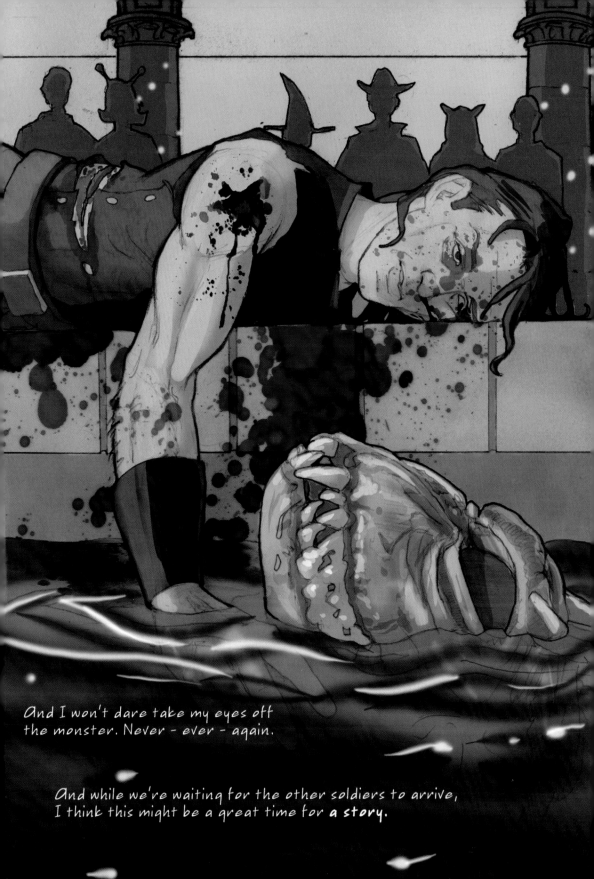

And I won't dare take my eyes off the monster. Never - ever - again.

And while we're waiting for the other soldiers to arrive, I think this might be a great time for **a story.**

You'll like this one, it's about **a dragon...**

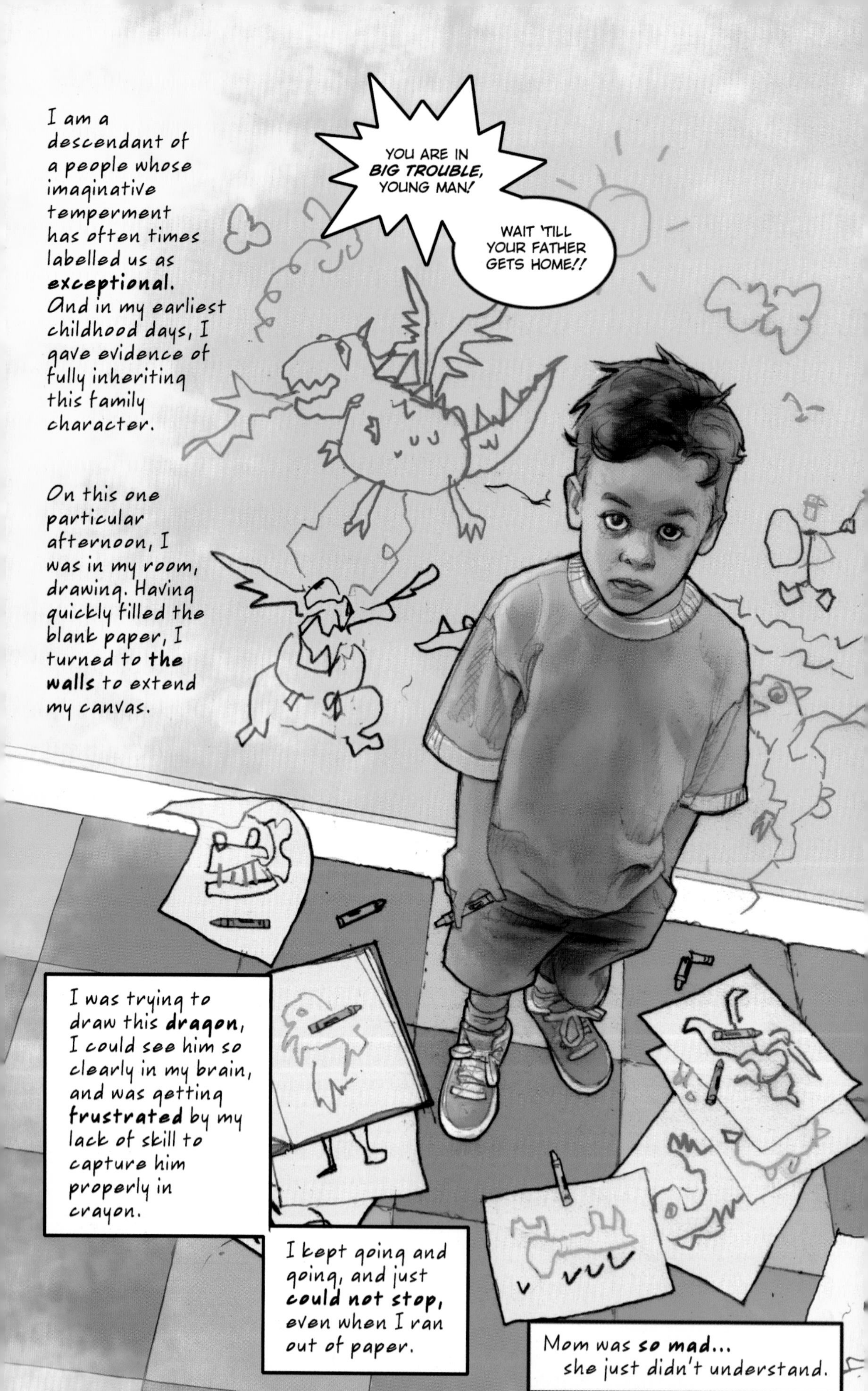
I am a descendant of a people whose imaginative temperment has often times labelled us as **exceptional.** And in my earliest childhood days, I gave evidence of fully inheriting this family character.
On this one particular afternoon, I was in my room, drawing. Having quickly filled the blank paper, I turned to **the walls** to extend my canvas.
YOU ARE IN *BIG TROUBLE,* YOUNG MAN!
WAIT 'TILL YOUR FATHER GETS HOME!!
I was trying to draw this **dragon,** I could see him so clearly in my brain, and was getting **frustrated** by my lack of skill to capture him properly in crayon.
I kept going and going, and just **could not stop,** even when I ran out of paper.
Mom was **so mad...** she just didn't understand.

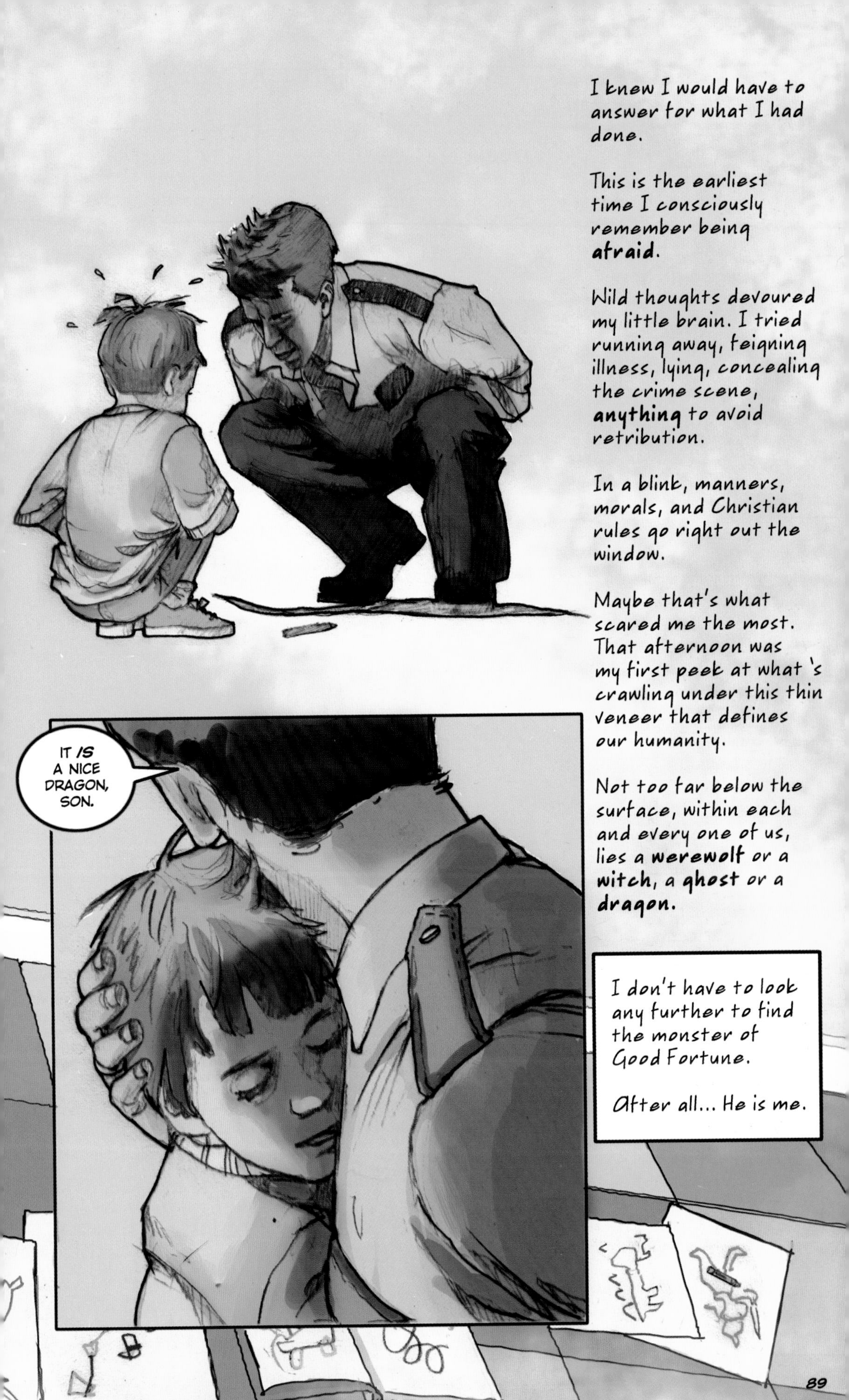
I knew I would have to answer for what I had done.
This is the earliest time I consciously remember being **afraid**.
Wild thoughts devoured my little brain. I tried running away, feigning illness, lying, concealing the crime scene, **anything** to avoid retribution.
In a blink, manners, morals, and Christian rules go right out the window.
Maybe that's what scared me the most. That afternoon was my first peek at what's crawling under this thin veneer that defines our humanity.
Not too far below the surface, within each and every one of us, lies a **werewolf** or a **witch**, a **ghost** or a **dragon**.
IT *IS* A NICE DRAGON, SON.
I don't have to look any further to find the monster of Good Fortune.
After all... He is me.

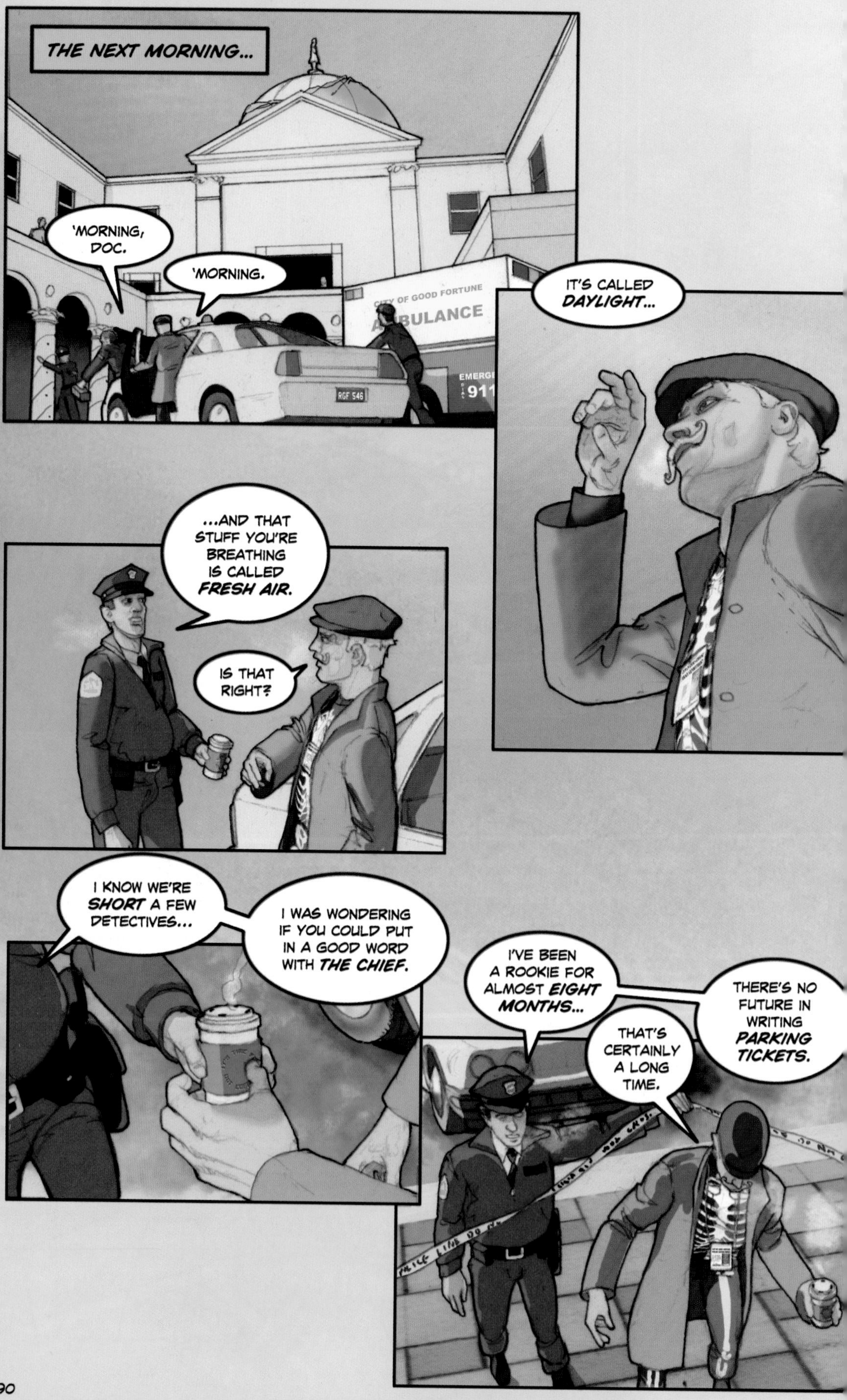
THE NEXT MORNING...
'MORNING, DOC.
'MORNING.
CITY OF GOOD FORTUNE
AMBULANCE
EMERGENCY
911
RGF 546
IT'S CALLED DAYLIGHT...
...AND THAT STUFF YOU'RE BREATHING IS CALLED FRESH AIR.
IS THAT RIGHT?
I KNOW WE'RE SHORT A FEW DETECTIVES...
I WAS WONDERING IF YOU COULD PUT IN A GOOD WORD WITH THE CHIEF.
I'VE BEEN A ROOKIE FOR ALMOST EIGHT MONTHS...
THAT'S CERTAINLY A LONG TIME.
THERE'S NO FUTURE IN WRITING PARKING TICKETS.

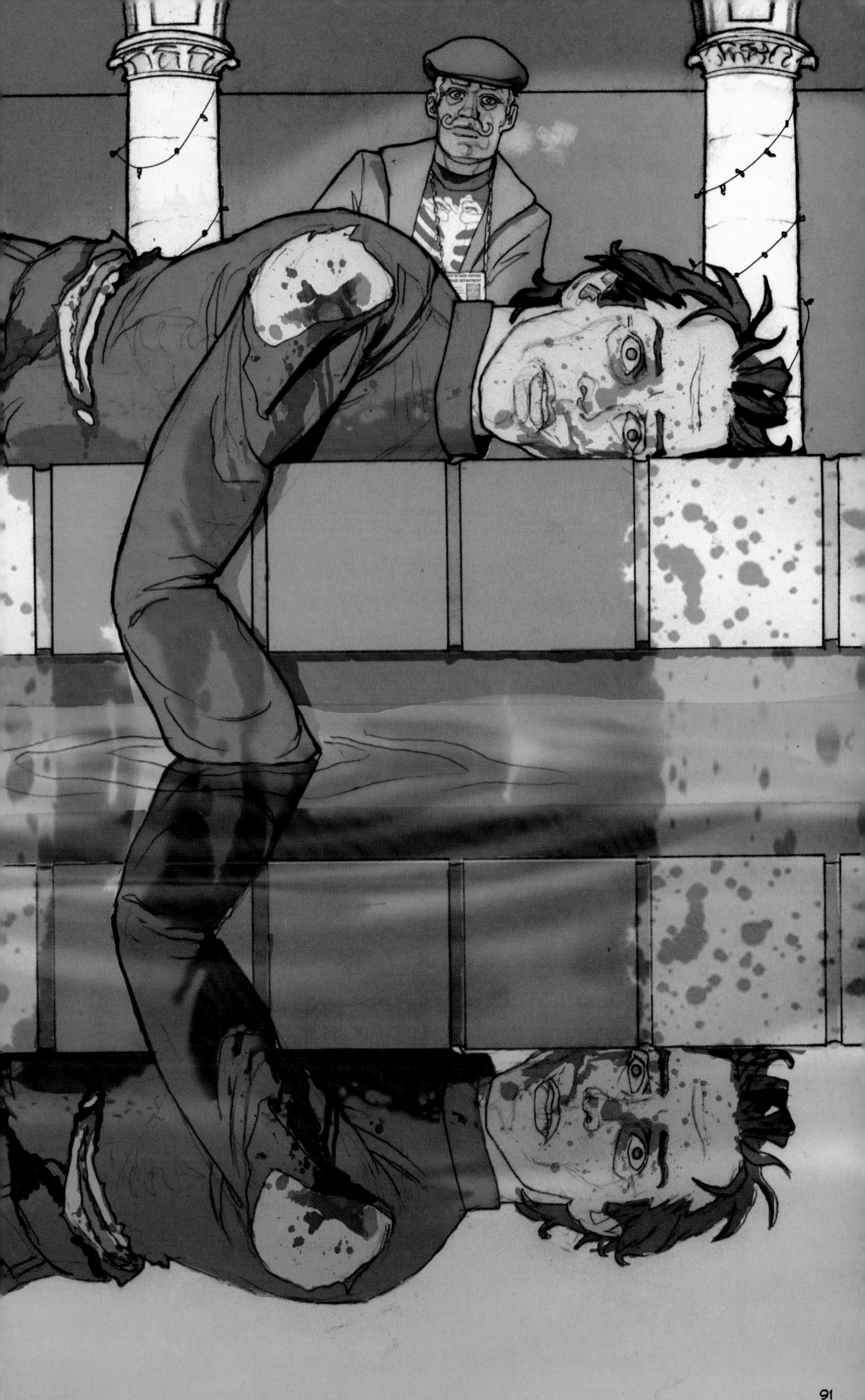

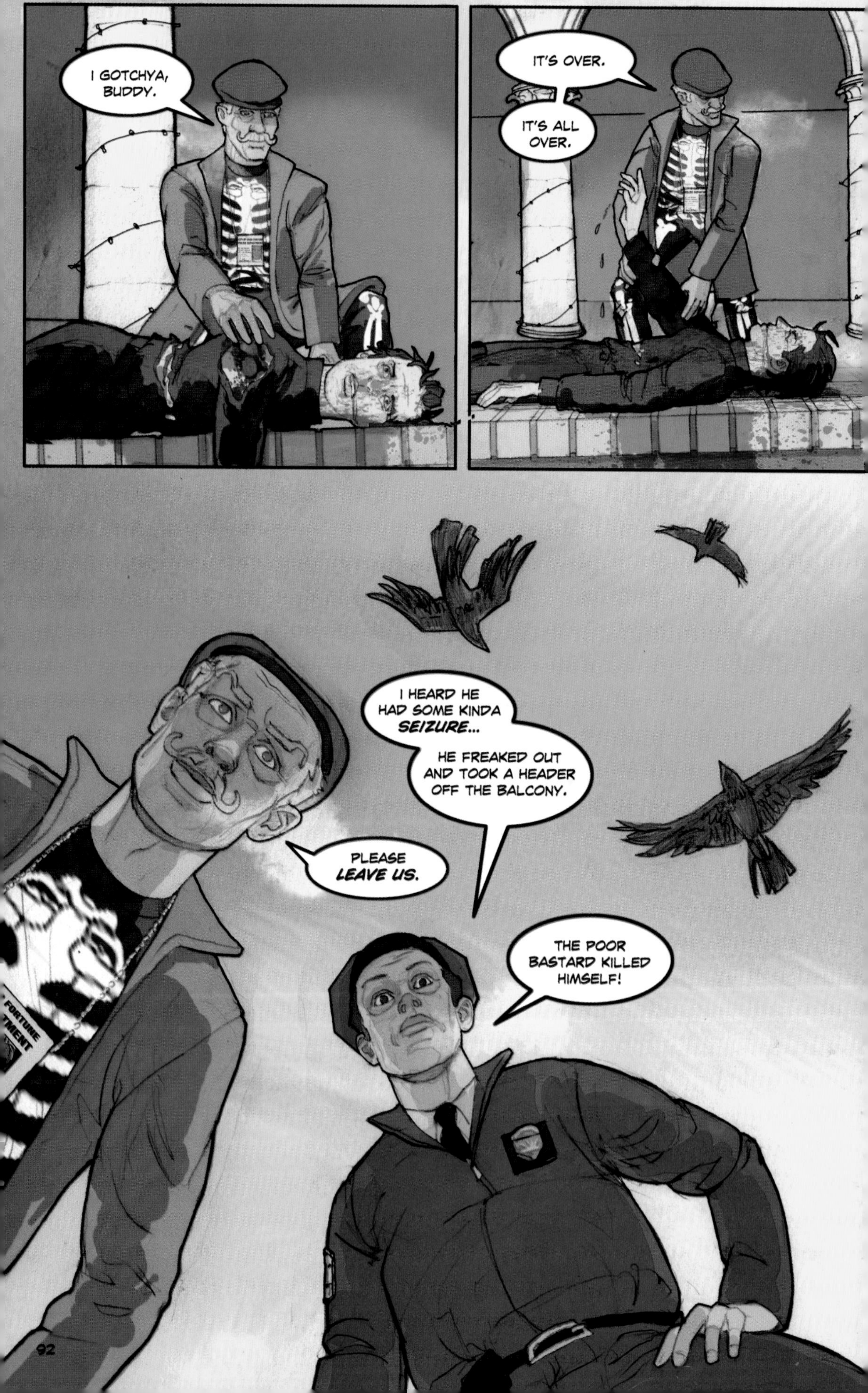
I GOTCHYA, BUDDY.
IT'S OVER.
IT'S ALL OVER.
I HEARD HE HAD SOME KINDA *SEIZURE...*
HE FREAKED OUT AND TOOK A HEADER OFF THE BALCONY.
PLEASE *LEAVE US.*
THE POOR BASTARD KILLED HIMSELF!

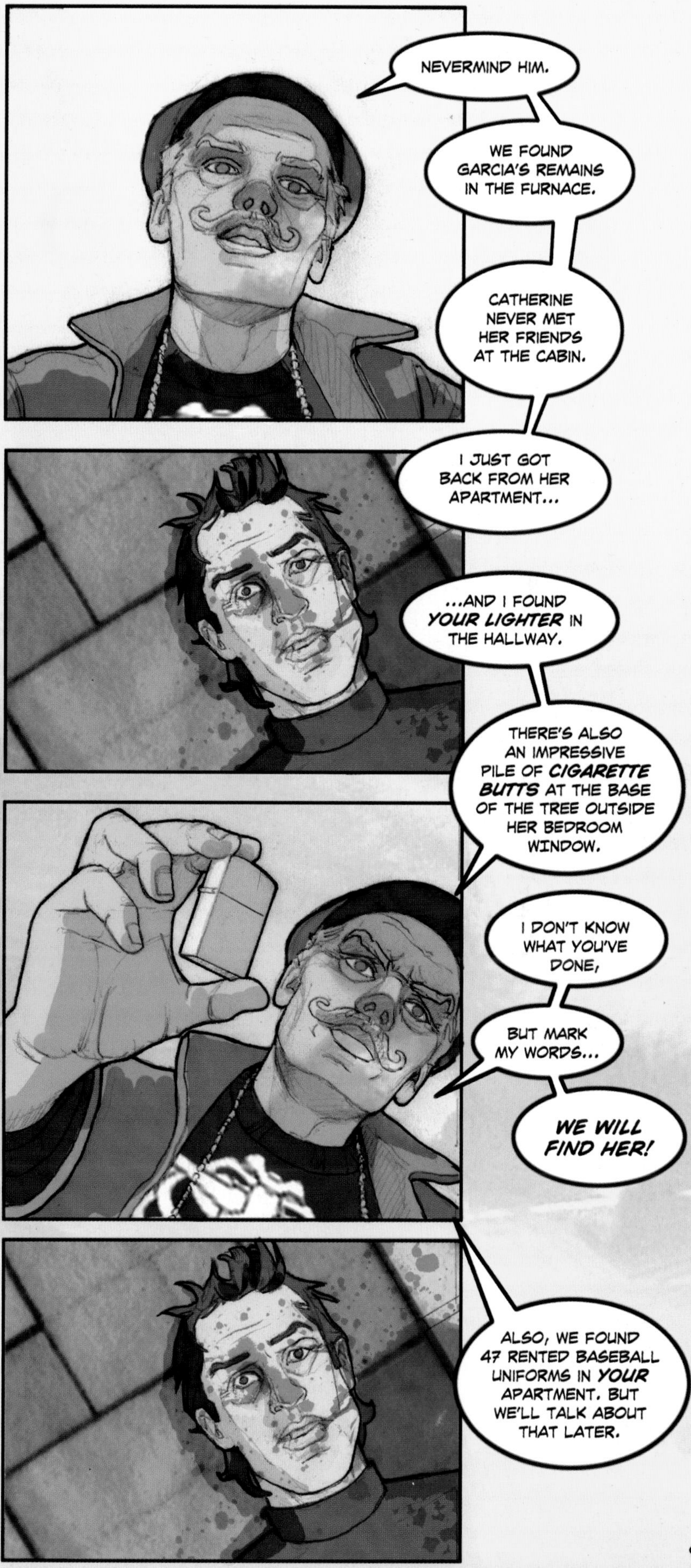
NEVERMIND HIM.
WE FOUND GARCIA'S REMAINS IN THE FURNACE.
CATHERINE NEVER MET HER FRIENDS AT THE CABIN.
I JUST GOT BACK FROM HER APARTMENT...
...AND I FOUND *YOUR LIGHTER* IN THE HALLWAY.
THERE'S ALSO AN IMPRESSIVE PILE OF *CIGARETTE BUTTS* AT THE BASE OF THE TREE OUTSIDE HER BEDROOM WINDOW.
I DON'T KNOW WHAT YOU'VE DONE,
BUT MARK MY WORDS...
WE WILL FIND HER!
ALSO, WE FOUND 47 RENTED BASEBALL UNIFORMS IN *YOUR* APARTMENT. BUT WE'LL TALK ABOUT THAT LATER.

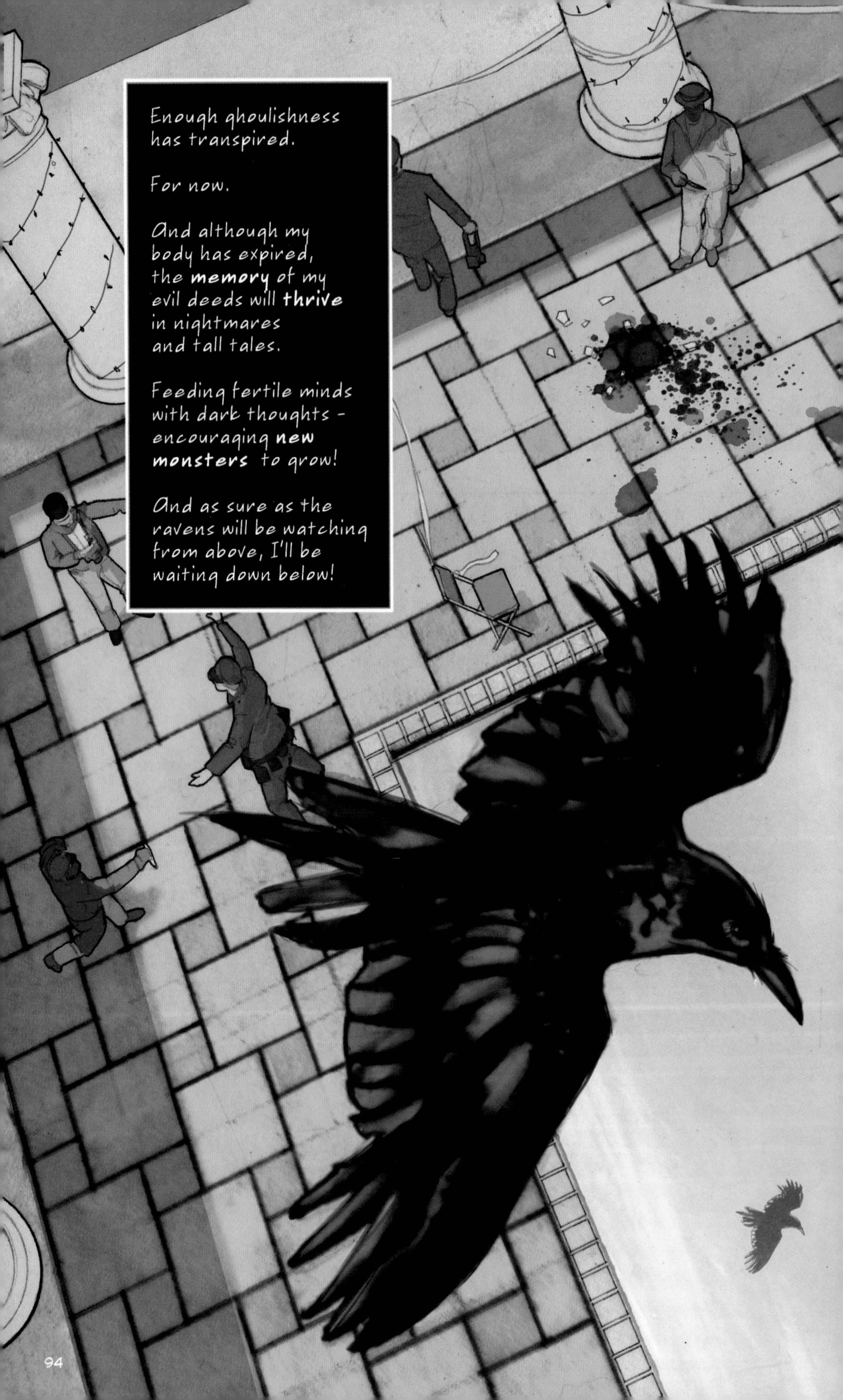
Enough ghoulishness has transpired.
For now.
And although my body has expired, the **memory** of my evil deeds will **thrive** in nightmares and tall tales.
Feeding fertile minds with dark thoughts - encouraging **new monsters** to grow!
And as sure as the ravens will be watching from above, I'll be waiting down below!

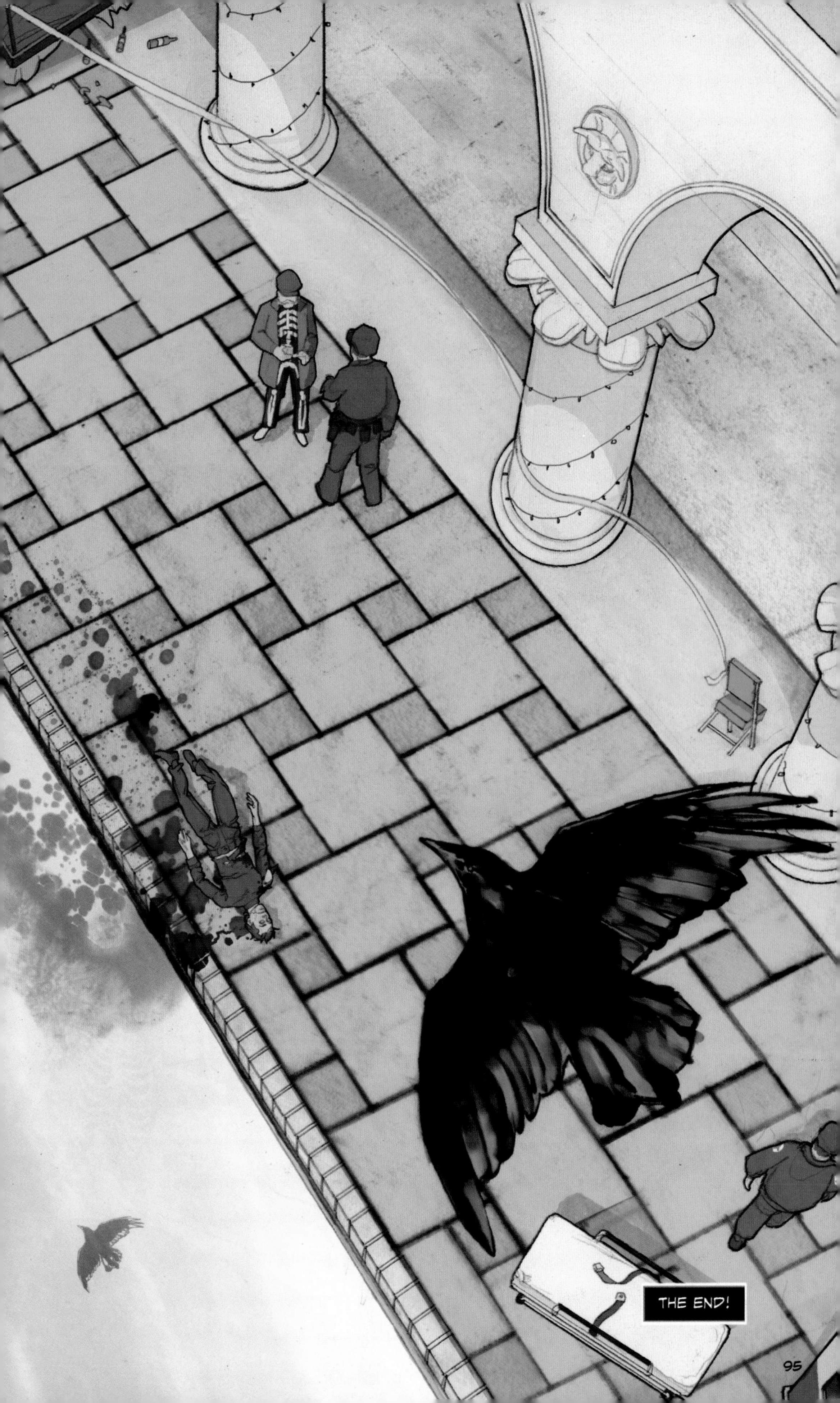
THE END!

INTERLUDE

Edgar Allan Poe believed that within each of us lurks the ability to commit fallacious acts, and that every moment holds the possibility for sanity to crumble into madness. His stories and poems explore the unexplainable desires and dark secrets of our humanity.

This supplemental section presents the five tales of mystery and imagination most influential to *Ravenous*. While *Ravenous* is not a direct adaptation of any one of Poe's short stories, it is an intricate web of many story lines, themes, and elements. They may be summarized as follows...

The irrational act of murdering someone loved and adored. *The Tell-Tale Heart.*

A man struggling to survive in the face of despair, knowing he and his community have been damned to unspeakable tortures. *The Pit & The Pendulum.*

The folly of human nature to fear and fight the inevitability of death. *The Masque of the Red Death.*

The duality that lies within each of us, the perpetual struggle between mannered order and unbridled mayhem.   *William Wilson.*

A man consumed with sorrow over the loss of a lover. *The Raven.*

Each of these ideas are explored in the following distinguished works of Edgar Allan Poe. Each defines a facet of the dark side of the human soul. Weave them together, and they become *Ravenous*.

The Tell-Tale Heart

TRUE! - nervous - very, very dreadfully nervous I had been and am; but why *will* you say that I am mad? The disease had sharpened my senses - not destroyed - not dulled them. Above all was the sense of hearing acute. I heard all things in the heaven and in the earth. I heard many things in hell. How, then, am I mad? Hearken! and observe how healthily - how calmly I can tell you the whole story.

It is impossible to say how first the idea entered my brain; but once conceived, it haunted me day and night. Object there was none. Passion there was none. I loved the old man. He had never wronged me. He had never given me insult. For his gold I had no desire. I think it was his eye! yes, it was this! He had the eye of a vulture - a pale blue eye, with a film over it. Whenever it fell upon me, my blood ran cold; and so by degrees - very gradually - I made up my mind to take the life of the old man, and thus rid myself of the eye for ever.

Now this is the point. You fancy me mad. Madmen know nothing. But you should have seen *me*. You should have seen how wisely I proceeded - with what caution - with what foresight - with what dissimulation I went to work! I was never kinder to the old man than during the whole week before I killed him. And every night, about midnight, I turned the latch of his door and opened it - oh so gently! And then, when I had made an opening sufficient for my head, I put in a dark lantern, all closed, closed, that no light shone out, and then I thrust in my head. Oh, you would have laughed to see how cunningly I thrust it in! I moved it slowly - very, very slowly, so that I might not disturb the old man's sleep. It took me an hour to place my whole head within the opening so far that I could see him as he lay upon his bed. Ha! - would a madman have been so wise as this? And then, when my head was well in the room, I undid the lantern cautiously-oh, so cautiously - cautiously (for the hinges creaked) - I undid it just so much that a single thin ray fell upon the vulture eye. And this I did for seven long nights - every night just at midnight - but I found the eye always closed; and so it was impossible to do the work; for it was not the old man who vexed me, but his Evil Eye. And every morning, when the day broke, I went boldly into the chamber, and spoke courageously to him, calling him by name in a hearty tone, and inquiring how he had passed the night. So you see he would have been a very profound old man, indeed, to suspect that every night, just at twelve, I looked in upon him while he slept.

Upon the eighth night I was more than usually cautious in opening the door. A watch's minute-hand moves more quickly than did mine. Never before that night had I *felt* the extent of my own powers - of my sagacity. I could scarcely contain my feelings of triumph. To think that there I was, opening the door, little by little, and he not even to dream of my secret deeds or thoughts. I fairly chuckled at the idea; and perhaps he heard me; for he moved on the bed suddenly, as if startled. Now you may think that I drew back - but no. His room was as black as pitch with the thick darkness, (for the shutters were close fastened, through fear of robbers), and so I knew that he could not see the opening of the door, and I kept pushing it on steadily, steadily.

I had my head in, and was about to open the lantern, when my thumb slipped upon the tin fastening, and the old man sprang up in bed, crying out - "Who's there?"

I kept quite still and said nothing. For a whole hour I did not move a muscle, and in the meantime I did not hear him lie down. He was still sitting up in the bed listening; - just as I have done, night after night, hearkening to the death-watches in the wall.

Presently I heard a slight groan, and I knew it was the groan of mortal terror. It was not a groan of pain or of grief - oh, no! - it was the low stifled sound that arises from the bottom of the soul when overcharged with awe. I knew the sound well. Many a night, just at midnight, when all the world slept, it has welled up from my own bosom, deepening, with its dreadful echo, the terrors that distracted me. I say I knew it well. I knew what the old man felt, and pitied him, although I chuckled at heart. I knew that he had been lying awake ever since the first slight noise, when he had turned in the bed. His fears had been ever since growing upon him. He had been trying to fancy them causeless, but could not. He had been saying to himself - "It is nothing but the wind in the chimney - it is only a mouse crossing the floor," or "it is merely a cricket which has made a single chirp." Yes, he had been trying to comfort himself with these suppositions: but he had found all in vain. *All in vain*; because Death, in approaching him had stalked with his black shadow before him, and enveloped the victim. And it was the mournful influence of the unperceived shadow that caused him to feel - although he neither saw nor heard - to *feel* the presence of my head within the room.

When I had waited a long time, very patiently, without hearing him lie down, I resolved to open a little - a very, very little crevice in the lantern. So I opened it - you cannot imagine how stealthily, stealthily - until, at length a simple dim ray, like the thread of the spider, shot from out the crevice and fell full upon the vultur e eye.

It was open - wide, wide open - and I grew furious as I gazed upon it. I saw it with perfect distinctness - all a dull blue, with a hideous veil over it that chilled the very marrow in my bones; but I could see nothing else of the old man's face or person: for I had directed the ray as if by instinct, precisely upon the damned spot.

And have I not told you that what you mistake for madness is but over-acuteness of the sense? - now, I say, there came to my ears a low, dull, quick sound, such as a watch

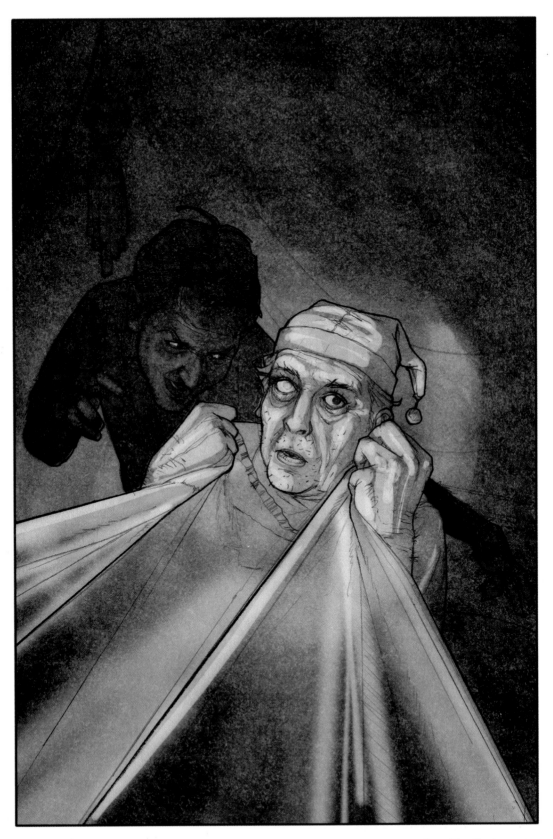

For a whole hour I did not move a muscle, and in the meantime I did not hear him lie down.

makes when enveloped in cotton. I knew *that* sound well, too. It was the beating of the old man's heart. It increased my fury, as the beating of a drum stimulates the soldier into courage.

But even yet I refrained and kept still. I scarcely breathed. I held the lantern motionless. I tried how steadily I could maintain the ray upon the eve. Meantime the hellish tattoo of the heart increased. It grew quicker and quicker, and louder and louder every instant. The old man's terror *must* have been extreme! It grew louder, I say, louder every moment! - do you mark me well? I have told you that I am nervous: so I am. And now at the dead hour of the night, amid the dreadful silence of that old house, so strange a noise as this excited me to uncontrollable terror. Yet, for some minutes longer I refrained and stood still. But the beating grew louder, louder! I thought the heart must burst. And now a new anxiety seized me - the sound would be heard by a neighbour! The old man's hour had come! With a loud yell, I threw open the lantern and leaped into the room. He shrieked once - once only. In an instant I dragged him to the floor, and pulled the heavy bed over him. I then smiled gaily, to find the deed so far done. But, for many minutes, the heart beat on with a muffled sound. This, however, did not vex me; it would not be heard through the wall. At length it ceased. The old man was dead. I removed the bed and examined the corpse. Yes, he was stone, stone dead. I placed my hand upon the heart and held it there many minutes. There was no pulsation. He was stone dead. His eye would trouble me no more.

If still you think me mad, you will think so no longer when I describe the wise precautions I took for the concealment of the body. The night waned, and I worked hastily, but in silence. First of all I dismembered the corpse. I cut off the head and the arms and the legs.

I then took up three planks from the flooring of the chamber, and deposited all between the scantlings. I then replaced the boards so cleverly, so cunningly, that no human eye - not even *his* - could have detected any thing wrong. There was nothing to wash out - no stain of any kind - no blood-spot whatever. I had been too wary for that. A tub had caught all - ha! ha!

When I had made an end of these labors, it was four o'clock - still dark as midnight. As the bell sounded the hour, there came a knocking at the street door. I went down to open it with a light heart, - for what had I *now* to fear? There entered three men, who introduced themselves, with perfect suavity, as officers of the police. A shriek had been heard by a neighbour during the night; suspicion of foul play had been aroused; information had been lodged at the police office, and they (the officers) had been deputed to search the premises.

I smiled, - for *what* had I to fear? I bade the gentlemen welcome. The shriek, I said, was my own in a dream. The old man, I mentioned, was absent in the country. I took my visitors all over the house. I bade them search - search *well*. I led them, at length, to *his* chamber. I showed them his treasures, secure, undisturbed. In the enthusiasm of my confidence, I brought chairs into the room, and desired them *here* to rest from their fatigues, while I myself, in the wild audacity of my perfect triumph, placed my own seat upon the very spot beneath which reposed the corpse of the victim.

The officers were satisfied. My *manner* had convinced them. I was singularly at ease. They sat, and while I answered cheerily, they chatted of familiar things. But, ere long, I felt myself getting pale and wished them gone. My head ached, and I fancied a ringing in my ears: but still they sat and still they chatted. The ringing became more distinct: - It continued and became more distinct: I talked more freely to get rid of the feeling: but it continued and gained definiteness - until, at length, I found that the noise was *not* within my ears.

No doubt I now grew *very* pale; - but I talked more fluently, and with a heightened voice. Yet the sound increased - and what could I do? It was *a low, dull, quick sound - much such a sound as a watch makes when enveloped in cotton.* I gasped for breath - and yet the officers heard it not.

I talked more quickly - more vehemently; but the noise steadily increased. I arose and argued about trifles, in a high key and with violent gesticulations; but the noise steadily increased. Why *would* they not be gone? I paced the floor to and fro with heavy strides, as if excited to fury by the observations of the men - but the noise steadily increased. Oh God! what *could* I do? I foamed - I raved - I swore! I swung the chair upon which I had been sitting, and grated it upon the boards, but the noise arose over all and continually increased. It grew louder - louder - *louder!* And still the men chatted pleasantly, and smiled. Was it possible they heard not? Almighty God! - no, no! They heard! - they suspected! - *they knew!* - they were making a mockery of my horror!-this I thought, and this I think. But anything was better than this agony! Anything was more tolerable than this derision! I could bear those hypocritical smiles no longer! I felt that I must scream or die! and now - again! - hark! louder! louder! louder! *louder!*

"Villains!" I shrieked, "dissemble no more! I admit the deed! - tear up the planks! here, here! - it is the beating of his hideous heart!"

The Pit & The Pendulum

Impia tortorum longos hic turba furores
Sanguinis innocui, non satiata, aluit.
Sospite nunc patria, fracto nunc funeris antro,
Mors ubi dira fuit vita salusque patent.

*[Quatrain composed for the gates of a market to be erected
upon the site of the Jacobin Club House at Paris.]*

I WAS sick -- sick unto death with that long agony; and when they at length unbound
me, and I was permitted to sit, I felt that my senses were leaving me. The sentence --
the dread sentence of death -- was the last of distinct accentuation which reached my
ears. After that, the sound of the inquisitorial voices seemed merged in one dreamy
indeterminate hum. It conveyed to my soul the idea of *revolution* -- perhaps from its
association in fancy with the burr of a mill-wheel. This only for a brief period; for
presently I heard no more. Yet, for a while, I saw; but with how terrible an exaggeration!
I saw the lips of the black-robed judges. They appeared to me white -- whiter than
the sheet upon which I trace these words -- and thin even to grotesqueness; thin with
the intensity of their expression of firmness -- of immoveable resolution -- of stern
contempt of human torture. I saw that the decrees of what to me was Fate were still
issuing from those lips. I saw them writhe with a deadly locution. I saw them fashion
the syllables of my name; and I shuddered because no sound succeeded. I saw, too,
for a few moments of delirious horror, the soft and nearly imperceptible waving of
the sable draperies which enwrapped the walls of the apartment. And then my vision
fell upon the seven tall candles upon the table. At first they wore the aspect of charity,
and seemed white and slender angels who would save me; but then, all at once, there
came a most deadly nausea over my spirit, and I felt every fibre in my frame thrill as
if I had touched the wire of a galvanic battery, while the angel forms became
meaningless spectres, with heads of flame, and I saw that from them there would be

no help. And then there stole into my fancy, like a rich musical note, the thought of what sweet rest there must be in the grave. The thought came gently and stealthily, and it seemed long before it attained full appreciation; but just as my spirit came at length properly to feel and entertain it, the figures of the judges vanished, as if magically from before me; the tall candles sank into nothingness; their flames went out utterly; the blackness of darkness supervened; all sensations appeared swallowed up in a mad rushing descent as of the soul into Hades. Then silence, and stillness, night were the universe.

I had swooned; but still will not say that all of consciousness was lost. What of it there remained I will not attempt to define, or even to describe; yet all was not lost. In the deepest slumber -- no! In delirium -- no! In a swoon -- no! In death -- no! even in the grave all *is not* lost. Else there is no immortality for man. Arousing from the most profound of slumbers, we break the gossamer web of *some* dream. Yet in a second afterward, (so frail may that web have been) we remember not that we have dreamed. In the return to life from the swoon there are two stages; first, that of the sense of mental or spiritual; secondly, that of the sense of physical, existence. It seems probable that if, upon reaching the second stage, we could recall the impressions of the first, we should find these impressions eloquent in memories of the gulf beyond. And that gulf is -- what? How at least shall we distinguish its shadows from those of the tomb? But if the impressions of what I have termed the first stage, are not, at will, recalled, yet, after long interval, do they not come unbidden, while we marvel whence they come? He who has never swooned, is not he who finds strange palaces and wildly familiar faces in coals that glow; is not he who beholds floating in mid-air the sad visions that the many may not view; is not he who ponders over the perfume of some novel flower -- is not he whose brain grows bewildered with the meaning of some musical cadence which has never before arrested his attention.

Amid frequent and thoughtful endeavors to remember; amid earnest struggles to regather some token of the state of seeming nothingness into which my soul had lapsed, there have been moments when I have dreamed of success; there have been brief, very brief periods when I have conjured up remembrances which the lucid reason of a later epoch assures me could have had reference only to that condition of seeming unconsciousness. These shadows of memory tell, indistinctly, of tall figures that lifted and bore me in silence down -- down -- still down -- till a hideous dizziness oppressed me at the mere idea of the interminableness of the descent. They tell also of a vague horror at my heart, on account of that heart's unnatural stillness. Then comes a sense of sudden motionlessness throughout all things; as if those who bore me (a ghastly train!) had outrun, in their descent, the limits of the limitless, and paused from the wearisomeness of their toil. After this I call to mind flatness and dampness; and then all is *madness* -- the madness of a memory which busies itself among forbidden things.

Very suddenly there came back to my soul motion and sound -- the tumultuous motion of the heart, and, in my ears, the sound of its beating. Then a pause in which all is blank. Then again sound, and motion, and touch -- a tingling sensation pervading my frame. Then the mere consciousness of existence, without thought -- a condition which lasted long. Then, very suddenly, thought, and shuddering terror, and earnest endeavor to comprehend my true state. Then a strong desire to lapse into insensibility. Then a rushing revival of soul and a successful effort to move. And now a full memory of the trial, of the judges, of the sable draperies, of the sentence, of the sickness, of the swoon. Then entire forgetfulness of all that followed; of all that a later day and much earnestness of endeavor have enabled me vaguely to recall.

So far, I had not opened my eyes. I felt that I lay upon my back, unbound. I reached out my hand, and it fell heavily upon something damp and hard. There I suffered it to remain for many minutes, while I strove to imagine where and *what* I could be. I longed, yet dared not to employ my vision. I dreaded the first glance at objects around me. It was not that I feared to look upon things horrible, but that I grew aghast lest there should be *nothing* to see. At length, with a wild desperation at heart, I quickly unclosed my eyes. My worst thoughts, then, were confirmed. The blackness of eternal night encompassed me. I struggled for breath. The intensity of the darkness seemed to oppress and stifle me. The atmosphere was intolerably close. I still lay quietly, and made effort to exercise my reason. I brought to mind the inquisitorial proceedings, and attempted from that point to deduce my real condition. The sentence had passed; and it appeared to me that a very long interval of time had since elapsed. Yet not for a moment did I suppose myself actually dead. Such a supposition, notwithstanding what we read in fiction, is altogether inconsistent with real existence; -- but where and in what state was I? The condemned to death, I knew, perished usually at the *auto-da-fés*, and one of these had been held on the very night of the day of my trial. Had I been remanded to my dungeon, to await the next sacrifice, which would not take place for many months? This I at once saw could not be. Victims had been in immediate demand. Moreover, my dungeon, as well as all the condemned cells at Toledo, had stone floors, and light was not altogether excluded.

A fearful idea now suddenly drove the blood in torrents upon my heart, and for a brief period, I once more relapsed into insensibility. Upon recovering, I at once started to my feet, trembling convulsively in every fibre. I thrust my arms wildly above and around me in all directions. I felt nothing; yet dreaded to move a step, lest I should be impeded by the walls of a *tomb*. Perspiration burst from every pore, and stood in cold big beads upon my forehead. The agony of suspense grew at length intolerable, and I cautiously moved forward, with my arms extended, and my eyes straining from their sockets, in the hope of catching some faint ray of light. I proceeded for many paces; but still all was blackness and vacancy. I breathed more freely. It seemed evident that mine was not, at least, the most hideous of fates.

And now, as I still continued to step cautiously onward, there came thronging upon my recollection a thousand vague rumors of the horrors of Toledo. Of the dungeons there had been strange things narrated -- fables I had always deemed them -- but yet strange, and too ghastly to repeat, save in a whisper. Was I left to perish of starvation in this subterranean world of darkness; or what fate, perhaps even more fearful, awaited me? That the result would be death, and a death of more than customary bitterness, I knew too well the character of my judges to doubt. The mode and the hour were all that occupied or distracted me.

My outstretched hands at length encountered some solid obstruction. It was a wall, seemingly of stone masonry -- very smooth, slimy, and cold. I followed it up; stepping with all the careful distrust with which certain antique narratives had inspired me. This process, however, afforded me no means of ascertaining the dimensions of my dungeon; as I might make its circuit, and return to the point whence I set out, without being aware of the fact; so perfectly uniform seemed the wall. I therefore sought the knife which had been in my pocket, when led into the inquisitorial chamber; but it was gone; my clothes had been exchanged for a wrapper of coarse serge. I had thought of forcing the blade in some minute crevice of the masonry, so as to identify my point of departure. The difficulty, nevertheless, was but trivial; although, in the disorder of my fancy, it seemed at first insuperable. I tore a part of the hem from the robe and placed the fragment at full length, and at right angles to the wall. In groping my way around the prison, I could not fail to encounter this rag upon completing the circuit. So, at least I thought: but I had not counted upon the extent of the dungeon, or upon my own weakness. The ground was moist and slippery. I staggered onward for some time, when I stumbled and fell. My excessive fatigue induced me to remain prostrate; and sleep soon overtook me as I lay.

Upon awaking, and stretching forth an arm, I found beside me a loaf and a pitcher with water. I was too much exhausted to reflect upon this circumstance, but ate and drank with avidity. Shortly afterward, I resumed my tour around the prison, and with much toil came at last upon the fragment of the serge. Up to the period when I fell I had counted fifty-two paces, and upon resuming my walk, I had counted forty-eight more; -- when I arrived at the rag. There were in all, then, a hundred paces; and, admitting two paces to the yard, I presumed the dungeon to be fifty yards in circuit. I had met, however, with many angles in the wall, and thus I could form no guess at the shape of the vault; for vault I could not help supposing it to be.

I had little object -- certainly no hope -- these researches; but a vague curiosity prompted me to continue them. Quitting the wall, I resolved to cross the area of the enclosure. At first I proceeded with extreme caution, for the floor, although seemingly of solid material, was treacherous with slime. At length, however, I took courage, and did not hesitate to step firmly; endeavoring to cross in as direct a line as possible. I had advanced some ten or twelve paces in this manner, when the remnant of the torn hem of my robe became entangled between my legs. I stepped on it, and fell violently on my face.

In the confusion attending my fall, I did not immediately apprehend a somewhat startling circumstance, which yet, in a few seconds afterward, and while I still lay prostrate, arrested my attention. It was this: my chin rested upon the floor of the prison, but my lips and the upper portion of my head, although seemingly at a less

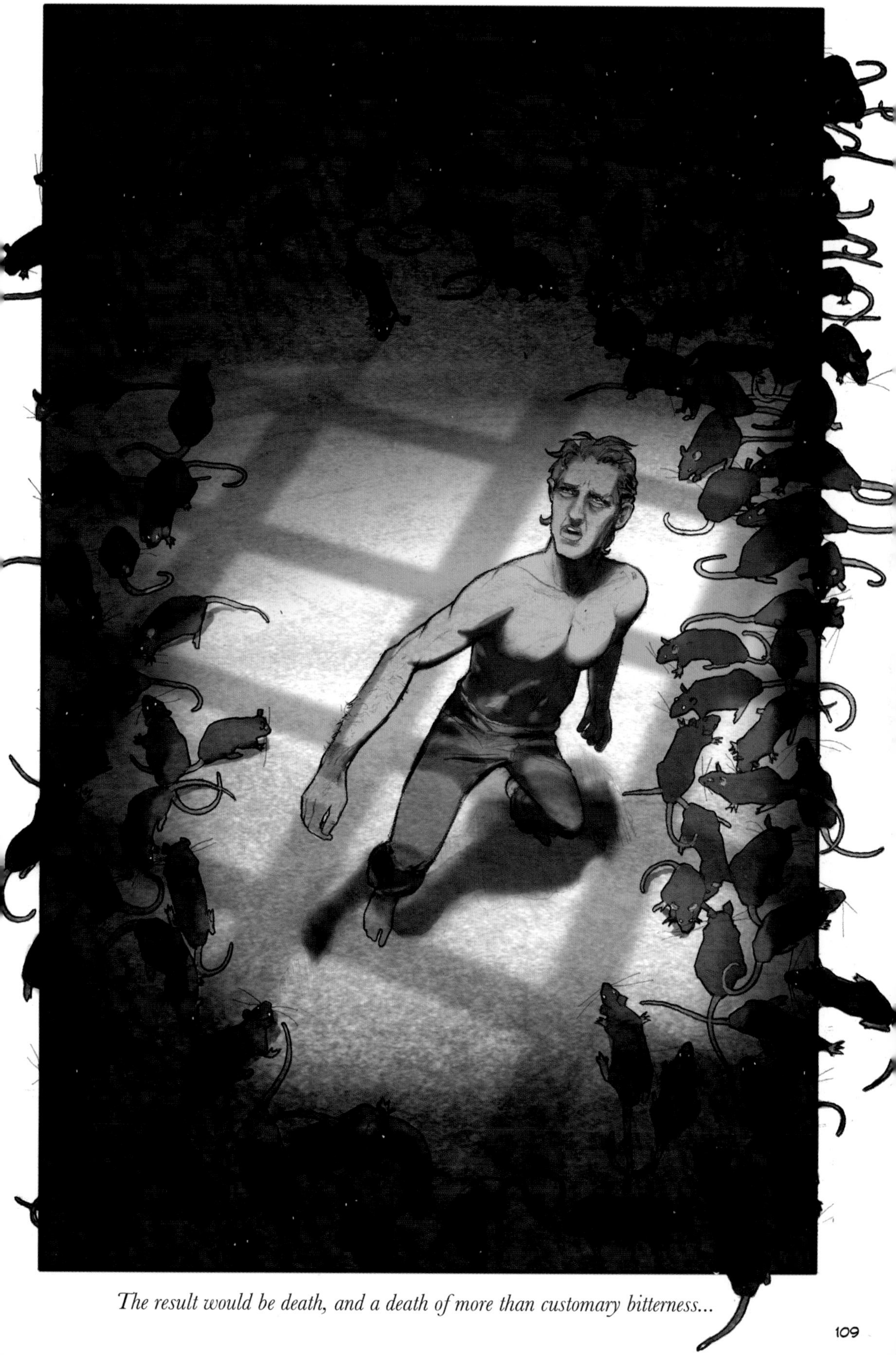

The result would be death, and a death of more than customary bitterness...

elevation than the chin, touched nothing. At the same time my forehead seemed bathed in a clammy vapor, and the peculiar smell of decayed fungus arose to my nostrils. I put forward my arm, and shuddered to find that I had fallen at the very brink of a circular pit, whose extent, of course, I had no means of ascertaining at the moment. Groping about the masonry just below the margin, I succeeded in dislodging a small fragment, and let it fall into the abyss. For many seconds I hearkened to its reverberations as it dashed against the sides of the chasm in its descent; at length there was a sullen plunge into water, succeeded by loud echoes. At the same moment there came a sound resembling the quick opening, and as rapid closing of a door overhead, while a faint gleam of light flashed suddenly through the gloom, and as suddenly faded away.

I saw clearly the doom which had been prepared for me, and congratulated myself upon the timely accident by which I had escaped. Another step before my fall, and the world had seen me no more. And the death just avoided, was of that very character which I had regarded as fabulous and frivolous in the tales respecting the Inquisition. To the victims of its tyranny, there was the choice of death with its direst physical agonies, or death with its most hideous moral horrors. I had been reserved for the latter. By long suffering my nerves had been unstrung, until I trembled at the sound of my own voice, and had become in every respect a fitting subject for the species of torture which awaited me.

Shaking in every limb, I groped my way back to the wall -- resolving there to perish rather than risk the terrors of the wells, of which my imagination now pictured many in various positions about the dungeon. In other conditions of mind I might have had courage to end my misery at once by a plunge into one of these abysses; but now I was the veriest of cowards. Neither could I forget what I had read of these pits -- that the *sudden* extinction of life formed no part of their most horrible plan.

Agitation of spirit kept me awake for many long hours; but at length I again slumbered. Upon arousing, I found by my side, as before, a loaf and a pitcher of water. A burning thirst consumed me, and I emptied the vessel at a draught. It must have been drugged; for scarcely had I drunk, before I became irresistibly drowsy. A deep sleep fell upon me, a sleep like that of death. How long it lasted of course, I know not; but when, once again, I unclosed my eyes, the objects around me were visible. By a wild sulphurous lustre, the origin of which I could not at first determine, I was enabled to see the extent and aspect of the prison.

In its size I had been greatly mistaken. The whole circuit of its walls did not exceed twenty-five yards. For some minutes this fact occasioned me a world of vain trouble; vain indeed -- for what could be of less importance, under the terrible circumstances which environed me, then the mere dimensions of my dungeon? But my soul took a wild interest in trifles, and I busied myself in endeavors to account for the error I had committed in my measurement. The truth at length flashed upon me. In my first attempt at exploration I had counted fifty-two paces, up to the period when I fell; I must then have been within a pace or two of the fragment of serge; in fact, I had nearly performed the circuit of the vault. I then slept, and upon awaking, I must have returned upon my steps -- thus supposing the circuit nearly double what it actually was. My confusion of mind prevented me from observing that I began my tour with the wall to the left, and ended it with the wall to the right.

I had been deceived, too, in respect to the shape of the enclosure. In feeling my way I had found many angles, and thus deduced an idea of great irregularity; so potent is the effect of total darkness upon one arousing from lethargy or sleep! The angles were simply those of a few slight depressions, or niches, at odd intervals. The general shape of the prison was square. What I had taken for masonry seemed now to be iron, or some other metal, in huge plates, whose sutures or joints occasioned the depression. The entire surface of this metallic enclosure was rudely daubed in all the hideous and repulsive devices to which the charnel superstition of the monks has given rise. The figures of fiends in aspects of menace, with skeleton forms, and other more really fearful images, overspread and disfigured the walls. I observed that the outlines of these monstrosities were sufficiently distinct, but that the colors seemed faded and blurred, as if from the effects of a damp atmosphere. I now noticed the floor, too, which was of stone. In the centre yawned the circular pit from whose jaws I had escaped; but it was the only one in the dungeon.

All this I saw indistinctly and by much effort -- for my personal condition had been greatly changed during slumber. I now lay upon my back, and at full length, on a species of low framework of wood. To this I was securely bound by a long strap resembling a surcingle. It passed in many convolutions about my limbs and body, leaving at liberty only my head, and my left arm to such extent that I could, by dint of much exertion, supply myself with food from an earthen dish which lay by my side on the floor. I saw, to my horror, that the pitcher had been removed. I say to my horror; for I was consumed with intolerable thirst. This thirst it appeared to be the design of my persecutors to stimulate -- for the food in the dish was meat pungently seasoned.

Looking upward, I surveyed the ceiling of my prison. It was some thirty or forty feet overhead, and constructed much as the side walls. In one of its panels a very singular figure riveted my whole attention. It was the painted figure of Time as he is commonly represented, save that, in lieu of a scythe, he held what, at a casual glance, I supposed to be the pictured image of a huge pendulum such as we see on antique clocks. There was something, however, in the appearance of this machine which caused me to regard it more attentively. While I gazed directly upward at it (for its position was immediately over my own) I fancied that I saw it in motion. In an instant afterward the fancy was confirmed. Its sweep was brief, and of course slow. I watched it for some minutes, somewhat in fear, but more in wonder. Wearied at length with observing its dull movement, I turned my eyes upon the other objects in the cell.

A slight noise attracted my notice, and, looking to the floor, I saw several enormous rats traversing it. They had issued from the well, which lay just within view to my right. Even then, while I gazed, they came up in troops, hurriedly, with ravenous eyes, allured by the scent of the meat. From this it required much effort and attention to scare them away. It might have been half an hour, perhaps even an hour, (for in cast my I could take but imperfect note of time) before I again cast my eyes upward. What I then saw confounded and amazed me. The sweep of the pendulum had increased in extent by nearly a yard. As a natural consequence , its velocity was also much greater. But what mainly disturbed me was the idea that had perceptibly *descended*. I now observed -- with what horror it is needless to say -- that its nether extremity was formed of a crescent of glittering steel, about a foot in length from horn to horn; the horns upward, and the under edge evidently as keen as that of a razor. Like a razor also, it seemed massy and heavy, tapering from the edge into a solid and broad structure above. It was appended to a weighty rod of brass, and the whole *hissed* as it swung through the air.

I could no longer doubt the doom prepared for me by monkish ingenuity in torture. My cognizance of the pit had become known to the inquisitorial agents -- *the pit*, whose horrors had been destined for so bold a recusant as myself -- *the pit*, typical of hell, and regarded by rumor as the Ultima Thule of all their punishments. The plunge into this pit I had avoided by the merest of accidents, I knew that surprise, or entrapment into torment, formed an important portion of all the grotesquerie of these dungeon deaths. Having failed to fall, it was no part of the demon plan to hurl me into the abyss; and thus (there being no alternative) a different and a milder destruction awaited me. Milder! I half smiled in my agony as I thought of such application of such a term.

What boots it to tell of the long, long hours of horror more than mortal, during which I counted the rushing vibrations of the steel! Inch by inch -- line by line -- with a descent only appreciable at intervals that seemed ages -- down and still down it came! Days passed -- it might have been that many days passed -- ere it swept so closely over me as to fan me with its acrid breath. The odor of the sharp steel forced itself into my nostrils. I prayed -- I wearied heaven with my prayer for its more speedy descent. I grew frantically mad, and struggled to force myself upward against the sweep of the fearful scimitar. And then I fell suddenly calm, and lay smiling at the glittering death, as a child at some rare bauble.

There was another interval of utter insensibility; it was brief; for, upon again lapsing into life there had been no perceptible descent in the pendulum. But it might have been long; for I knew there were demons who took note of my swoon, and who could have arrested the vibration at pleasure. Upon my recovery, too, I felt very -- oh, inexpressibly sick and weak, as if through long inanition. Even amid the agonies of that period, the human nature craved food. With painful effort I outstretched my left arm as far as my bonds permitted, and took possession of the small remnant which had been spared me by the rats. As I put a portion of it within my lips, there rushed to my mind a half formed thought of joy -- of hope. Yet what business had I with hope? It was, as I say, a half formed thought -- man has many such which are never completed. I felt that it was of joy -- of hope; but felt also that it had perished in its formation. In vain I struggled to perfect -- to regain it. Long suffering had nearly annihilated all my ordinary powers of mind. I was an imbecile -- an idiot.

The vibration of the pendulum was at right angles to my length. I saw that the crescent was designed to cross the region of the heart. It would fray the serge of my robe -- it would return and repeat its operations -- again -- and again. Notwithstanding its terrifically wide sweep (some thirty feet or more) and the its hissing vigor of its descent, sufficient to sunder these very walls of iron, still the fraying of my robe would be all that, for several minutes, it would accomplish. And at this thought I paused. I dared not go further than this reflection. I dwelt upon it with a pertinacity of attention -- as if, in so dwelling, I could arrest here the descent of the steel. I forced myself to ponder upon the sound of the crescent as it should pass across the garment -- upon the peculiar thrilling sensation which the friction of cloth produces on the nerves. I pondered upon all this frivolity until my teeth were on edge.

Down -- steadily down it crept. I took a frenzied pleasure in contrasting its downward with its lateral velocity. To the right -- to the left -- far and wide -- with the shriek of a damned spirit! to my heart, with the stealthy pace of the tiger! I alternately laughed and howled as the one or the other idea grew predominant.

Down -- certainly, relentlessly down! It vibrated within three inches of my bosom! I struggled violently -- furiously -- to free my left arm. This was free only from the elbow to the hand. I could reach the latter, from the platter beside me, to my mouth, with great effort, but no farther. Could I have broken the fastenings above the elbow, I would have seized and attempted to arrest the pendulum. I might as well have attempted to arrest an avalanche!

Down -- still unceasingly -- still inevitably down! I gasped and struggled at each vibration. I shrunk convulsively at its every sweep. My eyes followed its outward or upward whirls with the eagerness of the most unmeaning despair; they closed themselves spasmodically at the descent, although death would have been a relief, oh! how unspeakable! Still I quivered in every nerve to think how slight a sinking of the machinery would precipitate that keen, glistening axe upon my bosom. It was *hope* that prompted the nerve to quiver -- the frame to shrink. It was *hope* -- the hope that triumphs on the rack -- that whispers to the death-condemned even in the dungeons of the Inquisition.

I saw that some ten or twelve vibrations would bring the steel in actual contact with my robe, and with this observation there suddenly came over my spirit all the keen, collected calmness of despair. For the first time during many hours -- or perhaps days -- I thought. It now occurred to me that the bandage, or surcingle, which enveloped me, was unique. I was tied by no separate cord. The first stroke of the razorlike crescent athwart any portion of the band, would so detach it that it might be unwound from my person by means of my left hand. But how fearful, in that case, the proximity of the steel! The result of the slightest struggle how deadly! Was it likely, moreover, that the minions of the torturer had not foreseen and provided for this possibility!

Was it probable that the bandage crossed my bosom in the track of the pendulum? Dreading to find my faint, and, as it seemed, in last hope frustrated, I so far elevated my head as to obtain a distinct view of my breast. The surcingle enveloped my limbs and body close in all directions -- *save in the path of the destroying crescent.*

Scarcely had I dropped my head back into its original position, when there flashed upon my mind what I cannot better describe than as the unformed half of that idea of deliverance to which I have previously alluded, and of which a moiety only floated indeterminately through my brain when I raised food to my burning lips. The whole thought was now present -- feeble, scarcely sane, scarcely definite, -- but still entire. I proceeded at once, with the nervous energy of despair, to attempt its execution.

For many hours the immediate vicinity of the low framework upon which I lay, had been literally swarming with rats. They were wild, bold, ravenous -- their red eyes glaring upon me as if they waited but for motionlessness on my part to make me their prey. "To what food," I thought, "have they been accustomed in the well?"

They had devoured, in spite of all my efforts to prevent them, all but a small remnant of the contents of the dish. I had fallen into an habitual see-saw, or wave of the hand about the platter: and, at length, the unconscious uniformity of the movement deprived it of effect. In their voracity the vermin frequently fastened their sharp fangs in my fingers. With the particles of the oily and spicy viand which now remained, I thoroughly rubbed the bandage wherever I could reach it; then, raising my hand from the floor, I lay breathlessly still.

At first the ravenous animals were startled and terrified at the change -- at the cessation of movement. They shrank alarmedly back; many sought the well. But this was only for a moment. I had not counted in vain upon their voracity. Observing that I remained without motion, one or two of the boldest leaped upon the frame-work, and smelt at the surcingle. This seemed the signal for a general rush. Forth from the well they hurried in fresh troops. They clung to the wood -- they overran it, and leaped in hundreds upon my person. The measured movement of the pendulum disturbed them not at all. Avoiding its strokes they busied themselves with the anointed bandage. They pressed -- they swarmed upon me in ever accumulating heaps. They writhed upon my throat; their cold lips sought my own; I was half stifled by their thronging pressure; disgust, for which the world has no name, swelled my bosom, and chilled, with a heavy clamminess, my heart. Yet one minute, and I felt that the struggle would be over. Plainly I perceived the loosening of the bandage. I knew that in more than one place it must be already severed. With a more than human resolution I lay *still.*

Nor had I erred in my calculations -- nor had I endured in vain. I at length felt that I was *free.* The surcingle hung in ribands from my body. But the stroke of the pendulum already pressed upon my bosom. It had divided the serge of the robe. It had cut through the linen beneath. Twice again it swung, and a sharp sense of pain shot through every nerve. But the moment of escape had arrived. At a wave of my hand

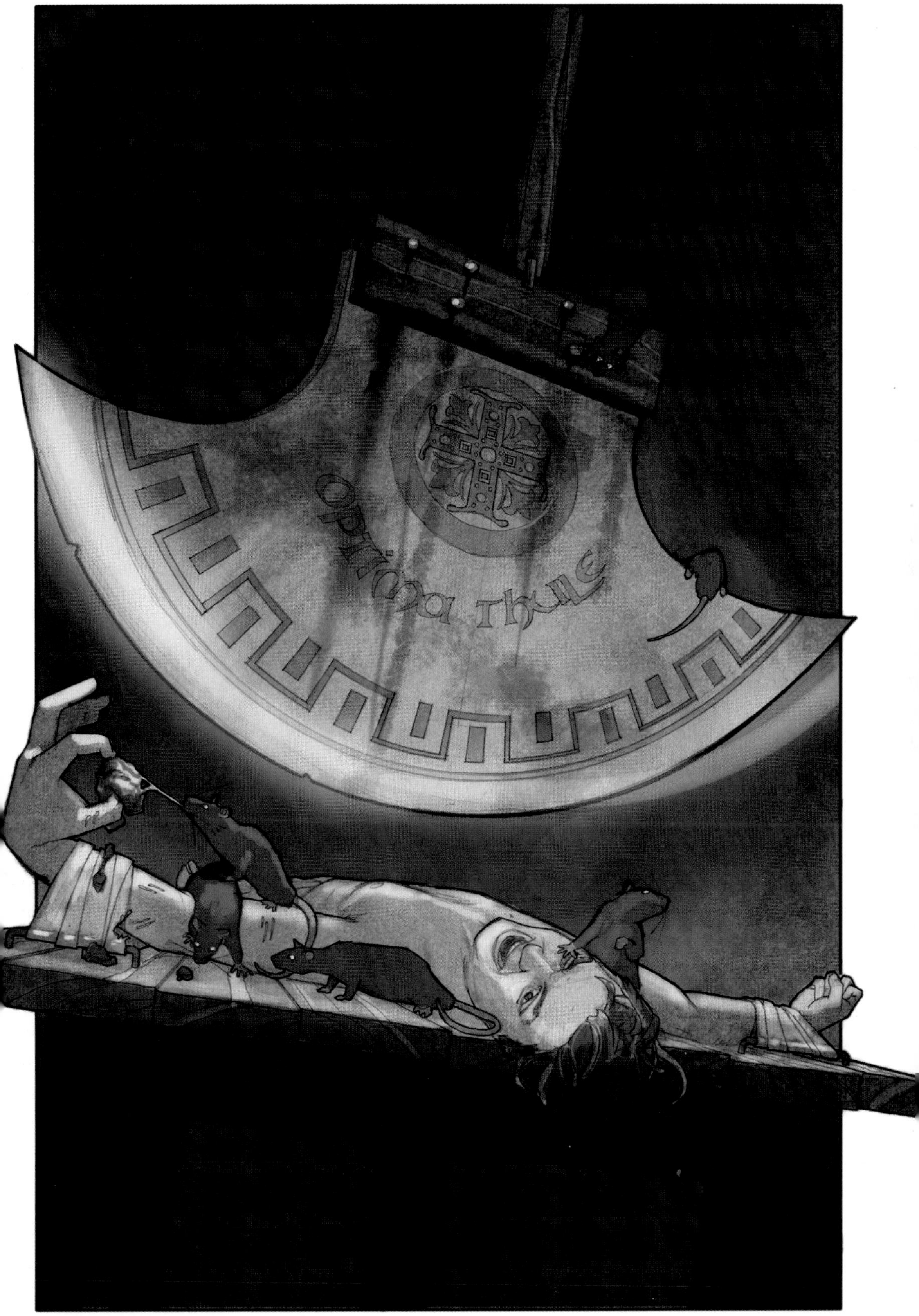
OPTIMA THULE

..the framework upon which I lay, had been literally swarming with rats. They were wild, bold, ravenous -

my deliverers hurried tumultuously away. With a steady movement -- cautious, sidelong, shrinking, and slow -- I slid from the embrace of the bandage and beyond the reach of the scimitar. For the moment, at least, I *was free.*

Free! -- and in the grasp of the Inquisition! I had scarcely stepped from my wooden bed of horror upon the stone floor of the prison, when the motion of the hellish machine ceased and I beheld it drawn up, by some invisible force, through the ceiling. This was a lesson which I took desperately to heart. My every motion was undoubtedly watched. Free! -- I had but escaped death in one form of agony, to be delivered unto worse than death in some other. With that thought I rolled my eyes nervously around on the barriers of iron that hemmed me in. Something unusual -- some change which, at first, I could not appreciate distinctly -- it was obvious, had taken place in the apartment. For many minutes of a dreamy and trembling abstraction, I busied myself in vain, unconnected conjecture. During this period, I became aware, for the first time, of the origin of the sulphurous light which illumined the cell. It proceeded from a fissure, about half an inch in width, extending entirely around the prison at the base of the walls, which thus appeared, and were, completely separated from the floor. I endeavored, but of course in vain, to look through the aperture.

As I arose from the attempt, the mystery of the alteration in the chamber broke at once upon my understanding. I have observed that, although the outlines of the figures upon the walls were sufficiently distinct, yet the colors seemed blurred and indefinite. These colors had now assumed, and were momentarily assuming, a startling and most intense brilliancy, that gave to the spectral and fiendish portraitures an aspect that might have thrilled even firmer nerves than my own. Demon eyes, of a wild and ghastly vivacity, glared upon me in a thousand directions, where none had been visible before, and gleamed with the lurid lustre of a fire that I could not force my imagination to regard as unreal.

Unreal! -- Even while I breathed there came to my nostrils the breath of the vapour of heated iron! A suffocating odour pervaded the prison! A deeper glow settled each moment in the eyes that glared at my agonies! A richer tint of crimson diffused itself over the pictured horrors of blood. I panted! I gasped for breath! There could be no doubt of the design of my tormentors -- oh! most unrelenting! oh! most demoniac of men! I shrank from the glowing metal to the centre of the cell. Amid the thought of the fiery destruction that impended, the idea of the coolness of the well came over my soul like balm. I rushed to its deadly brink. I threw my straining vision below. The glare from the enkindled roof illumined its inmost recesses. Yet, for a wild moment, did my spirit refuse to comprehend the meaning of what I saw. At length it forced -- it wrestled its way into my soul -- it burned itself in upon my shuddering reason. Oh! for a voice to speak! -- oh! horror! -- oh! any horror but this! With a shriek, I rushed from the margin, and buried my face in my hands -- weeping bitterly. The heat rapidly increased, and once again I looked up, shuddering as with a fit of the ague. There had been a second change in the cell -- and now the change was obviously in the *form.* As before, it was in vain that I, at first, endeavoured to appreciate or understand what was taking place. But not long was I left in doubt. The Inquisitorial vengeance had been hurried by my twofold escape, and there was to be no more dallying with the King of Terrors. The room had been square. I saw that two of its iron angles were now acute -- two, consequently, obtuse. The fearful difference quickly increased with a low rumbling or moaning sound. In an instant the apartment had shifted its form into that of a lozenge. But the alteration stopped not here-I neither hoped nor desired it to stop. I could have clasped the red walls to my bosom as a garment of eternal peace. "Death," I said, "any death but that of the pit!" Fool! might I have not known that *into the pit* it was the object of the burning iron to urge me? Could I resist its glow? or, if even that, could I withstand its pressure And now, flatter and flatter grew the lozenge, with a rapidity that left me no time for contemplation. Its centre, and of course, its greatest width, came just over the yawning gulf. I shrank back -- but the closing walls pressed me resistlessly onward. At length for my seared and writhing body there was no longer an inch of foothold on the firm floor of the prison. I struggled no more, but the agony of my soul found vent in one loud, long, and final scream of despair. I felt that I tottered upon the brink -- I averted my eyes --

There was a discordant hum of human voices! There was a loud blast as of many trumpets! There was a harsh grating as of a thousand thunders! The fiery walls rushed back! An outstretched arm caught my own as I fell, fainting, into the abyss. It was that of General Lasalle. The French army had entered Toledo. The Inquisition was in the hands of its enemies.

The Masque of The Red Death

THE "Red Death" had long devastated the country. No pestilence had ever been so fatal, or so hideous. Blood was its Avatar and its seal -- the redness and the horror of blood. There were sharp pains, and sudden dizziness, and then profuse bleeding at the pores, with dissolution. The scarlet stains upon the body and especially upon the face of the victim, were the pest ban which shut him out from the aid and from the sympathy of his fellow-men. And the whole seizure, progress and termination of the disease, were the incidents of half an hour.

But the Prince Prospero was happy and dauntless and sagacious. When his dominions were half-depopulated, he summoned to his presence a thousand hale and light-hearted friends from among the knights and dames of his court, and with these retired to the deep seclusion of one of his castellated abbeys. This was an extensive and magnificent structure, the creation of the prince's own eccentric yet august taste. A strong and lofty wall girdled it in. This wall had gates of iron. The courtiers, having entered, brought furnaces and massy hammers and welded the bolts. They resolved to leave means neither of ingress or egress to the sudden impulses of despair or of frenzy from within. The abbey was amply provisioned. With such precautions the courtiers might bid defiance to contagion. The external world could take care of itself. In the meantime it was folly to grieve, or to think. The prince had provided all the appliances of pleasure. There were buffoons, there were improvisatori, there were ballet-dancers, there were musicians, there was Beauty, there was wine. All these and security were within. Without was the "Red Death."

It was toward the close of the fifth or sixth month of his seclusion, and while the pestilence raged most furiously abroad, that the Prince Prospero entertained his thousand friends at a masked ball of the most unusual magnificence.

It was a voluptuous scene, that masquerade. But first let me tell of the rooms in which it was held. There were seven -- an imperial suite. In many palaces, however, such suites form a long and straight vista, while the folding doors slide back nearly to the walls on either hand, so that the view of the whole extent is scarcely impeded. Here the case was very different; as might have been expected from the duke's love of the *bizarre*. The apartments were so irregularly disposed that the vision embraced but little more than one at a time. There was a sharp turn at every twenty or thirty yards, and at each turn a novel effect. To the right and left, in the middle of each wall, a tall and narrow Gothic window looked out upon a closed corridor which pursued the windings of the suite. These windows were of stained glass whose color varied in accordance with the prevailing hue of the decorations of the chamber into which it opened. That at the eastern extremity was hung, for example, in blue -- and vividly blue were its windows. The second chamber was purple in its ornaments and tapestries, and here the panes were purple. The third was green throughout, and so were the casements. The fourth was furnished and lighted with orange -- the fifth with white -- the sixth with violet. The seventh apartment was closely shrouded in black velvet tapestries that hung all over the ceiling and down the walls, falling in heavy folds upon a carpet of the same material and hue. But in this chamber only, the color of the windows failed to correspond with the decorations. The panes here were scarlet -- a deep blood color. Now in no one of the seven apartments was there any lamp or candelabrum, amid the profusion of golden ornaments that lay scattered to and fro or depended from the roof. There was no light of any kind emanating from lamp or candle within the suite of chambers. But in the corridors that followed the suite, there stood, opposite to each window, a heavy tripod, bearing a brazier of fire that protected its rays through the tinted glass and so glaringly illumined the room. And thus were produced a multitude of gaudy and fantastic appearances. But in the western or black chamber the effect of the fire-light that streamed upon the dark hangings through the blood-tinted panes, was ghastly in the extreme, and produced so wild a look upon the countenances of those who entered, that there were few of the company bold enough to set foot within its precincts at all.

It was in this apartment, also, that there stood against the western wall, a gigantic clock of ebony. Its pendulum swung to and fro with a dull, heavy, monotonous clang; and when the minute-hand made the circuit of the face, and the hour was to be stricken, there came from the brazen lungs of the clock a sound which was clear and loud and deep and exceedingly musical, but of so peculiar a note and emphasis that, at each lapse of an hour, the musicians of the orchestra were constrained to pause, momentarily in their performance, to hearken to the sound; and thus the waltzers perforce ceased their evolutions; and there was a brief disconcert of the whole gay company; and, while the chimes of the clock yet rang, it was observed that the giddiest grew pale, and the more aged and sedate passed their hands over their brows as if in confused reverie or meditation. But when the echoes had fully ceased, a light laughter at once pervaded the assembly; the musicians looked at each other and smiled as if at their own nervousness and folly, and made whispering vows, each to the other, that the next chiming of the clock should produce in them no similar emotion; and then, after the lapse of sixty minutes, (which embrace three thousand and six hundred seconds of the Time that flies,) there came yet another chiming of the clock, and then were the same disconcert and tremulousness and meditation as before.

But, in spite of these things, it was a gay and magnificent revel. The tastes of the duke were peculiar. He had a fine eye for colors and effects. He disregarded the *decora* of mere fashion. His plans were bold and fiery, and his conceptions glowed with barbaric lustre. There are some who would have thought him mad. His followers felt that he was not. It was necessary to hear and see and touch him to be *sure* that he was not.

He had directed, in great part, the moveable embellishments of the seven chambers, upon occasion of this great *fete*; and it was his own guiding taste which had given character to the masqueraders. Be sure they were grotesque. There were much glare and glitter and piquancy and phantasm -- much of what has been since seen in *Hernani*. There were arabesque figures with unsuited limbs and appointments. There were delirious fancies such as the madman fashions. There was much of the beautiful, much of the wanton, much of the *bizarre*, something of the terrible, and not a little of that which might have excited disgust. To and fro in the seven chambers there stalked, in fact, a multitude of dreams. And these -- the dreams -- writhed in and about, taking hue from the rooms, and causing the wild music of the orchestra to seem as the echo of their steps. And, anon, there strikes the ebony clock which stands in the hall of the velvet. And then, for a moment, all is still, and all is silent save the voice of the clock. The dreams are stiff-frozen as they stand. But the echoes of the chime die away -- they have endured but an instant -- and a light, half-subdued laughter floats after them as they depart. And now again the music swells, and the dreams live, and writhe to and fro more merrily than ever, taking hue from the many-tinted windows through which stream the rays from the tripods. But to the chamber which lies most westwardly of the seven, there are now none of the maskers who venture; for the night is waning away; and there flows a ruddier light through the blood-colored panes; and the blackness of the sable drapery appals; and to him whose foot falls upon the sable carpet, there comes from the near clock of ebony a muffled peal more solemnly emphatic than any which reaches *their* ears who indulge in the more remote gaieties of the other apartments

But these other apartments were densely crowded, and in them beat feverishly the heart of life. And the revel went whirlingly on, until at length there commenced the sounding of midnight upon the clock. And then the music ceased, as I have told; and the evolutions of the waltzers were quieted; and there was an uneasy cessation of all things as before. But now there were twelve strokes to be sounded by the bell of the clock; and thus it happened, perhaps, that more of thought crept, with more of time, into the meditations of the thoughtful among those who revelled. And thus, too, it happened, perhaps, that before the last echoes of the last chime had utterly sunk into silence, there were many individuals in the crowd who had found leisure to become aware of the presence of a masked figure which had arrested the attention of no single individual before. And the rumor of this new presence having spread itself whisperingly around, there arose at length from the whole company a buzz, or murmur, expressive of disapprobation and surprise -- then, finally, of terror, of horror, and of disgust.

In an assembly of phantasms such as I have painted, it may well be supposed that no ordinary appearance could have excited such sensation. In truth the masquerade license of the night was nearly unlimited; but the figure in question had out-Heroded Herod, and gone beyond the bounds of even the prince's indefinite decorum. There are chords in the hearts of the most reckless which cannot be touched without emotion. Even with the utterly lost, to whom life and death are equally jests, there are matters of which no jest can be made. The whole company, indeed, seemed now deeply to feel that in the costume and bearing of the stranger neither wit nor propriety existed. The figure was tall and gaunt, and shrouded from head to foot in the habiliments of the grave. The mask which concealed the visage was made so nearly to resemble the countenance of a stiffened corpse that the closest scrutiny must have had difficulty in detecting the cheat. And yet all this might have been endured, if not approved, by the mad revellers around. But the mummer had gone so far as to assume the type of the Red Death. His vesture was dabbled in *blood* -- and his broad brow, with all the features of the face, was besprinkled with the scarlet horror.

When the eyes of Prince Prospero fell upon this spectral image (which with a slow and solemn movement, as if more fully to sustain its *role*, stalked to and fro among the waltzers) he was seen to be convulsed, in the first moment with a strong shudder either of terror or distaste; but, in the next, his brow reddened with rage.

"Who dares," - he demanded hoarsely of the courtiers who stood near him -- "who dares insult us with this blasphemous mockery? Seize him and unmask him -- that we may know whom we have to hang at sunrise , from the battlements!"

It was in the eastern or blue chamber in which stood the Prince Prospero as he uttered these words. They rang throughout the seven rooms loudly and clearly -- for the prince was a bold and robust man, and the music had become hushed at the waving of his hand.

It was in the blue room where stood the prince, with a group of pale courtiers by his side. At first, as he spoke, there was a slight rushing movement of this group in the direction of the intruder, who at the moment was also near at hand, and now, with deliberate and stately step, made closer approach to the speaker. But from a certain nameless awe with which the mad assumptions of the mummer had inspired the whole party, there were found none who put forth hand to seize him; so that, unimpeded, he passed within a yard of the prince's person; and, while the vast assembly, as if with one impulse, shrank from the centres of the rooms to the walls, he made his way uninterruptedly, but with the same solemn and measured step which had distinguished him from the first, through the blue chamber to the purple -- through the purple to the green -- through the green to the orange -- through this again to the white -- and even thence to the violet, ere a decided movement had been made to arrest him. It was then, however, that the Prince Prospero, maddening with rage and the shame of his own momentary cowardice, rushed hurriedly through the six chambers, while none followed him on account of a deadly terror that had seized upon all. He bore aloft a drawn dagger, and had approached, in rapid impetuosity, to within three or four feet of the retreating figure, when the latter, having attained the extremity of the

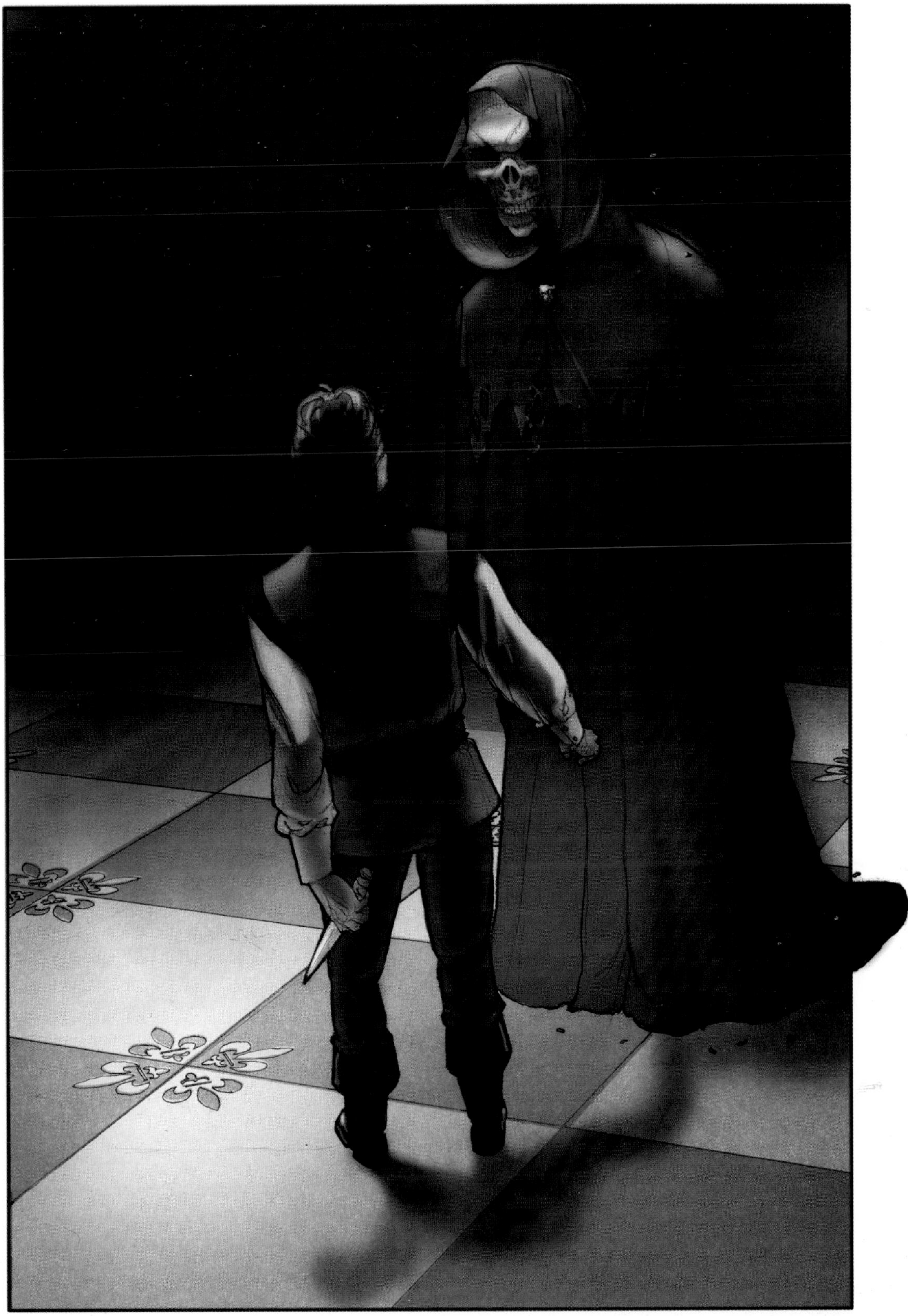

The figure was tall and gaunt, and shrouded from head to foot in the habiliments of the grave.

velvet apartment, turned suddenly and confronted his pursuer. There was a sharp cry -- and the dagger dropped gleaming upon the sable carpet, upon which, instantly afterwards, fell prostrate in death the Prince Prospero. Then, summoning the wild courage of despair, a throng of the revellers at once threw themselves into the black apartment, and, seizing the mummer, whose tall figure stood erect and motionless within the shadow of the ebony clock, gasped in unutterable horror at finding the grave-cerements and corpse-like mask which they handled with so violent a rudeness, untenanted by any tangible form.

And now was acknowledged the presence of the Red Death. He had come like a thief in the night. And one by one dropped the revellers in the blood-bedewed halls of their revel, and died each in the despairing posture of his fall. And the life of the ebony clock went out with that of the last of the gay. And the flames of the tripods expired. And Darkness and Decay and the Red Death held illimitable dominion over all.

William Wilson

What say of it? what say of CONSCIENCE grim,
That spectre in my path?

Chamberlayne's *Pharronida.*

LET me call myself, for the present, William Wilson. The fair page now lying before me need not be sullied with my real appellation. This has been already too much an object for the scorn -- for the horror -- for the detestation of my race. To the uttermost regions of the globe have not the indignant winds bruited its unparalleled infamy? Oh, outcast of all outcasts most abandoned! -- to the earth art thou not for ever dead? to its honors, to its flowers, to its golden aspirations? -- and a cloud, dense, dismal, and limitless , does it not hang eter nally betw een th y hopes and hea ven?

I would not, if I could, here or to-day, embody a record of my later years of unspeakable misery, and unpardonable crime. This epoch -- these later years -- took unto themselves a sudden elevation in turpitude, whose origin alone it is my present purpose to assign. Men usually grow base by degrees. From me, in an instant, all virtue dropped bodily as a mantle. From comparatively trivial wickedness I passed, with the stride of a giant, into more than the enormities of an Elah-Gabalus. What chance -- what one event brought this evil thing to pass, bear with me while I relate. Death approaches; and the shadow which foreruns him has thrown a softening influence over my spirit. I long, in passing through the dim valley, for the sympathy -- I had nearly said for the pity -- of my fellow men. I would fain have them believe that I have been, in some measure, the slave of circumstances beyond human control. I would wish them to seek out for me, in the details I am about to give, some little oasis of *fatality* amid a wilderness of error. I would have them allow -- what they cannot refrain from allowing -- that, although temptation may have erewhile existed as great, man was never *thus*, at least, tempted before -- certainly, never *thus* fell. And is it therefore that he has never thus suffered? Have I not indeed been living in a dream? And am I not now dying a victim to the horror and the mystery of the wildest of all sublunary visions? I am the descendant of a race whose imaginative and easily excitable temperament has at all times rendered them remarkable; and, in my earliest infancy, I gave evidence of having fully inherited the family character. As I advanced in years it was more strongly developed; becoming, for many reasons, a cause of serious disquietude to my friends, and of positive injury to myself. I grew self-willed, addicted to the wildest caprices, and a prey to the most ungovernable passions. Weak-minded, and beset with constitutional infirmities akin to my own, my parents could do but little to check the evil propensities which distinguished me. Some feeble and ill-directed efforts resulted in complete failure on their part, and, of course, in total triumph on mine. Thenceforward my voice was a household law; and at an age when few children have abandoned their leading-strings, I was left to the guidance of my own will, and became, in all but name, the master of my own actions.

My earliest recollections of a school-life, are connected with a large, rambling, Elizabethan house, in a misty-looking village of England, where were a vast number of gigantic and gnarled trees, and where all the houses were excessively ancient. In truth, it was a dream-like and spirit-soothing place, that venerable old town. At this moment, in fancy, I feel the refreshing chilliness of its deeply-shadowed avenues, inhale the fragrance of its thousand shrubberies, and thrill anew with undefinable delight, at the deep hollow note of the church-bell, breaking, each hour, with sullen and sudden roar, upon the stillness of the dusky atmosphere in which the fretted Gothic steeple lay imbedded and asleep.

It gives me, perhaps, as much of pleasure as I can now in any manner experience, to dwell upon minute recollections of the school and its concerns. Steeped in misery as I am -- misery, alas! only too real -- I shall be pardoned for seeking relief, however slight and temporary, in the weakness of a few rambling details. These, moreover, utterly trivial, and even ridiculous in themselves, assume, to my fancy, adventitious importance, as connected with a period and a locality when and where I recognize the first ambiguous monitions of the destiny which afterwards so fully overshadowed me. Let me then remember.

The house, I have said, was old and irregular. The grounds were extensive, and a high and solid brick wall, topped with a bed of mortar and broken glass, encompassed the whole. This prison-like rampart formed the limit of our domain; beyond it we saw but thrice a week -- once every Saturday afternoon, when, attended by two ushers, we were permitted to take brief walks in a body through some of the neighbouring fields -- and twice during Sunday, when we were paraded in the same formal manner to the morning and evening service in the one church of the village. Of this church the principal of our school was pastor. With how deep a spirit of wonder and perplexity was I wont to regard him from our remote pew in the gallery, as, with step solemn and slow, he ascended the pulpit! This reverend man, with countenance so demurely benign, with robes so glossy and so clerically flowing, with wig so minutely powdered, so rigid and so vast, -- -could this be he who, of late, with sour visage, and in snuffy habiliments, administered, ferule in hand, the Draconian laws of the academy? Oh, gigantic paradox, too utterly monstrous for solution!

At an angle of the ponderous wall frowned a more ponderous gate. It was riveted and studded with iron bolts, and surmounted with jagged iron spikes. What impressions of deep awe did it inspire! It was never opened save for the three periodical egressions and ingressions already mentioned; then, in every creak of its mighty hinges, we found a plenitude of mystery -- a world of matter for solemn remark, or for more solemn meditation.

The extensive enclosure was irregular in form, having many capacious recesses. Of these, three or four of the largest constituted the play-ground. It was level, and covered with fine hard gravel. I well remember it had no trees, nor benches, nor anything similar within it. Of course it was in the rear of the house. In front lay a small parterre, planted with box and other shrubs; but through this sacred division we passed only upon rare occasions indeed -- such as a first advent to school or final departure thence, or perhaps, when a parent or friend having called for us, we joyfully took our way home for the Christmas or Midsummer holidays.

But the house! -- how quaint an old building was this! -- to me how veritably a palace of enchantment! There was really no end to its windings -- to its incomprehensible subdivisions. It was difficult, at any given time, to say with certainty upon which of its two stories one happened to be. From each room to every other there were sure to be found three or four steps either in ascent or descent. Then the lateral branches were innumerable -- inconceivable -- and so returning in upon themselves, that our most exact ideas in regard to the whole mansion were not very far different from those with which we pondered upon infinity. During the five years of my residence here, I was never able to ascertain with precision, in what remote locality lay the little sleeping apartment assigned to myself and some eighteen or twenty other scholars.

The school-room was the largest in the house -- I could not help thinking, in the world. It was very long, narrow, and dismally low, with pointed Gothic windows and a ceiling of oak. In a remote and terror-inspiring angle was a square enclosure of eight or ten feet, comprising the *sanctum*, "during hours," of our principal, the Reverend Dr. Bransby. It was a solid structure, with massy door, sooner than open which in the absence of the "Dominic," we would all have willingly perished by the *peine forte et dure*. In other angles were two other similar boxes, far less reverenced, indeed, but still greatly matters of awe. One of these was the pulpit of the "classical" usher, one of the "English and mathematical." Interspersed about the room, crossing and recrossing in endless irregularity, were innumerable benches and desks, black, ancient, and time-worn, piled desperately with much-bethumbed books, and so beseamed with initial letters, names at full length, grotesque figures, and other multiplied efforts of the knife, as to have entirely lost what little of original form might have been their portion in days long departed. A huge bucket with water stood at one extremity of the room, and a clock of stupendous dimensions at the other.

Encompassed by the massy walls of this venerable academy, I passed, yet not in tedium or disgust, the years of the third lustrum of my life. The teeming brain of childhood requires no external world of incident to occupy or amuse it; and the apparently dismal monotony of a school was replete with more intense excitement than my riper youth has derived from luxury, or my full manhood from crime. Yet I must believe that my first mental development had in it much of the uncommon -- even much of the *outre*. Upon mankind at large the events of very early existence rarely leave in mature age any definite impression. All is gray shadow -- a weak and irregular remembrance -- an indistinct regathering of feeble pleasures and phantasmagoric pains. With me this is not so. In childhood I must have felt with the energy of a man what I now find stamped upon memory in lines as vivid, as deep, and as durable as the *exergues* of the Carthaginian medals.

Yet in fact -- in the fact of the world's view -- how little was there to remember! The morning's awakening, the nightly summons to bed; the connings, the recitations; the periodical half-holidays, and perambulations; the play-ground, with its broils, its pastimes, its intrigues; -- these, by a mental sorcery long forgotten, were made to involve a wilderness of sensation, a world of rich incident, an universe of varied emotion, of excitement the most passionate and spirit-stirring. *"Oh, le bon temps, que ce siecle de fer!"*

In truth, the ardor, the enthusiasm, and the imperiousness of my disposition, soon rendered me a marked character among my schoolmates, and by slow, but natural gradations, gave me an ascendancy over all not greatly older than myself; -- over all with a single exception. This exception was found in the person of a scholar, who, although no relation, bore the same Christian and surname as myself; -- a circumstance, in fact, little remarkable; for, notwithstanding a noble descent, mine was one of those everyday appellations which seem, by prescriptive right, to have been, time out of mind, the common property of the mob. In this narrative I have therefore designated myself as William Wilson, -- a fictitious title not very dissimilar to the real. My namesake alone, of those who in school phraseology constituted "our set," presumed to compete with me in the studies of the class -- in the sports and broils of the play-ground -- to refuse implicit belief in my assertions, and submission to my will -- indeed, to interfere with my arbitrary dictation in any respect whatsoever. If there is on earth a supreme and unqualified despotism, it is the despotism of a master mind in boyhood over the less energetic spirits of its companions.

Wilson's rebellion was to me a source of the greatest embarrassment; -- the more so as, in spite of the bravado with which in public I made a point of treating him and his pretensions, I secretly felt that I feared him, and could not help thinking the equality which he maintained so easily with myself, a proof of his true superiority; since not to be overcome cost me a perpetual struggle. Yet this superiority -- even this equality -- was in truth acknowledged by no one but myself; our associates, by some unaccountable

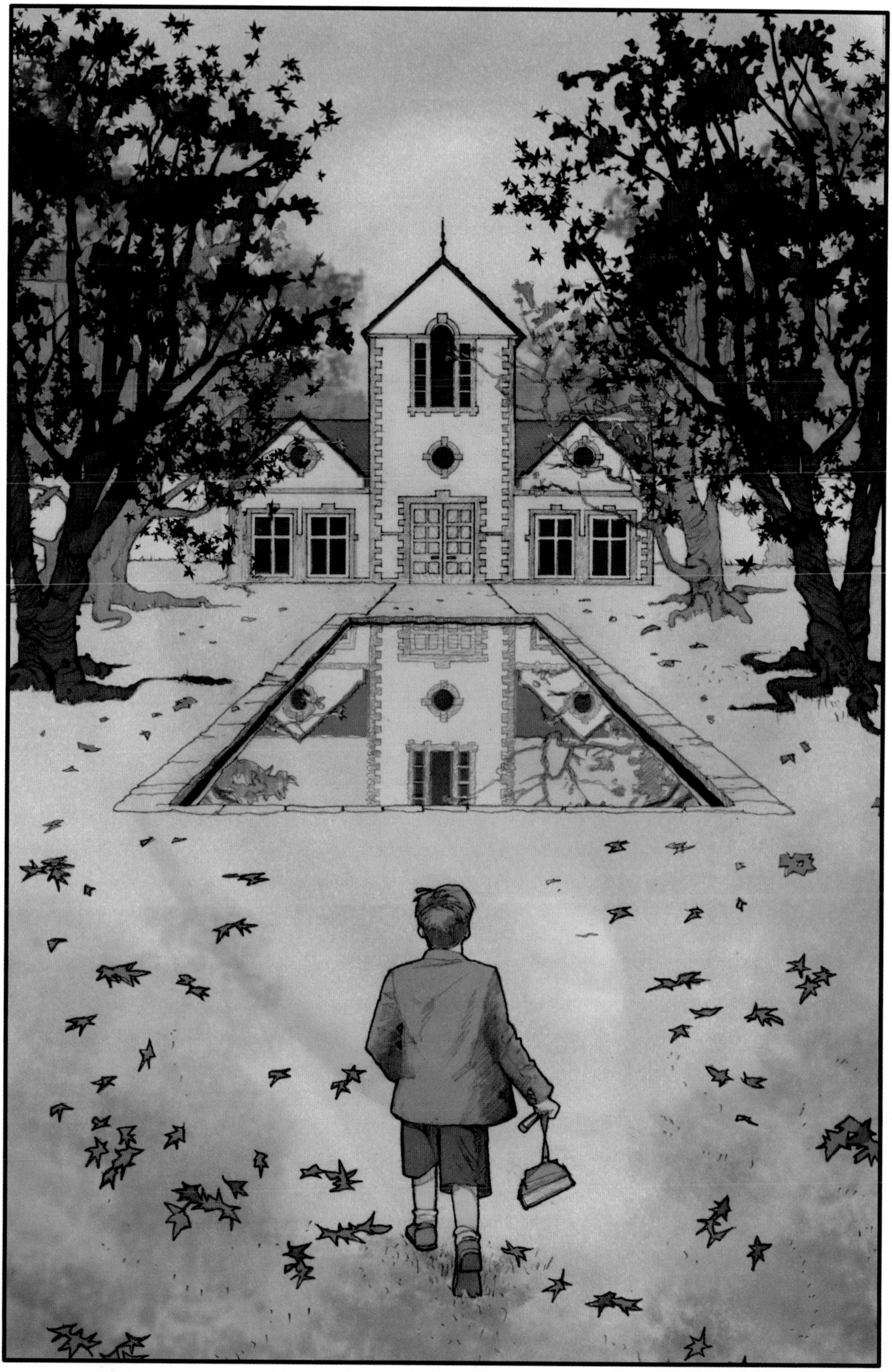

In truth, it was a dream-like and spirit-soothing place, that venerable old town.

EDGAR ALLAN POE

blindness, seemed not even to suspect it. Indeed, his competition, his resistance, and especially his impertinent and dogged interference with my purposes, were not more pointed than private. He appeared to be destitute alike of the ambition which urged, and of the passionate energy of mind which enabled me to excel. In his rivalry he might have been supposed actuated solely by a whimsical desire to thwart, astonish, or mortify myself; although there were times when I could not help observing, with a feeling made up of wonder, abasement, and pique, that he mingled with his injuries, his insults, or his contradictions, a certain most inappropriate, and assuredly most unwelcome *affectionateness* of manner. I could only conceive this singular behavior to arise from a consummate self-conceit assuming the vulgar airs of patronage and protection.

Perhaps it was this latter trait in Wilson's conduct, conjoined with our identity of name, and the mere accident of our having entered the school upon the same day, which set afloat the notion that we were brothers, among the senior classes in the academy. These do not usually inquire with much strictness into the affairs of their juniors. I have before said, or should have said, that Wilson was not, in the most remote degree, connected with my family. But assuredly if we *had* been brothers we must have been twins; for, after leaving Dr. Bransby's, I casually learned that my namesake was born on the nineteenth of January, 1813 -- and this is a somewhat remarkable coincidence; for the day is precisely that of my own nativity.

It may seem strange that in spite of the continual anxiety occasioned me by the rivalry of Wilson, and his intolerable spirit of contradiction, I could not bring myself to hate him altogether. We had, to be sure, nearly every day a quarrel in which, yielding me publicly the palm of victory, he, in some manner, contrived to make me feel that it was he who had deserved it; yet a sense of pride on my part, and a veritable dignity on his own, kept us always upon what are called "speaking terms," while there were many points of strong congeniality in our tempers, operating to awake me in a sentiment which our position alone, perhaps, prevented from ripening into friendship It is difficult, indeed, to define, or even to describe, my real feelings towards him. They formed a motley and heterogeneous admixture; -- some petulant animosity, which was not yet hatred, some esteem, more respect, much fear, with a world of uneasy curiosity. To the moralist it will be unnecessary to say, in addition, that Wilson and myself were the most inseparable of companions.

It was no doubt the anomalous state of affairs existing between us, which turned all my attacks upon him, (and they were many, either open or covert) into the channel of banter or practical joke (giving pain while assuming the aspect of mere fun) rather than into a more serious and determined hostility. But my endeavours on this head were by no means uniformly successful, even when my plans were the most wittily concocted; for my namesake had much about him, in character, of that unassuming and quiet austerity which, while enjoying the poignancy of its own jokes, has no heel of Achilles in itself, and absolutely refuses to be laughed at. I could find, indeed, but one vulnerable point, and that, lying in a personal peculiarity, arising, perhaps, from constitutional disease, would have been spared by any antagonist less at his wit's end than myself; -- my rival had a weakness in the faucal or guttural organs, which precluded him from raising his voice at any time *above a very low whisper.* Of this defect I did not fall to take what poor advantage lay in my power.

Wilson's retaliations in kind were many; and there was one form of his practical wit that disturbed me beyond measure. How his sagacity first discovered at all that so petty a thing would vex me, is a question I never could solve; but, having discovered, he habitually practised the annoyance. I had always felt aversion to my uncourtly patronymic, and its very common, if not plebeian praenomen. The words were venom in my ears; and when, upon the day of my arrival, a second William Wilson came also to the academy, I felt angry with him for bearing the name, and doubly disgusted with the name because a stranger bore it, who would be the cause of its two-fold repetition, who would be constantly in my presence, and whose concerns, in the ordinary routine of the school business, must inevitably, on account of the detestable coincidence, be often confounded with my own.

The feeling of vexation thus engendered grew stronger with every circumstance tending to show resemblance, moral or physical, between my rival and myself. I had not then discovered the remarkable fact that we were of the same age; but I saw that we were of the same height, and I perceived that we were even singularly alike in general contour of person and outline of feature. I was galled, too, by the rumor touching a relationship, which had grown current in the upper forms. In a word, nothing could more seriously disturb me (although I scrupulously concealed such disturbance,) than any allusion to a similarity of mind, person, or condition existing between us. But, in truth, I had no reason to believe that (with the exception of the matter of relationship, and in the case of Wilson himself) this similarity had ever been made a subject of comment, or even observed at all by our schoolfellows. That *he* observed it in all its bearings, and as fixedly as I, was apparent; but that he could discover in such circumstances so fruitful a field of annoyance, can only be attributed, as I said before, to his more than ordinary penetration.

His cue, which was to perfect an imitation of myself, lay both in words and in actions; and most admirably did he play his part. My dress it was an easy matter to copy; my gait and general manner were, without difficulty, appropriated; in spite of his constitutional defect, even my voice did not escape him. My louder tones were, of course, unattempted, but then the key, it was identical; *and his singular whisper, it grew the very echo of my own.*

How greatly this most exquisite portraiture harassed me, (for it could not justly be termed a caricature,) I will not now venture to describe. I had but one consolation -- in the fact that the imitation, apparently, was noticed by myself alone, and that I had to endure only the knowing and strangely sarcastic smiles of my namesake himself. Satisfied with having produced in my bosom the intended effect, he seemed to chuckle in secret over the sting he had inflicted, and was characteristically disregardful of the public applause which the success of his witty endeavours might have so easily elicited. That the school, indeed, did not feel his design, perceive its accomplishment, and participate in his sneer, was, for many anxious months, a riddle I could not resolve. Perhaps the *gradation* of his copy rendered it not so readily perceptible; or, more possibly, I owed my security to the master air of the copyist, who, disdaining the letter (which in a painting is all the obtuse can see) gave but the full spirit of his original for my individual contemplation and chagrin.

I have already more than once spoken of the disgusting air of patronage which he assumed toward me, and of his frequent officious interference withy my will. This interference often took the ungracious character of advice; advice not openly given, but hinted or insinuated. I received it with a repugnance which gained strength as I grew in years. Yet, at this distant day, let me do him the simple justice to acknowledge that I can recall no occasion when the suggestions of my rival were on the side of those errors or follies so usual to his immature age and seeming inexperience; that his moral sense, at least, if not his general talents and worldly wisdom, was far keener than my own; and that I might, to-day, have been a better, and thus a happier man, had I less frequently rejected the counsels embodied in those meaning whispers which I then but too cordially hated and too bitterly despised.

As it was, I at length grew restive in the extreme under his distasteful supervision, and daily resented more and more openly what I considered his intolerable arrogance. I have said that, in the first years of our connexion as schoolmates, my feelings in regard to him might have been easily ripened into friendship: but, in the latter months of my residence at the academy, although the intrusion of his ordinary manner had, beyond doubt, in some measure, abated, my sentiments, in nearly similar proportion, partook very much of positive hatred. Upon one occasion he saw this, I think, and afterwards avoided, or made a show of avoiding me.

It was about the same period, if I remember aright, that, in an altercation of violence with him, in which he was more than usually thrown off his guard, and spoke and acted with an openness of demeanor rather foreign to his nature, I discovered, or fancied I discovered, in his accent, his air, and general appearance, a something which first startled, and then deeply interested me, by bringing to mind dim visions of my earliest infancy -- wild, confused and thronging memories of a time when memory herself was yet unborn. I cannot better describe the sensation which oppressed me than by saying that I could with difficulty shake off the belief of my having been acquainted with the being who stood before me, at some epoch very long ago -- some point of the past even infinitely remote. The delusion, however, faded rapidly as it came; and I mention it at all but to define the day of the last conversation I there held with my singular namesake.

The huge old house, with its countless subdivisions, had several large chambers communicating with each other, where slept the greater number of the students. There were, however (as must necessarily happen in a building so awkwardly planned), many little nooks or recesses, the odds and ends of the structure; and these the economic ingenuity of Dr. Bransby had also fitted up as dormitories; although, being the merest closets, they were capable of accommodating but a single individual. One of these small apartments was occupied by Wilson.

One night, about the close of my fifth year at the school, and immediately after the altercation just mentioned, finding every one wrapped in sleep, I arose from bed, and, lamp in hand, stole through a wilderness of narrow passages from my own bedroom to that of my rival. I had long been plotting one of those ill-natured pieces of practical wit at his expense in which I had hitherto been so uniformly unsuccessful. It was my intention, now, to put my scheme in operation, and I resolved to make him feel the whole extent of the malice with which I was imbued. Having reached his closet, I noiselessly entered, leaving the lamp, with a shade over it, on the outside. I advanced a step, and listened to the sound of his tranquil breathing. Assured of his being asleep, I returned, took the light, and with it again approached the bed. Close curtains were around it, which, in the prosecution of my plan, I slowly and quietly withdrew, when the bright rays fell vividly upon the sleeper, and my eyes, at the same moment, upon his countenance. I looked; -- and a numbness, an iciness of feeling instantly pervaded my frame. My breast heaved, my knees tottered, my whole spirit became possessed with an objectless yet intolerable horror. Gasping for breath, I lowered the lamp in still nearer proximity to the face. Were these -- *these* the lineaments of William Wilson? I saw, indeed, that they were his, but I shook as if with a fit of the ague in fancying they were not. What *was* there about them to confound me in this manner? I gazed; -- while my brain reeled with a multitude of incoherent thoughts. Not thus he appeared -- assuredly not *thus* -- in the vivacity of his waking hours. The same name! the same contour of person! the same day of arrival at the academy! And then his dogged and meaningless imitation of my gait, my voice, my habits, and my manner! Was it, in truth, within the bounds of human possibility, that *what I now saw* was the result, merely, of the habitual practice of this sarcastic imitation? Awe-stricken, and with a creeping shudder, I extinguished the lamp, passed silently from the chamber, and left, at once, the halls of that old academy, never to enter them again.

After a lapse of some months, spent at home in mere idleness, I found myself a student at Eton. The brief interval had been sufficient to enfeeble my remembrance of the events at Dr. Bransby's, or at least to effect a material change in the nature of the feelings with which I remembered them. The truth -- the tragedy -- of the drama was no more. I could now find room to doubt the evidence of my senses; and seldom called up the subject at all but with wonder at extent of human credulity, and a smile at the vivid force of the imagination which I hereditarily possessed. Neither was this species of scepticism likely to be diminished by the character of the life I led at Eton. The vortex of thoughtless folly into which I there so immediately and so recklessly plunged, washed away all but the froth of my past hours, engulfed at once every solid or serious impression, and left to memory only the veriest levities of a former existence.

I do not wish, however, to trace the course of my miserable profligacy here -- a profligacy which set at defiance the laws, while it eluded the vigilance of the institution. Three years of folly, passed without profit, had but given me rooted habits of vice, and added, in a somewhat unusual degree, to my bodily stature, when, after a week of soulless dissipation, I invited a small party of the most dissolute students to a secret carousal in my chambers. We met at a late hour of the night; for our debaucheries were to be faithfully protracted until morning. The wine flowed freely, and there were not wanting other and perhaps more dangerous seductions; so that the gray dawn had already faintly appeared in the east, while our delirious extravagance was at its height. Madly flushed with cards and intoxication, I was in the act of insisting upon a toast of more than wonted profanity, when my attention was suddenly diverted by the violent, although partial unclosing of the door of the apartment, and by the eager voice of a servant from without. He said that some person, apparently in great haste, demanded to speak with me in the hall.

Wildly excited with wine, the unexpected interruption rather delighted than surprised me. I staggered forward at once, and a few steps brought me to the vestibule of the building. In this low and small room there hung no lamp; and now no light at all was admitted, save that of the exceedingly feeble dawn which made its way through the semi-circular window. As I put my foot over the threshold, I became aware of the figure of a youth about my own height, and habited in a white kerseymere morning frock, cut in the novel fashion of the one I myself wore at the moment. This the faint light enabled me to perceive; but the features of his face I could not distinguish. Upon my entering he strode hurriedly up to me, and, seizing me by. the arm with a gesture of petulant impatience, whispered the words "William Wilson!" in my ear.

I grew perfectly sober in an instant.

There was that in the manner of the stranger, and in the tremulous shake of his uplifted finger, as he held it between my eyes and the light, which filled me with unqualified amazement; but it was not this which had so violently moved me. It was the pregnancy of solemn admonition in the singular, low, hissing utterance; and, above all, it was the character, the tone, *the key*, of those few, simple, and familiar, yet *whispered* syllables, which came with a thousand thronging memories of bygone days, and struck upon my soul with the shock of a galvanic battery. Ere I could recover the use of my senses he was gone.

Although this event failed not of a vivid effect upon my disordered imagination, yet was it evanescent as vivid. For some weeks, indeed, I busied myself in earnest inquiry, or was wrapped in a cloud of morbid speculation. I did not pretend to disguise from my perception the identity of the singular individual who thus perseveringly interfered with my affairs, and harassed me with his insinuated counsel. But who and what was this Wilson? -- and whence came he? -- and what were his purposes? Upon neither of these points could I be satisfied; merely ascertaining in regard to him, that a sudden accident in his family had caused his removal from Dr. Bransby's academy on the afternoon of the day in which I myself had eloped. But in a brief period I ceased to think upon the subject; my attention being all absorbed in a contemplated departure for Oxford. Thither I soon went; the uncalculating vanity of my parents furnishing me with an outfit and annual establishment, which would enable me to indulge at will in the luxury already so dear to my heart, -- to vie in profuseness of expenditure with the haughtiest heirs of the wealthiest earldoms in Great Britain.

Excited by such appliances to vice, my constitutional temperament broke forth with redoubled ardor, and I spurned even the common restraints of decency in the mad infatuation of my revels. But it were absurd to pause in the detail of my extravagance. Let it suffice, that among spendthrifts I out-Heroded Herod, and that, giving name to a multitude of novel follies, I added no brief appendix to the long catalogue of vices then usual in the most dissolute university of Europe.

It could hardly be credited, however, that I had, even here, so utterly fallen from the gentlemanly estate, as to seek acquaintance with the vilest arts of the gambler by profession, and, having become an adept in his despicable science, to practise it habitually as a means of increasing my already enormous income at the expense of the weak-minded among my fellow-collegians. Such, nevertheless, was the fact. And the very enormity of this offence against all manly and honourable sentiment proved, beyond doubt, the main if not the sole reason of the impunity with which it was committed. Who, indeed, among my most abandoned associates, would not rather have disputed the clearest evidence of his senses, than have suspected of such courses, the gay, the frank, the generous William Wilson -- the noblest and most commoner at Oxford -- him whose follies (said his parasites) were but the follies of youth and unbridled fancy -- whose errors but inimitable whim -- whose darkest vice but a careless and dashing extravagance?

I had been now two years successfully busied in this way, when there came to the university a young *parvenu* nobleman, Glendinning -- rich, said report, as Herodes Atticus -- his riches, too, as easily acquired. I soon found him of weak intellect, and, of course, marked him as a fitting subject for my skill. I frequently engaged him in play, and contrived, with the gambler's usual art, to let him win considerable sums, the more effectually to entangle him in my snares. At length, my schemes being ripe, I met him (with the full intention that this meeting should be final and decisive) at the chambers of a fellow-commoner (Mr. Preston), equally intimate with both, but who, to do him Justice, entertained not even a remote suspicion of my design. To give to this a better colouring, I had contrived to have assembled a party of some eight or ten, and was solicitously careful that the introduction of cards should appear accidental, and originate in the proposal of my contemplated dupe himself. To be brief upon a vile topic, none of the low finesse was omitted, so customary upon similar occasions that it is a just matter for wonder how any are still found so besotted as to fall its victim.

We had protracted our sitting far into the night, and I had at length effected the manoeuvre of getting Glendinning as my sole antagonist. The game, too, was my favorite *ecarte*. The rest of the company, interested in the extent of our play, had abandoned their own cards, and were standing around us as spectators. The *parvenu*, who had been induced by my artifices in the early part of the evening, to drink deeply, now shuffled, dealt, or played, with a wild nervousness of manner for which his intoxication, I thought, might partially, but could not altogether account. In a very short period he had become my debtor to a large amount, when, having taken a long draught of port, he did precisely what I had been coolly anticipating -- he proposed to double our already extravagant stakes. With a well-feigned show of reluctance, and not until after my repeated refusal had seduced him into some angry words which gave a color of *pique* to my compliance, did I finally comply. The result, of course, did but prove how entirely the prey was in my toils; in less than an hour he had quadrupled his debt. For some time his countenance had been losing the florid tinge lent it by the wine; but now, to my astonishment, I perceived that it had grown to a pallor truly fearful. I say to my astonishment. Glendinning had been represented to my eager inquiries as immeasurably wealthy; and the sums which he had as yet lost, although in themselves vast, could not, I supposed, very seriously annoy, much less so violently affect him. That he was overcome by the wine just swallowed, was the idea which most readily presented itself; and, rather with a view to the preservation of my own character in the eyes of my associates, than from any less interested motive, I was about to insist, peremptorily, upon a discontinuance of the play, when some expressions at my elbow from among the company, and an ejaculation evincing utter despair on the part of Glendinning gave me to understand that I had effected his total ruin under circumstances which, rendering him an object for the pity of all, should have protected him from the ill offices even of a fiend.

What now might have been my conduct it is difficult to say. The pitiable condition of my dupe had thrown an air of embarrassed gloom over all; and, for some moments, a profound silence was maintained, during which I could not help feeling my cheeks tingle with the many burning glances of scorn or reproach cast upon me by the less abandoned of the party. I will even own that an intolerable weight of anxiety was for a brief instant lifted from my bosom by the sudden and extraordinary interruption which ensued. The wide, heavy folding doors of the apartment were all at once thrown open, to their full extent, with a vigorous and rushing impetuosity that extinguished, as if by magic, every candle in the room. Their light, in dying, enabled us just to perceive that a stranger had entered, about my own height, and closely muffled in a cloak. The darkness, however, was now total; and we could only *feel* that he was standing in our midst. Before any one of us could recover from the extreme astonishment into which this rudeness had thrown all, we heard the voice of the intruder.

"Gentlemen," he said, in a low, distinct, and never-to-be-forgotten *whisper* which thrilled to the very marrow of my bones, "Gentlemen, I make no apology for this behaviour, because in thus behaving, I am but fulfilling a duty. You are, beyond doubt, uninformed of the true character of the person who has to-night won at *ecarte* a large sum of money from Lord Glendinning. I will therefore put you upon an expeditious and decisive plan of obtaining this very necessary information. Please to examine, at your leisure, the

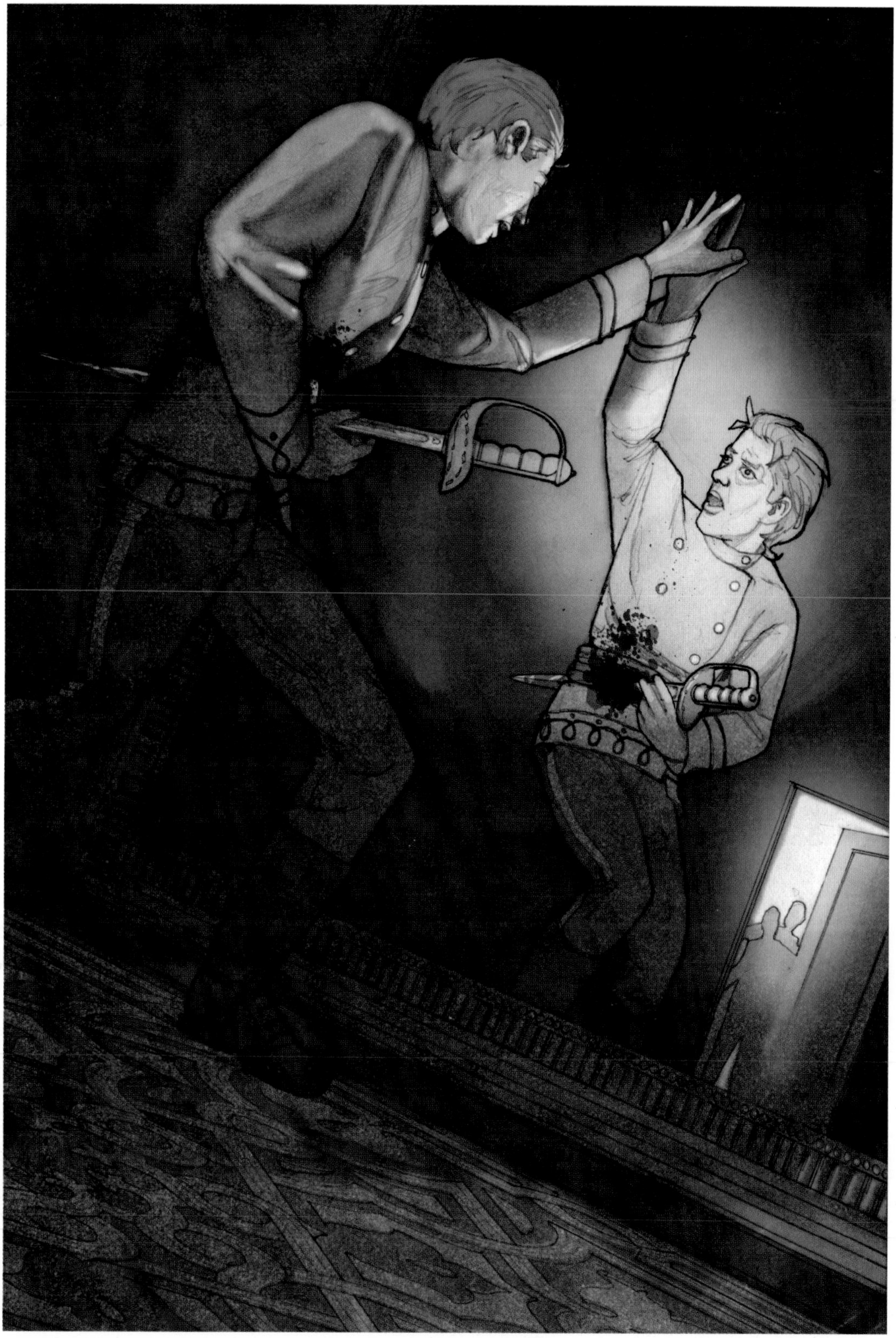

...and, in my death, see by this image, which is thine own, how utterly thou hast murdered thyself.

inner linings of the cuff of his left sleeve, and the several little packages which may be found in the somewhat capacious pockets of his embroidered morning wrapper."

While he spoke, so profound was the stillness that one might have heard a pin drop upon the floor. In ceasing, he departed at once, and as abruptly as he had entered. Can I -- shall I describe my sensations? -- must I say that I felt all the horrors of the damned? Most assuredly I had little time given for reflection. Many hands roughly seiz ed me upon the spot, and lights wer e immedia tely re-pr ocur ed. A search ensued. In the lining of my sleeve were found all the court cards essential in *ecarte*, and, in the pockets of my wrapper, a number of packs, facsimiles of those used at our sittings, with the single exception that mine were of the species called, technically, *arrondees*; the honours being slightly convex at the ends, the lower cards slightly convex at the sides. In this disposition, the dupe who cuts, as customary, at the length of the pack, will invariably find that he cuts his antagonist an honor; while the gambler, cutting at the breadth, will, as certainly cut nothing for his victim which may count in the records of the game.

Any burst of indignation upon this discovery would have affected me less than the silent contempt, or the sarcastic composure, with which it was received.

"Mr. Wilson," said our host, stooping to remove from beneath his feet an exceedingly luxurious cloak of rare furs, "Mr. Wilson, this is your property." (The weather was cold; and, upon quitting my own room, I had thrown a cloak over my dressing-wrapper, putting it off upon reaching the scene of play.) "I presume it is supererogatory to seek here" (eyeing the folds of the garment with a bitter smile) "for any farther evidence of your skill. Indeed, we have had enough. You will see the necessity, I hope, of quitting Oxford -- at all events, of quitting instantly my chambers."

Abased, humbled to the dust as I then was, it is probable that I should have resented this galling language by immediate personal violence, had not my whole attention been at the moment arrested by a fact of the most startling character. The cloak which I had worn was of a rare description of fur; how rare, how extravagantly costly, I shall not venture to say. Its fashion, too, was of my own fantastic invention; for I was fastidious to an absurd degree of coxcombry, in matters of this frivolous nature. When, therefore, Mr. Preston reached me that which he had picked up upon the floor, and near the folding doors of the apartment, it was with an astonishment nearly bordering upon terror, that I perceived my own already hanging on my arm, (where I had no doubt unwittingly placed it), and that the one presented me was but its exact counterpart in every, in even the minutest possible particular. The singular being who had so disastrously exposed me, had been muffled, I remembered, in a cloak; and none had been worn at all by any of the members of our party with the exception of myself. Retaining some presence of mind, I took the one offered me by Preston; placed it, unnoticed, over my own; left the apartment with a resolute scowl of defiance; and, next morning ere dawn of day, commenced a hurried journey from Oxford to the continent, in a perfect agony of horror and of shame.

I fled in vain. My evil destiny pursued me as if in exultation, and proved, indeed, that the exercise of its mysterious dominion had as yet only begun. Scarcely had I set foot in Paris ere I had fresh evidence of the detestable interest taken by this Wilson in my concerns. Years flew, while I experienced no relief. Villain! -- at Rome, with how untimely, yet with how spectral an officiousness, stepped he in between me and my ambition! At Vienna, too -- at Berlin -- and at Moscow! Where, in truth, had I not bitter cause to curse him within my heart? From his inscrutable tyranny did I at length flee, panic-stricken, as from a pestilence; and to the very ends of the earth *I fled in vain.*

And again, and again, in secret communion with my own spirit, would I demand the questions "Who is he? -- whence came he? -- and what are his objects?" But no answer was there found. And then I scrutinized, with a minute scrutiny, the forms, and the methods, and the leading traits of his impertinent supervision. But even here there was very little upon which to base a conjecture. It was noticeable, indeed, that, in no one of the multiplied instances in which he had of late crossed my path, had he so crossed it except to frustrate those schemes, or to disturb those actions, which, if fully carried out, might have resulted in bitter mischief. Poor justification this, in truth, for an authority so imperiously assumed! Poor indemnity for natural rights of self-agency so pertinaciously, so insultingly denied!

I had also been forced to notice that my tormentor, for a very long period of time, (while scrupulously and with miraculous dexterity maintaining his whim of an identity of apparel with myself) had so contrived it, in the execution of his varied interference with my will, that I saw not, at any moment, the features of his face. Be Wilson what he might, this, at least, was but the veriest of affectation, or of folly. Could he, for an instant, have supposed that, in my admonisher at Eton -- in the destroyer of my honor at Oxford, -- in him who thwarted my ambition at Rome, my revenge at Paris, my passionate love at Naples, or what he falsely termed my avarice in Egypt, -- that in this, my arch-enemy and evil genius, could fall to recognise the William Wilson of my school boy days, -- the namesake, the companion, the rival, -- the hated and dreaded rival at Dr. Bransby's? Impossible! -- But let me hasten to the last eventful scene of the drama.

Thus far I had succumbed supinely to this imperious domination. The sentiment of deep awe with which I habitually regarded the elevated character, the majestic wisdom, the apparent omnipresence and omnipotence of Wilson, added to a feeling of even terror, with which certain other traits in his nature and assumptions inspired me, had operated, hitherto, to impress me with an idea of my own utter weakness and helplessness, and to suggest an implicit, although bitterly reluctant submission to his arbitrary will. But, of late days, I had given myself up entirely to wine; and its maddening influence upon my hereditary temper rendered me more and more impatient of control. I began to murmur, -- to hesitate, -- to resist. And was it only fancy which induced me to believe that, with the increase of my own firmness, that of my tormentor underwent a proportional diminution? Be this as it may, I now began to feel the inspiration of a burning hope, and at length nurtured in my secret thoughts a stern and desperate resolution that I would submit no longer to be enslaved.

It was at Rome, during the Carnival of 18 -- , that I attended a masquerade in the palazzo of the Neapolitan Duke Di Broglio. I had indulged more freely than usual in the excesses of the wine-table; and now the suffocating atmosphere of the crowded rooms irritated me beyond endurance. The difficulty, too, of forcing my way through the mazes of the company contributed not a little to the ruffling of my temper; for I was anxiously seeking, (let me not say with what unworthy motive) the young, the gay, the beautiful wife of the aged and doting Di Broglio. With a too unscrupulous confidence she had previously communicated to me the secret of the costume in which she would be habited, and now, having caught a glimpse of her person, I was hurrying to make my way into her presence. -- At this moment I felt a light hand placed upon my shoulder , and that ever-remember ed, low, damnab le *whisper* within my ear.

In an absolute phrenzy of wrath, I turned at once upon him who had thus interrupted me, and seized him violently by tile collar. He was attired, as I had expected, in a costume altogether similar to my own; wearing a Spanish cloak of blue velvet, begirt about the waist with a crimson belt sustaining a rapier. A mask of black silk entirely covered his face.

"Scoundrel!" I said, in a voice husky with rage, while every syllable I uttered seemed as new fuel to my fury, "scoundrel! impostor! accursed villain! you shall not -- you *shall not* dog me unto death! Follow me, or I stab you where you stand!" -- and I broke my way from the ball-room into a small ante-chamber adjoining-- dragging him unresistingly with me as I went.

Upon entering, I thrust him furiously from me. He staggered against the wall, while I closed the door with an oath, and commanded him to draw. He hesitated but for an instant; then, with a slight sigh, drew in silence, and put himself upon his defence.

The contest was brief indeed. I was frantic with every species of wild excitement, and felt within my single arm the energy and power of a multitude. In a few seconds I forced him by sheer strength against the wainscoting, and thus, getting him at mercy, plunged my sword, with brute ferocity, repeatedly through and through his bosom.

At that instant some person tried the latch of the door. I hastened to prevent an intrusion, and then immediately returned to my dying antagonist. But what human language can adequately portray *that* astonishment, that horror which possessed me at the spectacle then presented to view? The brief moment in which I averted my eyes had been sufficient to produce, apparently, a material change in the arrangements at the upper or farther end of the room. A large mirror, -- so at first it seemed to me in my confusion -- now stood where none had been perceptible before; and, as I stepped up to it in extremity of terror, mine own image, but with features all pale and dabbled in blood, advanced to meet me with a feeble and tottering gait.

Thus it appeared, I say, but was not. It was my antagonist -- it was Wilson, who then stood before me in the agonies of his dissolution. His mask and cloak lay, where he had thrown them, upon the floor. Not a thread in all his raiment -- not a line in all the marked and singular lineaments of his face which was not, even in the most absolute identity, *mine own!*

It was Wilson; but he spoke no longer in a whisper, and I could have fancied that I myself was speaking while he said:

"You have conquered, and I yield. Yet, henceforward art thou also dead -- dead to the World, to Heaven and to Hope! In me didst thou exist -- and, in my death, see by this image, which is thine own, how utterly thou hast murdered thyself."

The Raven

Once upon a midnight dreary, while I pondered, weak and weary,
Over many a quaint and curious volume of forgotten lore--
While I nodded, nearly napping, suddenly there came a tapping,
As of some one gently rapping--rapping at my chamber door.
"'Tis some visitor," I muttered, "tapping at my chamber door--
Only this and nothing more."

Ah, distinctly I remember, it was in the bleak December,
And each separate dying ember wrought its ghost upon the floor.
Eagerly I wished the morrow;--vainly I had sought to borrow
From my books surcease of sorrow--sorrow for the lost Lenore--
For the rare and radiant maiden whom the angels name Lenore--
Nameless here for evermore.

And the silken sad uncertain rustling of each purple curtain
Thrilled me--filled me with fantastic terrors never felt before;
So that now, to still the beating of my heart, I stood repeating,
"'Tis some visitor entreating entrance at my chamber door--
Some late visitor entreating entrance at my chamber door;--
This it is, and nothing more."

Presently my soul grew stronger; hesitating then no longer,
"Sir," said I, "or Madam, truly your forgiveness I implore;
But the fact is I was napping, and so gently you came rapping,
And so faintly you came tapping--tapping at my chamber door,
That I scarce was sure I heard you"--here I opened wide the door:--
Darkness there, and nothing more.

Deep into that darkness peering, long I stood there wondering, fearing,
Doubting, dreaming dreams no mortal ever dared to dream before;
But the silence was unbroken, and the darkness gave no token,
And the only word there spoken was the whispered word, "Lenore!"
This I whispered, and an echo murmured back the word, "Lenore!"
Merely this, and nothing more.

Back into the chamber turning, all my soul within me burning,
Soon I heard again a tapping, somewhat louder than before.
"Surely," said I, "surely that is something at my window lattice;
Let me see, then, what thereat is, and this mystery explore--
Let my heart be still a moment, and this mystery explore;--
'Tis the wind and nothing more."

Open here I flung the shutter, when, with many a flirt and flutter,
In there stepped a stately Raven of the saintly days of yore;
Not the least obeisance made he: not an instant stopped or stayed he;
But, with mien of lord or lady, perched above my chamber door--
Perched upon a bust of Pallas just above my chamber door--
Perched, and sat, and nothing more.

Then this ebony bird beguiling my sad fancy into smiling,
By the grave and stern decorum of the countenance it wore,
"Though thy crest be shorn and shaven, thou," I said, "art sure no craven,
Ghastly grim and ancient Raven wandering from the Nightly shore--
Tell me what thy lordly name is on the Night's Plutonian shore."
Quoth the Raven, "Nevermore."

Much I marvelled this ungainly fowl to hear discourse so plainly,
Though its answer little meaning--little relevancy bore;
For we cannot help agreeing that no living human being
Ever yet was blessed with seeing bird above his chamber door--
Bird or beast upon the sculptured bust above his chamber door,
With such name as "Nevermore."

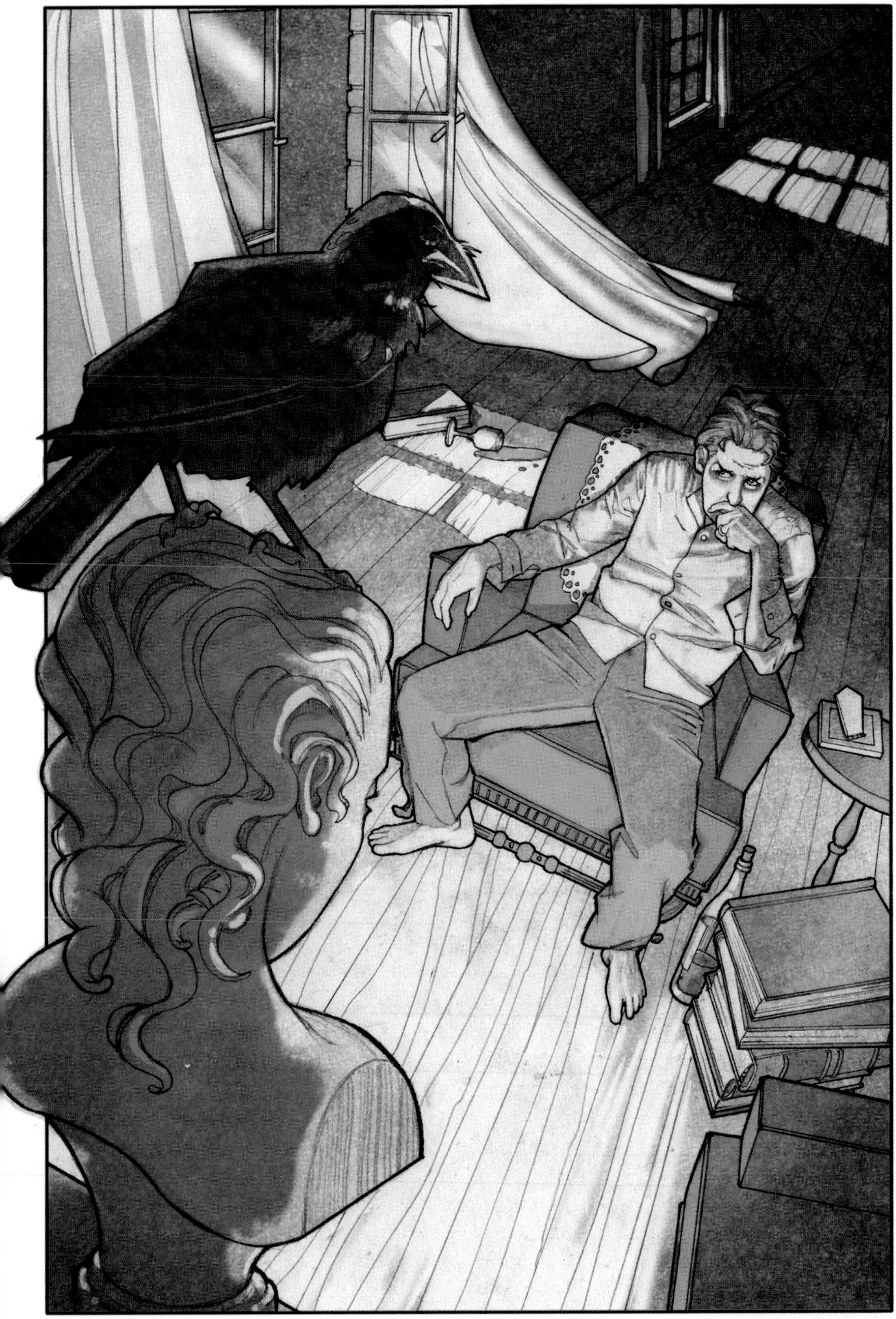

On the morrow he will leave me, as my hopes have flown before. Then the bird said, "Nevermore."

But the Raven, sitting lonely on that placid bust, spoke only
That one word, as if his soul in that one word he did outpour.
Nothing further then he uttered--not a feather then he fluttered--
Till I scarcely more than muttered, "Other friends have flown before--
On the morrow he will leave me, as my hopes have flown before."
Then the bird said, "Nevermore."

Startled at the stillness broken by reply so aptly spoken,
"Doubtless," said I, "what it utters is its only stock and store,
Caught from some unhappy master whom unmerciful disaster
Followed fast and followed faster till his songs one burden bore--
Till the dirges of his Hope the melancholy burden bore
Of 'Never--nevermore.'"

But the Raven still beguiling all my sad soul into smiling,
Straight I wheeled a cushioned seat in front of bird and bust and door;
Then, upon the velvet sinking, I betook myself to linking
Fancy unto fancy, thinking what this ominous bird of yore--
What this grim, ungainly, ghastly, gaunt, and ominous bird of yore
Meant in croaking "Nevermore."

This I sat engaged in guessing, but no syllable expressing
To the fowl whose fiery eyes now burned into my bosom's core;
This and more I sat divining, with my head at ease reclining
On the cushion's velvet lining that the lamp-light gloated o'er,
But whose velvet violet lining with the lamp-light gloating o'er,
She shall press, ah, nevermore!

Then, methought, the air grew denser, perfumed from an unseen censer
Swung by seraphim whose foot-falls tinkled on the tufted floor.
"Wretch," I cried, "thy God hath lent thee--by these angels he hath sent thee
Respite--respite aad nepenthe from thy memories of Lenore!
Quaff, oh quaff this kind nepenthe, and forget this lost Lenore!"
Quoth the Raven, "Nevermore."

"Prophet!" said I, "thing of evil!--prophet still, if bird or devil!--
Whether tempter sent, or whether tempest tossed thee here ashore,
Desolate yet all undaunted, on this desert land enchanted--
On this home by Horror haunted--tell me truly, I implore--
Is there--is there balm in Gilead?--tell me--tell me, I implore!"
Quoth the Raven, "Nevermore."

"Prophet!" said I, "thing of evil!--prophet still, if bird or devil!
By that heaven that bends above us--by that God we both adore--
Tell this soul with sorrow laden if, within the distant Aidenn,
It shall clasp a sainted maiden whom the angels name Lenore--
Clasp a rare and radiant maiden whom the angels name Lenore."
Quoth the Raven, "Nevermore."

"Be that word our sign of parting, bird or fiend!" I shrieked, upstarting--
"Get thee back into the tempest and the Night's Plutonian shore!
Leave no black plume as a token of that lie thy soul hath spoken!
Leave my loneliness unbroken!--quit the bust above my door!
Take thy beak from out my heart, and take thy form from off my door!"
Quoth the Raven, "Nevermore."

And the Raven, never flitting, still is sitting, still is sitting
On the pallid bust of Pallas just above my chamber door;
And his eyes have all the seeming of a demon's that is dreaming,
And the lamp-light o'er him streaming throws his shadow on the floor;
And my soul from out that shadow that lies floating on the floor
Shall be lifted--nevermore!

ALSO FROM THE CREATOR OF RAVENOUS

LITTLE RED HOT

PLEASE CALL ME CHANE!

SHE WAS THE MOST RUTHLESS BOUNTY HUNTER IN THE BIZ. HER EVIL EXPLOITS FUELLED RUMORS THAT SHE ONCE SHARED HER BED WITH THE DEVIL, LITERALLY. IN CHANE'S WORLD, EVIL IS PERSONIFIED SO CLEARLY, BUT GOOD IS NEVER QUITE DEFINED. CHANE IS CONSTANTLY PUT THROUGH THE RINGER AS SHE STRUGGLES TO FIND REDEMPTION.

EAGER TO PUT HER WICKED WAYS BEHIND, SHE'S QUICKLY LEARNING THAT'S NOT SUCH AN EASY THING TO DO.

FOR MORE INFO, PLEASE VISIT WWW.DAWNBROWN.NET

LITTLE RED HOT
WRITTEN & ILLUSTRATED BY DAWN BROWN
CHANE OF FOOLS
LITTLE RED HOT
CHANE OF FOOLS
LITTLE RED HOT BOUND
WRITTEN & ILLUSTRATED BY DAWN BROWN
LITTLE RED HOT
THE FOOLISH COLLECTION
WRITTEN & ILLUSTRATED BY
DAWN BROWN
LITTLE RED HOT BOUND
WRITTEN & ILLUSTRATED BY DAWN BROWN
LITTLE RED HOT BOUND

OWN A PIECE OF

RAVENOUS

ORIGINAL ART AND OTHER FUN STUFF IS AVAILABLE ON THE WEBSITE!

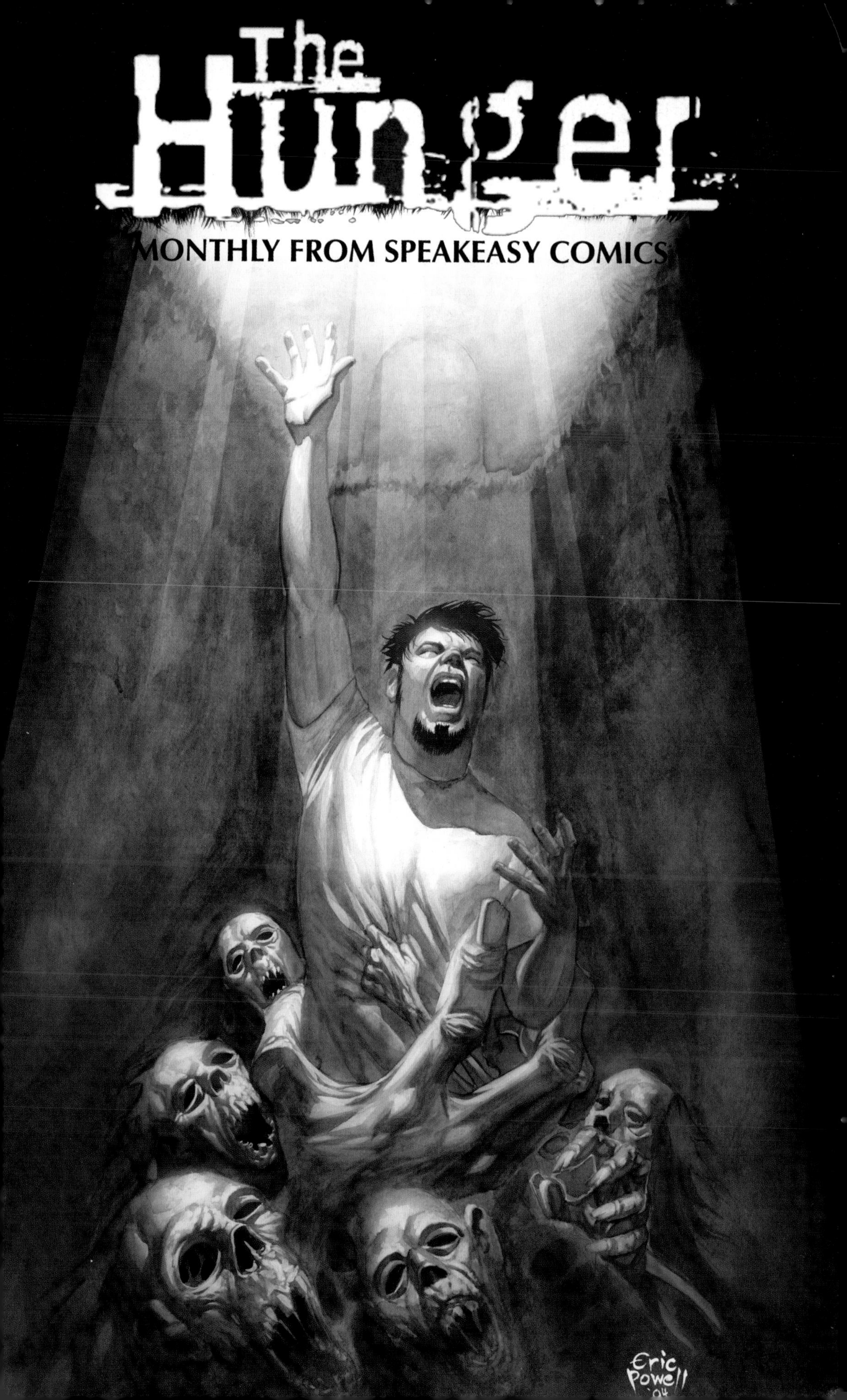
The Hunger
MONTHLY FROM SPEAKEASY COMICS
Eric Powell '04

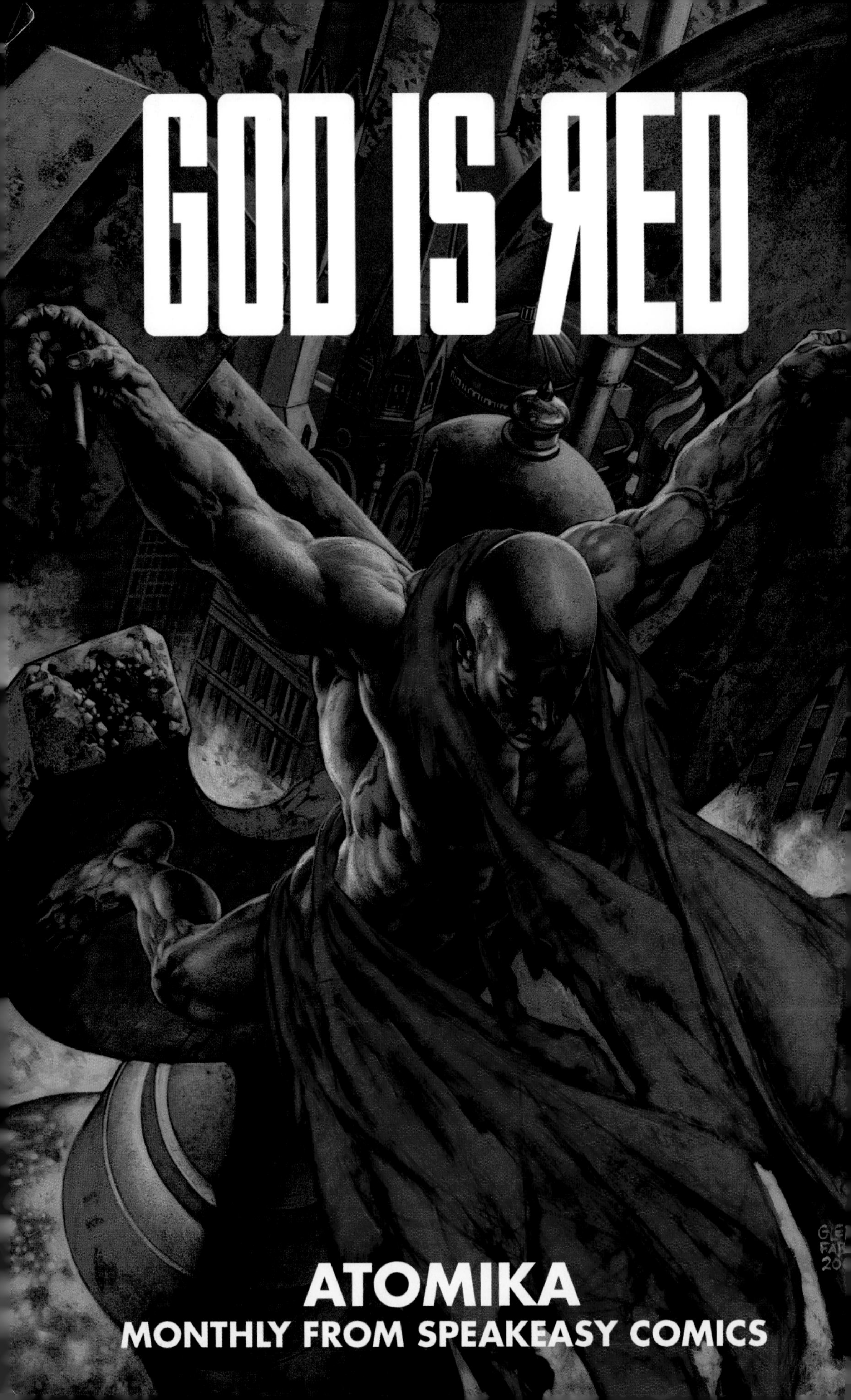
GOD IS RED
ATOMIKA
MONTHLY FROM SPEAKEASY COMICS

DAWN BROWN began her career in comics after a fateful meeting with Batman creator Bob Kane on the set of the film *Batman & Robin* in 1996. After many years working on movies as a set designer, Dawn was inspired to start developing stories of her own, and comics were the way they should be told. In 1998, she won the prestigious Xeric Grant for her debut mini-series, *Little Red Hot*, published by Image Comics. Another *Little Red Hot* series in 2001 led to a turn illustrating the cult-classic *Vampirella* for Harris Comics. She continues to design movie sets for Hollywood productions including *Planet of the Apes, Ocean's 11, Big Fish*, and *The Island*. Dawn lives in Los Angeles with her husband and their two crazy cats.